Making Sense
of the Constitution

Making Sense
of the Constitution

A Primer on the
Supreme Court
and Its
Struggle
to Apply Our
Fundamental Law

WALTER M. FRANK

Southern Illinois University Press
Carbondale and Edwardsville

Library of Congress Cataloging-in-Publication Data
Frank, Walter M., 1945–
Making sense of the constitution : a primer on
the Supreme Court and its struggle to apply our
fundamental law / Walter M. Frank.
    p. cm.
Includes bibliographical references and index.
ISBN-13: 978-0-8093-3083-6 (pbk. : alk. paper)
ISBN-10: 0-8093-3083-0 (pbk. : alk. paper)
ISBN-13: 978-0-8093-3084-3 (ebook)
ISBN-10: 0-8093-3084-9 (ebook)
1. Constitutional law—United States. 2. United States.
Supreme Court. I. Title.
KF4550.F678 2012
342.73—dc23   2011027008

Printed on recycled paper. ♻
The paper used in this publication meets the minimum
requirements of American National Standard for Information Sciences—Permanence of Paper for Printed
Library Materials, ANSI Z39.48-1992. ∞

For Lydia, David, and Rebecca
and
In memory of Honor

Contents

Acknowledgments

Many friends and colleagues have reviewed this manuscript and offered me their encouragement and comments for which I am very grateful. I do wish to single out Michael Zuckerman for special thanks. He was a gifted teacher when I took an undergraduate history course at the University of Pennsylvania with him more than four decades ago, and only a special person would receive an email totally out of the blue after the passage of that much time and respond with an astonishing set of comments and enthusiasm that made me really feel I was on the right track in attempting a volume of this scope. I also wish to thank my cousin, Jack Bronston, whose suggestions and support at an early stage in the process were very helpful and much appreciated. Finally, I would like to thank the anonymous readers for Southern Illinois University Press whose constructive criticisms, suggestions, and questions were of inestimable value.

Making Sense
of the Constitution

Introduction

On December 9, 2000, the United States Supreme Court decided a presidential election. The candidate of the losing party accepted the decision even though he had won a majority of the popular vote and even though the Court's decision seemed to many people a deliberately partisan act. Arguably, conservative justices had elected a conservative president with a decision violating their own cherished constitutional principles. Certainly, one could reasonably believe that this sudden change had something to do with achieving a skewed political outcome. Not only, however, did Vice President Gore accept the result, so did the vast majority of the American people. No angry mobs stormed the Court, and the country calmly resumed its business.

This was not the first time the nation stood by the Court when it might have done otherwise. During Franklin Roosevelt's first term, a conservative Supreme Court had declared unconstitutional key elements of his New Deal program. In response, President Roosevelt proposed that Congress allow him to appoint a new justice for each justice over the age of seventy then on the bench. The proposal would have given him six new appointments and a supportive Court. He had every reason to expect success, having just won a presidential election by 523 electoral votes to 8. Yet both Congress and the country reacted against the idea, fearing that it struck too strongly against the institutional integrity of the Court.

The Court's prestige and power has enabled it to reshape American life in significant ways, notwithstanding that the Constitution itself is silent on the Court's right to declare acts of Congress or the states unconstitutional.

In 1953 when Earl Warren became chief justice of the Supreme Court, abortion was illegal in almost every state, prayer in public schools was an accepted part of national life, rural populations enjoyed hugely disproportionate representation in both Congress and state legislatures, blacks in the South could not vote and lived in a system not much different from the apartheid of South Africa, women were given no special protection against discrimination because their proper place was still deemed to be the home, and police had no obligation to inform anyone of their constitutional rights. In the following two decades, Supreme Court decisions altered each of these facts.

The Warren Court era has cast a long shadow. For judicial conservatives, the Warren Court was akin to the pre–Wyatt Earp days of Dodge City, with black-robed justices running amuck through a defenseless Constitution. For many liberals, it remains the moment in time when the Constitution shone the brightest.

If you are reading this introduction, then you have already met the only requirement for enjoying this book—a genuine curiosity about the Supreme Court and how it goes about interpreting the Constitution. Drawing on many kinds of materials, we will explore how both constitutional law and the Court have evolved and where both stand today. At book's end, you should have a good understanding of the historical roots of the Constitution, the Bill of Rights, and the Fourteenth Amendment and how they have been interpreted; the role of the Court in our constitutional structure; the major themes in the development of constitutional law; the way today's Court works; the differing perspectives on constitutional interpretation and the materials the Court relies on to interpret the Constitution; and how the Court today has divided over some of our most controversial public issues.

This is a serious topic, but it is also fascinating and fun. We will not only see the Supreme Court as an institution but will see justices as individuals, how they relate to each other, and how they struggle to apply to issues of modern life a document written for an age that knew nothing of electric lights, modern transportation, computers, nuclear power, or email and had never heard of Freud, Marx, Darwin, or Einstein—a Court and a document that have had to grow with the nation, sometimes for better and sometimes for worse.

1. Some Foundational Ideas

A Functional Definition of Law

Oliver Wendell Holmes appears on almost every list of the Supreme Court's great justices. He spent the last fifty years of his life on the bench: twenty as a justice of the Supreme Judicial Court of Massachusetts and thirty on the United States Supreme Court. He wrote a classic book of legal scholarship and before that managed to get himself wounded in three separate Civil War battles, once finding himself briefly behind rapidly shifting enemy lines.

Holmes's experiences, among other things, led him to see law in very concrete terms. In 1897, in a seminal article in the *Harvard Law Review*, Holmes wrote: "The prophecies of what the courts will do in fact, and nothing more pretentious, are what I mean by the law."[1] Holmes asked his reader to imagine a man who cared nothing for ethics or morality. For such a person, the law only matters because it forces him to fit his behavior to the minimum set of standards needed to keep him out of jail. Holmes emphasized that his was not a cynical view of the law. He wasn't saying that law had nothing to do with morality. Quite the contrary, Holmes also wrote, "The law is the witness and external deposit of our moral life."[2] What Holmes was getting at was the connection between the purpose of law and the need to study and understand it, for it was up to lawyers, judges, and legislators to make the bad consequences of the law clear enough to restrain the unethical man's behavior.

Of course, predictability in the law is important for the honest man as well. Two businessmen, both upstanding citizens always wishing to do the right thing, may easily develop honest disagreements about their obligations under a contract. They too need a predictable set of rules to help them resolve their dispute.

If predictability, in Holmes's view, was the essential ingredient of law, it is also the essence of the rule of law; indeed, it is the point at which the two concepts intersect, for those things which are anathema to the rule of law—corruption, hidden judicial bias, secret government intervention—also destroy its predictability. To the extent that judges are paid off, or are favorably disposed to one party for reasons having nothing to do with their legal position, or are themselves afraid to render an honest opinion based on the law, there is no rule of law; rather what is ruling is greed, bias, or fear

There is another aspect of law: procedural fairness. Even if the substantive law is predictable, it will matter little if there are rules in place that prevent a party from fully presenting his case should it come to a lawsuit or prosecution. Here our Constitution makes its entrance, for, as we will see shortly, the Bill of Rights contains a very specific set of instructions designed to assure that every criminal defendant has a fair trial. Moreover, there is a much broader guarantee of procedural fairness contained in the Fifth Amendment's (and later the Fourteenth Amendment's) requirement that no person be deprived of life, liberty, or property without due process of law.

When the government acts in a way inconsistent with its obligations under the Constitution, it too is engaging in bad behavior. Consequently, constitutional law, in the sense that Holmes regarded the law, should be clear enough to restrain bad governmental behavior. Such governmental bad behavior occurs when government either violates an individual's constitutional rights or acts in a way inconsistent with its powers or authority under the Constitution. Deciding, of course, when such rights have been violated or such actions have been taken is not always easy. If it were, then the thousands of books and law review articles devoted to the subject, including this one, would be unnecessary.

If constitutional law is like ordinary law in Holmes's sense, it is also special in an important way that we should acknowledge before we immerse ourselves in its details.

The Special Nature of Constitutional Law

There are many ways to classify laws. Criminal law involves an accusation by a government that someone has violated its laws and needs to be punished either by going to jail or paying a fine. Civil law, on the other hand, largely involves actions by private parties where Party A complains that an action or omission of Party B has violated a legal duty owed to Party A. When a car accident occurs, the negligent driver will be sued for violating a duty owed to the public, including his or her victim, to drive safely. A distinction is often made between public and private law, with public law involving, at the national level, laws and regulations governing the highly complex set of administrative agencies dealing with the economy and the complex network of federal social programs, as opposed to private law governing matters such as contract relations and personal injuries.

Another way of classifying law is by identifying who makes it. *Common law* refers to judge-made law; *statutory law* to law made by legislatures and similar lawmaking bodies; and *constitutional law* can be fairly described as the fundamental law of society, whether it takes the form of one written document, or several, or even deeply entrenched customs and traditions. Our constitutional law, of course, emanates from the single document framed at the Constitutional Convention in 1787 and subsequently ratified by the states.

An important hierarchy exists among this last group of classifications. At the risk of oversimplification, statutory law may be said to trump common law, and constitutional law to trump both. The law of contracts, for example, was originally developed by common-law judges in England because, for many reasons, Parliament had not addressed the subject in legislation. Once, however, Parliament or any lawmaking body enacts legal rules the judges must apply those rules even if they disagree with them and would prefer another set of rules. Constitutional law represents the law to which both statutory and common law must conform.

In the United States, because we have a federal system, we have two sets of fundamental law: the United States Constitution and the various state constitutions. We will have much to say about federalism shortly. For the moment, we simply observe that when state law, including state constitutional law, is found to violate the U.S. Constitution, it is the U.S. Constitution that prevails.

But why is that the case? Just because a document declares itself to be supreme does not necessarily make it supreme. A document cannot establish its own legitimacy. That must come from some external set of events. In the case of our U.S. Constitution, that event was the ratification of the Constitution by the people, which expressed the fundamental idea that government draws its authority from the consent of the governed. "The consent of the governed" in turn embodies fundamental ideas about freedom, autonomy, and the dignity of the individual. What makes the Constitution special, however, is not exactly what has made our constitutional law special. If society never changed and everything were completely fixed, constitutional law would have long ago ceased to be a subject of much interest. A static society would have produced a frozen constitutional law.

Our constitutional law, however, has been anything but frozen because our history, with its many triumphs and tragedies, its eras of consensus and of conflict, has required a continuing examination of how our Constitution should be applied in an ever-evolving social, economic, technological, and political landscape. If there is one proposition that might unite virtually all students of constitutional law, it would be that how to apply the Constitution to the myriad of cases and controversies that bubble up from this cauldron has never been either self-evident or easy. Our constitutional law has been a never-ending final examination, asking us to define ourselves as a nation and to determine what government can legitimately expect and demand of us, and we, in turn, from it. Keith Whittington, an important constitutional scholar, has written: "A constitution, unlike a law, does not simply express legal rights and duties but also expresses normative sensibilities."[3] As you will see, our constitutional law has been for over two hundred years the laboratory for debating and testing our differing ideas about those sensibilities and how they may or may not be realized within the overall governmental structure created by the Constitution. It is the breadth, fundamental importance, and open-endedness of that debate that has made American constitutional law special.

Sometimes 9–0, Sometimes 5–4

There are nine justices on the Supreme Court. Sometimes, even on important constitutional cases, they agree unanimously, other times they divide much more closely, often by 5–4. Unanimous decisions will often result when the members of the Court agree on the general principles that are at stake in a particular case and how those principles apply to the facts and circumstances of the case. Such decisions are important because they show that there is a body of constitutional law settled enough to allow justices with very different constitutional approaches and political views to come together.

Let me provide two examples of cases that show justices uniting on matters when the public might not have expected such level of agreement. Not long ago the Court was asked to address the issue of access of military recruiters to university campuses—certainly an issue on which the general public might divide. Adding to it the question of the rights of gays and lesbians to serve in the military, one might expect an ideologically divided Court to be as quarrelsome as the rest of us. Nonetheless, in *Rumsfeld v. Forum for Academic and Institutional Rights, Inc.*,[4] a unanimous Court upheld the right of the federal government to withhold federal funds from universities that did not allow access to military recruiters because of disagreement with the military's policies regarding homosexuality. The case was brought by an association of law schools and law faculties and was based on First Amendment protection against compelled speech and the unconstitutional conditions doctrine, which the plaintiff claimed had been violated because the schools were forced to choose between surrendering First Amendment rights or losing federal funding. The decision in *Rumsfeld* was unanimous because all the justices agreed that the power granted to Congress to provide for the common defense by raising and supporting an army and a navy "includes the authority to require campus access for military recruiters."[5] Congress had not directly required access, but for the Court this was immaterial: "It is clear that a funding condition cannot be unconstitutional if it could be constitutionally imposed directly."[6] With these simple propositions agreed upon, the Court had little trouble reaching a unanimous decision.

Rumsfeld was a case in which the more liberal justices arguably did the unexpected. In *Crane v. Kentucky*,[7] the more conservative justices arguably went against form. In *Crane*, a trial judge had ruled in a murder case that the defendant's confession was voluntary and therefore admissible against him. Because he had found the confession voluntary, the trial judge excluded evidence offered by the defendant to cast doubt on the confession's believability. The Supreme Court unanimously overruled the trial judge's decision. Examining its prior cases, the Court stated that it had always held that the credibility of a confession was a separate issue from its voluntariness so that exclusion of the evidence was improper.

While unanimity on the Court does occur, nevertheless, it is striking how many of the Court's most important constitutional decisions have been decided by a vote of 5 to 4. Appendix 2 of this work provides a list of sixty-four constitutional law cases that, in the first decade of this century, have split the Court 5–4. Virtually every major constitutional law decision during this period was decided by this margin. While there is no comparable decade in the history of the Supreme Court, the fact is that a number of very important constitutional cases decided by the Court have also been decided by this margin. Some of the major ones are listed in Appendix 1.

It might seem premature to discuss why justices, who can sometimes agree completely, can also disagree so profoundly. Nevertheless, since some of the general factors at work introduce a number of important themes, it is worth at least touching upon these factors now as a way of getting our bearings.

There are many factors that pull the Court in the direction of 5–4 opinions.

First, constitutional law really matters. It affects how we live our lives, how we relate to each other, and how the balance between competing interests is to be struck on many important issues. Whenever anything is important, strong opinions develop that are not easily discarded in the interests of unanimity or good fellowship.

Second, the Constitution did not come with a set of instructions on how to interpret it. As a result, as we will see, particularly in Chapters 10 and 11, there are a number of different interpretive approaches to the Constitution.

Third, our constitutional structure contains tensions within it that are not easily resolved, and the Constitution itself raises questions not easily answered. Federalism and separation of powers are two key guiding principles of our constitutional structure. Both principles are of fundamental importance and both, as we will see, can be highly contested. When the president and Congress clash over their powers or when the issue pits the power of the national government versus the states, the constitutional text rarely provides a clear answer. The Court, therefore, whether or not it admits it, assumes the role of policy maker, an inherently ambiguous task, trying to strike the right balance between competing interests.

Fourth, constitutional law is not handed down from on high by an omniscient God. It is a product of human thought engaged in by individuals who bring to the task very different experiences and values.

Fifth, there is the text of the Constitution itself. The meaning of such phrases as "due process," "equal protection," "privileges and immunities," "unreasonable searches and seizures," and "interstate commerce" are hardly self-evident and can easily lead different justices to apply them differently.

A sixth factor involves the element of time. The fact is that constitutional law is a continuing exercise in applying old language to new situations, many of which could never have been contemplated by the Framers. To cite just a few examples, the constitutional rights of high school students in a public school system could hardly have been in the minds of the Framers at a time when public schools did not exist, nor, for the same reason, would the Constitutional Convention have thought about the applicability of the Eminent Domain clause to economic development projects or the extent of Congress's power to regulate the Internet. In short, time itself has rendered the Constitution a fairly uncooperative witness to its own meaning. Just how limited the text has become and how freely justices should feel to read emerging values and understandings into old language is one of the great dividing lines in constitutional debate.

Finally, and probably most important, there is the simple fact that justices themselves owe their jobs to the political branches, being appointed by the president with the approval of the Senate. Presidents look for justices whose thinking is compatible with their own. During eras when one party or point of view was dominant, there were fewer 5–4 decisions because justices sharing a similar outlook were appointed by like-minded presidents. Today, however, and at least since the advent of the New Deal, political power has gone back and forth. It should not be surprising, therefore, that the Supreme Court, its composition itself a product of the political process, should also reflect its political divisions. This is not to say that Supreme Court decisions are always unprincipled or that justices simply vote their feelings. We will see that the process is very complex, and certainly not all constitutional decisions are split 5–4. The fact remains, however, that in our democracy, a divided nation will often be reflected in a divided Court.

2. The Constitution and Its Amendments: An Overview

Framing, Debating, and Ratifying the Constitution
Why They Came

At the National Constitutional Center in Philadelphia, one can wander through a room filled with life-size statues of each of the delegates to the Constitutional Convention of 1787, going from Washington to Franklin to Madison and the other delegates, some in private thought, others deep in conversation. It is a slightly eerie experience. One wonders what they were thinking, how each of them came to be there, and what they would have thought of all the ink that has been spilt trying to fathom what they intended by the document they fashioned more than two centuries ago.

That we have a National Constitutional Center at all, a museum dedicated to our founding document, is not without significance. We are and have always been a nation of immigrants, defined not by a particular ethnicity but by the need to accommodate many ethnicities as well as religious beliefs. As one writer recently observed, "We are founded on ideas, not genetics, on aspirations, not the accidents of geography."[1] And our first big idea, the one that has stood us in the greatest stead, even as it has simultaneously locked us into a never-ending debate about the nature of our governing structure, was the Constitution itself, the expression of the revolutionary idea of a government, in Lincoln's words, "of the people, by the people and for the people."

The Constitution was hammered out during a hot, uncomfortable Philadelphia summer in 1787 at a time when many worried that events were spinning out of control. The problem seemed to be too much democracy, not too little. In the words of the historian Gordon Wood, "The economic and social instability engendered by the Revolution was finding political expression in the state legislatures at the very time they were larger, more representative, and more powerful than ever before in American history."[2] During the period 1780 to 1787, many laws were enacted in numerous states favoring the legal position of debtors and loose money in general. To

10

those who were better-off, the very notion of property rights seemed under siege and state legislatures too powerful in relation to their executive and judicial branches. This was very troubling to a generation well schooled in political principles. The absence of a meaningful central government was also leading to debilitating rivalries among the states, thwarting commercial progress and inviting foreign invasion. Continental security and what would today be called foreign policy matters were an important concern for the Framers and perhaps the public as well when one considers that the first group of the series of newspaper essays aimed at gaining support for the Constitution in the ratification struggle argued that a stronger central government was needed to protect against actions of foreign powers and better secure frontier settlements. The essays later became known as the Federalist Papers, which we will discuss further in a moment.

There was a central government in place, but it hardly deserved the name. It had been created by another document, the Articles of Confederation, agreed to by thirteen state legislatures in 1781. The Confederation government lacked the power to tax or to control trade without the unanimous consent of all the states; it had no federal executive or judicial branches; and it lacked even the power to pass legislation affecting individuals, so there was no direct relation between it and the people. In effect, the Articles had created not a nation but a league, one that, because of the requirement of complete unanimity, was, among other things, unable to retaliate against Britain for closing its ports in the West Indies to American ships by closing American ports to British ships. The Confederation was also unable, despite agreement among almost all the states, to effectuate a comprehensive revenue plan.

In 1786, western Massachusetts farmers, many of them former Revolutionary soldiers, now deeply in debt and facing debtors' prison, forcibly closed courts to prevent foreclosures on their mortgages. A conservative state legislature sent out General Benjamin Lincoln, himself a Revolutionary War hero, to put down what history knows as Shays Rebellion. Lincoln succeeded. Many of the leaders, including Daniel Shays, were sentenced to death but later pardoned. Shays Rebellion only added to the growing sense of a country in peril.

At the start of the 1780s, contemporary leaders, reflecting the earlier struggle with England, had feared monarchy and too powerful government. By 1787, they were worrying about preserving order and creating a rational system of government capable of protecting property interests. James Madison, among others, had become "a thorough nationalist, intent on subordinating the states as far as possible to the sovereignty of the central government."[3]

The men who gathered in Philadelphia (55 in total over the entire summer, including 35 lawyers) were not engaged in an abstract exercise in good government. Rather, they were intent on reversing a course of events that many found deeply disturbing. In the process, they also wanted to rekindle the sense of unity that had been forged during the Revolution. They believed, rightly so in the judgment of history, that the Articles of Confederation were too flawed simply to be amended. A new governmental structure was needed. Whether the "Framers" were on sound ground legally in deciding to scrap the Articles of Confederation and create a whole new structure is still debated among legal scholars, but it was events, not theory, that drove the creation of a new government. In the end, the Constitutional Convention was not just about America. Something deeper was at stake, something of which the Framers were well aware, for they also saw themselves on a larger stage, acting for all mankind in deciding, in the words of Alexander Hamilton, "the important question whether societies of men are really capable or not of establishing good government from reflection and choice, or whether they are forever destined to depend for their political constitutions on accident and force."[4]

The Constitutional Convention

The story of the Constitutional Convention has been told many times and need not be recounted here. (I recommend a few accounts of the convention in Suggestions for Further Reading). Understanding, however, how the document itself came to be written and why the convention succeeded are worth a brief discussion because it is difficult to fully understand the Constitution without understanding the process that gave it life.

The first order of business at the convention was the introduction of the Virginia Plan prepared by James Madison. The plan consisted of fifteen separate resolutions and reflected Madison's strong distrust of state legislatures in giving the national legislature, Congress, the power to veto any state laws that it deemed to "contravene" the Constitution. Under the Virginia Plan, there would be a House of Representatives whose membership was based on the proportion of population in each state, and that "House" would elect a Senate. The plan did not provide for a president but instead for the "institution" of a "national executive" to be chosen by the "national legislature." The plan also provided for a Council of Revision with the power to reject laws passed by Congress, subject to an override by a supermajority whose precise number was not set forth in the plan. Madison's plan, if adopted in substantially the form submitted, would likely have led eventually to a national government organized much more along parliamentary lines.

The Framers spent the first two months debating every element of the Virginia Plan. By the end of this period, the convention had adopted nineteen statements of principle, essentially refinements and amendments to the Virginia Plan.[5] At this point, the convention adjourned for a week and a half to allow a five-person Committee on Detail to turn the resolutions into a coherent document. The committee produced the first real draft of a constitution. Parenthetically, it should be noted that the committee itself made major changes to the resolutions, perhaps the most important being its recommendation to specifically enumerate the powers of Congress, a device that conservative members of the committee proposed to limit the scope of national power.

The draft produced by the Committee on Detail on August 6 moved the process forward but did not end debate, which continued for another five weeks, revising virtually every clause of the committee's handiwork on virtually every aspect of the new national government.[6] So difficult were some of the issues that the convention created several more committees, including one aptly named the Committee on Postponed Matters, to resolve difficult points. Finally, on September 8, the convention, its work nearly complete, appointed a Committee on Style to give the document its final shape. Here Gouverneur Morris, a major participant in the convention's deliberations and an ardent nationalist, steps forward. By all accounts, including his own, Morris wrote the final draft, reducing the twenty-three articles of the prior draft to a manageable seven and, in the words of one historian, "gathering together all the decisions on the legislature, executive and judiciary in such a way as to finally make the form of the new government clear."[7]

That clarity was achieved organizationally by devoting each of the first three articles to one of the three branches (legislative, executive, and judicial) of the national government, mirroring in the document's structure the distinct roles for each branch upon which the national government was based. Having created the governmental structure in the first three articles, the document addresses other matters deemed essential by the Framers in its remaining provisions, such as state comity (the Full Faith and Credit clause), the processes for amending the Constitution and for admitting new states into the Union, and the Supremacy clause establishing that the central government would be supreme within its proper sphere.

Gouverneur Morris also redrafted the Preamble, giving it "an emotional force that had been lacking in earlier drafts" and that "captured perfectly the nationalist vision of a supreme central government capable of knitting together a sprawling country and overcoming the petty divisions among its competitive states."[8] The words speak for themselves: "WE THE PEOPLE of the United States, in Order to form a more perfect Union, establish Justice, insure domestic Tranquility, provide for the common defense, promote the general Welfare, and secure the Blessings of Liberty to ourselves and our Posterity, do ordain and establish this Constitution for the United States of America." While the Preamble itself has not figured prominently in deciding specific cases, its bold vision has influenced many justices, including Justice Ginsburg, who in a discussion at Princeton University in October 2005 cited the expression of a desire to "form a more perfect union" in the Preamble as a kind of North Star for her own constitutional philosophy.

Many factors contributed to the convention's success. For one thing, the delegates were pragmatic, experienced politicians. Nearly all had served in colonial or state legislatures and a quarter of them had held important statewide positions.[9] Forty-one of them had served in the Continental Congress.[10] They had built consensus for a revolution, made it a success, and then established state governments based on republican principles. The delegates were well versed in political theory but were not imprisoned by it. In fact, the Constitution's most innovative feature—the principle of shared sovereignty—was widely regarded as impossible. Federalism arose, however, not from theory, but from the simple need to accommodate the desire for a much stronger national government with the political reality that the states themselves, each with their distinctive identities and histories, were not about to preside over their own funeral.

The convention, at the outset, also adopted some very sound procedural rules. The best known was the decision to hold meetings in complete secrecy, eliminating any motive for posturing inside the convention and minimizing pressures from the outside. There were other good rules as well. The delegates wanted to be free to change their minds, so from the start they rejected a rule that would have required the recording of roll call votes. As one delegate observed, "A record of the opinions of members would be an obstacle to a change of them on conviction."[11] The convention also adopted a rule to assure that delegates paid strict attention to the proceedings: "Every member, rising to speak, shall address the President and whilst he shall be speaking, none shall pass between them, or hold discourse with another, or read a book, pamphlet or paper, printed or manuscript."[12]

A critical factor in the convention's success was the willingness of the delegates to compromise their positions. It was this flexibility at crucial moments that kept the process from falling apart. To take the most famous example, the Virginia Plan favored the big states because it proposed that congressional representation be accomplished through election by the people with the size of a state's representation based on population. However, William Patterson, who proposed the contrasting New Jersey Plan, which was supported by the smaller states, argued that "If the sovereignty of the States is to be maintained, the Representatives must be drawn immediately from the States, not from the people: and we have no power to vary the idea of equal sovereignty."[13] To break the deadlock, Roger Sherman proposed what became known as the Connecticut Compromise, which essentially provided for one branch of Congress (the House of Representatives) to be organized as the Virginia Plan envisioned and the other branch (the Senate) as the New Jersey Plan envisioned. A number of the larger states opposed the compromise, and the convention came dangerously close to breaking up over the issue, but when it was put to a vote, 5 states voted in favor, and 4 against, accepting Sherman's compromise. The losing states (Virginia, Pennsylvania, South Carolina and Georgia) acceded to this defeat and, with the shape of Congress not as much to their liking, people like Madison became more willing to invest the executive with greater authority.

One other factor, perhaps the most important of all, accounted for the convention's success, as historian Jack Rakove explains: "On the principles of government a broad consensus reigned. Government existed for the good of the many, and to protect the liberty, property and equal rights of the citizen. The idea that representation would help the government to determine the common good was commonplace, and so was the belief that separation of powers was essential to the protection of rights."[14] Differences had to be worked out, divergent interests reconciled, but all within a critical mass of shared assumptions, including the need for a strong national government to replace, not merely amend, the Articles of Confederation.

A National Government

The Constitutional Convention, with all its compromises, did achieve its major objective, creation of a strong national government. This was accomplished, first, by declaration of national supremacy in the Constitution itself; second, by a ratification process for the Constitution that would protect that supremacy against future challenge; and third, by creation of a mechanism for enforcing that supremacy.

The first step was accomplished in the second paragraph of Article VI, which declares, "This Constitution, and the Laws of the United States . . . and all Treaties . . . the Supreme Law of the Land" and provides that "the Judges in every State shall be bound thereby, any Thing in the Constitution or Laws of any State to the Contrary notwithstanding." The second step required that the Constitution be ratified by the people, not by the state governments, because then, at least theoretically, it could be undone only by a vote of the people. The Framers achieved step two in Article VII, calling for ratification by "conventions" in which the delegates would be chosen by the people rather than by the state legislatures. The third step required a mechanism for enforcement of the Constitution as the supreme law of the land. As one eminent historian has written, "The framers never doubted the need for judicial enforcement of national law."[15] The Framers provided for that enforcement by the generous definition of national judicial power contained in Article III, the creation of the Supreme Court, and, if established by Congress, additional inferior federal courts.

Interestingly, one of the first major cases decided by the Supreme Court tested the Supremacy clause. In *Ware v. Hilton*,[16] the Court held that the commitments made under the Treaty of Paris superseded any conflicting state laws. The case was an important precursor to the more celebrated case of *Martin v. Hunter's Lessee* discussed in Chapter 4. Ironically, the lawyer in *Ware* who argued the losing state sovereignty position for Virginia was the celebrated John Marshall, who later, as chief justice, led the cause of judicial nationalism for more than three decades.

The national judicial power does not extend to declaring state laws or actions unconstitutional except if they violate the U.S. Constitution. It is up to the states to make and interpret their own laws and constitution. That is part of the essence of state sovereignty, which is still very much a part of our constitutional structure. Decisions of various state high courts, for example, regarding same-sex marriage[17] have not been reviewable by the U.S. Supreme Court for the simple reason that they have been based upon interpretations of their respective state constitutions.

The Ratification Struggle

The delegates to the Constitutional Convention never thought that they could declare a Constitution on their own. Instead, they decided that the assent of nine states would be needed before the Constitution would come into effect. A few days after the convention ended, the Constitution was formally read to the then existing "national" government, the Congress formed by the Articles of Confederation. On September 28, 1787, the Congress voted to send the proposed Constitution to the states with a recommendation that the states follow the ratification procedure in Article VII but without comment on the Constitution itself. The Confederation Congress had rejected a proposal that would have allowed the states to condition ratification on the acceptance of amendments, a mechanism that would have allowed each state to redraft the Constitution to its liking and, undoubtedly, would have required a second constitutional convention. The Constitution would be voted either up or down, nothing in between.

Opposition to the Constitution was strong in many states. The Anti-Federalists (the rather negative name given to the opposition) argued that the proposed central government was too strong, particularly in the absence of a written guarantee of individual rights. In several states, the Anti-Federalists tried to condition ratification on the passage of such a guarantee. They failed, but it was understood that one of the first orders of business of the new Government would be the drafting of amendments addressing their concerns.

The struggle over the Constitution was impassioned. In many ways it was not dissimilar to a modern presidential election, fought out state by state, with both sides employing every tactic at their disposal and with predictions of doom if the other side won; Anti-Federalists predicted loss of American liberty if the Constitution passed, and Federalists, disunion and foreign invasion if it did not. According to one distinguished historian, both sides feared the very public opinion they had to court: "Federalists feared that the parochial demagogues of state politics would use their mischievous influence to poison the public mind; while Anti-Federalists worried that the prestige of the Convention would be invoked to ask that the Constitution be adopted on trust."[18]

New Hampshire became the critical ninth state to ratify the Constitution. A viable, new nation, however, was still not assured, since neither New York nor Virginia had yet ratified the document. It was known from the outset that the battle in New York would be extremely close. Initially the Anti-Federalists had the upper hand. To gain support for the new Constitution, Alexander Hamilton, James Madison (who was in New York as a Virginia delegate to the still existing Congress under the Articles of Confederation) and John Jay published a series of essays in New York newspapers, under the pseudonym Publius. The articles amounted to a barrage of propaganda, three or four different articles sometimes appearing in the same week, in favor of the new government. The essays, now known as the Federalist Papers, were circulated widely throughout the states and became an important part of the ratification debate not only in New York but elsewhere. The essays achieved their short-term objective as New York and Virginia both ratified the Constitution in close votes. More importantly, they were written so brilliantly, with such detail and clarity, that they have become a major source for our understanding of the Constitution. The Federalist Papers have been cited as evidence of the original meaning of the Constitution more often than any other historical source.[19]

Who actually ratified the Constitution? The people as a whole or the people in each of the individual states? Prior to the Civil War, this was a matter of intense debate between the North and the South because of its implications respecting the right of secession. Even today, there are echoes of that dispute. Akhil Reed Amar of Yale Law School, for example, sees both national and state power as something conditionally bestowed by the people as a whole and still subject to "the people's" collective will. Amar finds support for his view, not only in the Constitution's Preamble with its forceful opening phrase, "We the People of the United States," but also in the references in the Ninth and Tenth Amendments to "rights retained by the people" and "rights reserved to the States respectively, or the people." Amar's notion of the Constitution as the creation of a unified American people leads him to argue that Article V is not the only mechanism for amending the Constitution and that it could also be amended in a national referendum by popular vote. This latter view is not widely shared, but the idea that the Constitution molded a nation, not just a collection of states, is widely embraced. On the other side, there are those who, while conceding that the people certainly ceded certain authority to a national government, emphasize they did so only in the context of state ratifications. Clarence Thomas, for example, finds no constitutional significance in viewing the people as part of an undifferentiated mass and regards it as bad history. "The ultimate source of the Constitution's authority," he has written, "is the consent of the people of each individual State, not the consent of the undifferentiated people of the Nation as a whole."[20]

The Constitution: How Successful? How Democratic?

Today, it is hard to conceive how stunning the Constitution was to a world then governed by kings, czars, and sultans. The Constitution "was not merely a text but a deed."[21] For the first time in history, a sovereign people had brought their own government into existence. The measure of the Framers' achievement is that a document written for a seaboard agrarian nation of 3 million people and designed to dampen public debate and discourage factional conflict, is still the governing blueprint for a world power with over 300 million people and an appetite for democracy and public conflict which the Framers thought might be its death knell.

Its success is no accident, for the Constitution is built on solid foundational principles: checks and balances, separation of powers, and federalism that have diffused but not paralyzed governmental power and provided room for experimentation at the state and local level. The Framers also struck the right balance in allowing for amendments to the Constitution but making the process a demanding one: two-thirds of both houses of Congress or of the legislatures of the states must propose amendments, which must then be approved by three-quarters of the state legislatures or state conventions.

For many, the idea of the Constitution itself as higher law, superior to all others, is the surpassing accomplishment of the Constitutional Convention. That concept, however, needs some qualification. Certainly, the Constitution is superior in the sense that it constrains and defines what government can and cannot do, but even the Framers themselves thought of the Constitution only as a beginning, a framework for a new nation that would undoubtedly require change, as provision for an amendment process clearly shows. They might not have predicted, for example, the extension of the voting franchise beyond what they originally envisioned, but most of them would hardly have disapproved of it as a matter of principle, given their overwhelming pragmatism and their strong sense of history.

A constitution does not guarantee success of any kind. At best, it can create a framework in which sound decisions can be made and power is not abused. It can create the setting in which history is made but does not determine what that history will be. Thus, when the Southern states felt political power slipping from their grasp, they seceded from the Union, and the original constitutional understanding, which had accepted the existence of slavery and made concessions designed to enhance the power of Southern states, collapsed. The result was the Civil War, a war that cost over 600,000 lives and is still the bloodiest in our history.

If the Constitution could not prevent the collapse of the original understanding, it did allow, after the passage of the post–Civil War amendments, particularly the Fourteenth Amendment, for the development of a new conceptual framework for individual rights and for the balance of power between the states and the national government: a new conceptual framework but still within the same basic governance structure that had been created in 1787. The creation of such a structure, sound enough to survive the Civil War with democracy intact yet flexible enough to allow a much-altered nation to go forward, may have been the Framers' greatest accomplishment, though it was achieved politically only at the cost of postponing the realization of black rights for another century.

Today some observers question whether the Constitution is up to the task of fulfilling the needs of a modern democracy. They point out, for example, that most of the older European democracies have adopted parliamentary systems and proportional representation, which encourage multiparty political systems and coalition government that seem better able to translate political rhetoric into legislative accomplishments.[22] By contrast, our current politics seem mired in ideological divisions that accentuate differences and even make cross-party friendships among politicians a rarity.

The continuing success of any constitutional enterprise is never fully assured since, as Sortoris Barber has noted, "A good constitution preserves doubt about its own success even as it works (with arguable success) to approximate its ends and maintain the capacity for constitutional reform."[23] Barber believes that an essential purpose of our Constitution has been to encourage healthy and respectful civic debate, a quality he worries is increasingly vanishing from our public discourse with consequences yet to be measured.

While this is a complex subject, our current problems cannot simply be laid at the doorstep of the Constitution. For one thing, nothing in the Constitution prevents a system of proportional representation in the House of Representatives since it is Congress, not the Constitution, which determines the manner in which representatives are elected. Our current winner-take-all district system is a product of federal legislation, not the Constitution.

On the other hand, it would be naïve not to recognize the manner in which our basic constitutional structure can make broad governmental action extremely difficult. Unlike parliamentary systems, our three political branches (the Senate, the House, and the presidency) are elected in different ways and by different constituencies, and not all at the same time. Most importantly, different political parties can simultaneously control different political branches. As this is being written, for example, the Democrats control the presidency, the Republicans the House of Representatives, and the Democrats (at least theoretically) the Senate. I say *theoretically* because the filibuster rule in the Senate requiring a supermajority of sixty senators to cut off debate on all proposed legislation other than budget matters means that neither party can enact legislation without some support from the opposition party. The simple fact is that our system encourages divided power, hardly a recipe for strong governmental action. In most countries, elections lead to one party assuming power and enacting its program which will then be judged in a subsequent election. For us, however, elections often simply lead to a continuation of party warfare, just one battle among many for control of the public agenda.

The Constitution was certainly not a perfect document. It was born in an atmosphere of crisis that required delegates to reconcile a host of conflicting state, regional, and economic interests. It might, from one vantage point, have been a "covenant with death" and "the devil's pact," as famously described by William Lloyd Garrison,[24] but it also would not likely have been signed (and certainly not ratified) by the four Southern states attending the convention (Georgia, North Carolina, South Carolina, and Virginia) or Maryland if some accommodation with the slave system had not been reached. Without even mentioning the word *slavery*, the Constitution fully protected Southern interests, requiring the return of fugitive slaves, barring Congress from prohibiting the slave trade until at least 1808 and allowing every slave to count as three-fifths of a person toward a state's population for determining the number of representatives to which it was entitled. Without these accommodations, there would have been no Constitution.

The Constitution was also not a democratic document *by modern standards*: Only the members of the House of Representatives were to be elected directly by the people; the Constitution guaranteed no one the right to vote (it still doesn't although it now forbids certain forms of discrimination). Senators were to be chosen by state legislatures and were to represent the interests of the states. The president was to be chosen by a "college" of electors envisioned to represent the better sort of people with the judgment necessary to find the right person. In each state, these electors would be chosen in such manner as their state legislature would decide. In the first presidential election only five states chose their electors by popular vote.

These provisions were no accident. Voting and governance were seen as best entrusted to those with a strong stake in society. Not only were their interests most affected by governmental decisions, but only property owners, not dependent on others, were believed to have the ability to arrive at independent decisions for the good of the community. Consider this statement of John Adams arguing *against* the extension of suffrage to non–property holders: "The same reasoning which will induce you to admit all men who have no property, to vote . . . will prove that you ought to admit women and children; for, generally speaking, women and children have as good judgments, and as independent minds, as those men wholly destitute of property; these last being to all intents and purposes as much dependent upon others, who will please to feed, clothe and employ them, as women are upon their husbands, or children on their parents."[25]

Adams's view needs to be understood in the context of his times. It reflects not a distrust of representative government but a belief that only voters free to vote their convictions could assure its success. Such voters, in Adams view, would assure a government in which "the many should have a full fair and perfect Representation."[26] Some States attempted to reconcile the tension between full representation and property ownership by discriminating among the officers for whom people could vote. In New York, for example, under the Constitution of 1777, property owners with a freehold valued at 50 to 250 pounds could vote for state assembly and Congress but only their wealthier brethren having freeholds of more than 250 pounds could vote as well for governor, lieutenant governor, and state senator.[27]

In his famous work *An Economic Interpretation of the Constitution of the United States*, Charles Beard argued that "the Constitution was essentially an economic document" in which almost all the members of the Constitutional Convention were "immediately, directly, and personally interested."[28] Many have questioned whether self-interest fully accounts for the Framers' motivations, and Beard himself later said that he never intended to argue economics as the sole motivation. At the time of its publication, however, that was how the book was often understood.

Admitting that the delegates were motivated in part by interests as well as ideals should not, in any event, minimize the Constitution's historic achievement in creating a democratic government. Voters, even if for the most part composed of propertied white males, were still choosing vital parts of their government, electing not only the House of Representatives but also the state legislatures that selected U.S. senators (and often presidential electors). The nature of the ratification process should also not be overlooked, particularly because, as Akhil Reed Amar has pointed out, many states allowed an unusually broad franchise for the ratification-convention elections held in 1787–88.[29]

The Constitution received its first real test in 1800 as the result of an electoral crisis that was itself the result of a technical error that almost reversed the expressed will of the people. Much to the surprise of many contemporaries, the new nation had been plagued with deep divisions from the outset. Two very different visions for the young republic vied for supremacy—the Jeffersonian dream of an honest, agrarian society composed of independent farmers versus the Hamiltonian hope for a powerful, commercial nation centered in its growing urban centers. This dichotomy led almost immediately to the emergence of two clearly identifiable factions competing for political power. The events of the French Revolution further enflamed this rivalry with Jeffersonians regarding it as the fulfillment of democratic hopes and the Federalists as confirmation of every fear they harbored about entrusting power to the people.

For the first twelve years of the Republic, the Federalists had maintained control of the government but in 1800 Jefferson defeated Adams in a very close and bitterly fought contest. Adams lost in part because his refusal to go to war with France, when he had every excuse for doing so, alienated many of his fellow Federalists. For them, this refusal amounted to inexcusable cowardice. Late in the campaign, Alexander Hamilton, a Federalist like Adams but a personal enemy, wrote a long public letter attacking Adams that sealed Adams's political fate.

Today we celebrate our peaceful transitions of power from one group to another. The loser is expected to be present at the inauguration, and the new president is expected to at least thank the outgoing president for his service to the country. Bi-partisanship is the watchword of the day. Jefferson was the first to try and capture this spirit when he noted in his inaugural address, "We are all Republicans, We are all Federalists." Jefferson's statement could not hide, however, the bitter feelings the election had engendered. Adams was not present at the inauguration, having left the capital "at four in the morning traveling by public stage under clear skies lit by a quarter-moon,"[30] and Jefferson made no reference to him. Nonetheless, power had been transferred without bloodshed.

Constitutionally, the election of 1800 was nearly a fiasco, reflecting how little the Founders had anticipated the emergence of permanent political factions. Under the Constitution as originally drafted, each presidential elector cast a vote for two individuals for president. There was no separate contest for vice president. The vice president was simply the person who had polled the second highest number of votes for president. The Republicans in the election of 1800 forgot to arrange for Jefferson (their presidential candidate) to get at least one more vote than Burr (their vice presidential candidate) so even though Jefferson and Burr beat their Federalist opponents, they inadvertently, tied for the presidency. As a result, the election, as the Constitution required, and still requires when no candidate gets a majority of electoral votes, was thrown into the House of Representatives. Jefferson eventually won only when a Federalist from Delaware, James Bayard (the only House member from Delaware who therefore controlled Delaware's vote), switched his vote to Jefferson after 36 deadlocked ballots. Burr, who might actually have become president had he been more willing to bargain with the Federalists,[31] ended up as Jefferson's vice president. The technical problem was fixed by the Twelfth Amendment to the Constitution, which provides for separate voting for president and vice president.

Through luck and circumstance, a constitutional crisis had been averted and the country and the world had its first peaceful transition of power resulting from a democratic, constitutionally organized election.

The Basic Structure

In the remainder of this chapter, we will examine the Bill of Rights and subsequent amendments to the Constitution. Before doing so, however, we should pause for a minute to consider the governmental structure created by the Constitution. As important as the Bill of Rights has been (and the later Fourteenth Amendment), it would not have meant much if the basic architecture of the constitutional system were deeply flawed, as the Articles of Confederation had been. During the ratification debate, *before* a Bill of Rights had been enacted, the Federalists had to convince voters that the Constitution, with its much heightened role for a central government, was not a threat to liberty. Their argument, distilled to its essence and most forcibly advanced in the Federalist Papers, was simply this: Liberty will not be threatened by the new government because no one faction or demagogue will be able to effectively control the machinery of government in such a way as to threaten liberty. It would be protected by the federal nature of constitutional structure in which power is shared between the national and state governments; by the fact that the executive, legislative, and judicial powers of the central government are allocated to three separate "Departments"; by the way that these departments act on each other through the system of checks and balances; and by the additional division of legislative authority into two separate branches, elected at different times and "as little connected with each other as the nature of their common functions and common dependence on the society will admit."[32] To note major checks and balances in the system, consider how Congress's power to impeach the president is divided between the House and Senate, how the president can veto laws passed by Congress but the Congress can override the veto by a two-thirds majority in each house, how the president is given responsibility for negotiating treaties, but the Senate must approve them by a two-thirds majority; how the president is the commander in chief, but only Congress can declare war; and how the president appoints ambassadors and Supreme Court justices but only with the approval of the Senate. Power sharing, of course, is also a key element of the federal system and, in this respect, argued Madison, "The Federal Constitution forms a happy combination. . . . the great and aggregate interests being referred to the national, the local and particular to the State legislatures."[33]

The Framers did not sentimentalize their own society. Indeed, in a passage from *Federalist No. 10*, Madison describes a world not much different from our own: "A zeal for different opinions concerning religion, concerning government and many other points . . . [and] an attachment to different leaders ambitiously contending for pre-eminence and power . . . have, in turn, divided mankind into parties, inflamed them with mutual animosity, and rendered them much more disposed to vex and oppress each other than to cooperate for their common good."[34]

Madison saw a society in which landed, manufacturing, mercantile, and moneyed interests would inevitably clash. He believed that reconciling or containing these "various and interfering interests" as the "principal task of modern legislation," a task that would inevitably involve "the spirit of party and faction in the necessary and ordinary operations of government."[35] Because Madison was not naïve about human nature, he also recognized that even, perhaps particularly, in a republican form of government, an "unjust and interested majority" could hold sway. For Madison, it was "the extent and proper structure of the Union"[36] that would contain these various forces.

We should note also here the views of Justice John Marshall Harlan, whose grandfather also served with great distinction on the Court. Appointed by President Eisenhower in 1955, Harlan saw federalism as the key guarantor of individual liberty, even more important than the enumeration of individual rights.[37] In Harlan's own words: "They [the Framers] staked their faith that liberty would prosper not primarily upon declarations of individual rights but upon the kind of government the Union was to have. And they determined that in a government of divided powers lay the best promise for realizing the free society it was their objective to achieve."[38]

Proposing and Ratifying the Bill of Rights

The constitution that emerged from Philadelphia said little about individual rights beyond providing for a right to trial by jury in criminal cases, forbidding passage of bills of attainder and ex post facto laws, prohibiting suspension of the writ of habeas corpus other than in cases of a rebellion or emergency involving public safety, and forbidding any state from impairing the obligation of contracts. The Bill of Rights was intended to remedy that omission. What if there had been no Bill of Rights? Would we have moved closer to a British system where tradition and custom form such a critical part of the unwritten constitution? Would the importance of the Supreme Court have diminished? Would natural law have played a more significant role in the development of constitutional law? Would we have developed the same robust commitment to freedom of expression and religious freedom? The questions are fascinating but speculative, for the Bill of Rights and the Fourteenth Amendment have created a textually based system of rights whose interpretation forms a major part of American constitutional law.

As the Constitutional Convention drew to a close, George Mason, a Virginia delegate and one of only three who refused in the end to sign the Constitution, had proposed to a weary group of delegates that a committee be appointed to draft a bill of rights. Not a single state voted for the proposal even though Mason assured them that it could be written in a matter of hours—an assurance he could have delivered on since the outline of a bill had already been prepared based on similar sets of guarantees in state constitutions.

The convention's lack of interest in a formal expression of rights—perplexing perhaps from our vantage point—is less so when one considers that the Framers were intent on creating a strong national government, not qualifying its powers. It was the ratifying conventions which exposed that the framers had made a glaring political miscalculation.

After the Constitution was ratified, while most Federalists still thought a Bill of Rights unnecessary or dangerous, they ended up supporting it, while many Anti-Federalists who had argued for a Bill of Rights during ratification, ended up opposing it. Ironically, the Bill of Rights became a defensive political measure, recommended to the states by a Federalist Congress at the behest of James Madison, who viewed it as the most effective way of forestalling a second Constitutional Convention, which he feared would undermine the work of the first one. By the time he began working on the bill, four states, including New York and Virginia, had already called for a second convention. Madison believed that the Bill of Rights "will kill the opposition everywhere, and by putting an end to disaffection to the Government itself, enable the administration to venture on measures not otherwise safe."[39] He also hoped that a Bill of Rights would induce Rhode Island and North Carolina to finally ratify the Constitution (it did).

The Bill of Rights was not just a matter of politics for Madison. Although originally somewhat skeptical of its necessity, he had by June of 1789 become convinced, partly as result of correspondence with Thomas Jefferson, of its wisdom. Madison envisioned a critical role for the judiciary in enforcing the Bill of Rights, arguing that "independent tribunals of justice will consider themselves in a peculiar manner the guardians of those rights" and would form an "impenetrable bulwark"[40] against unwarranted assumptions of legislative or executive power.

In drafting the bill, Madison had a delicate task: make the new national government more palatable to those who feared its power without compromising that power itself. In the process, he and the Congress had to reject proposals from the Anti-Federalists to limit the central government's powers and to subject representatives to instructions from their states. When, for example, Madison proposed the right of the people to peacefully assemble, which is now part of the First Amendment, a South Carolina congressman attempted to add an express right of the people to instruct their representatives in Congress. Congress embraced the right of assembly but rejected the proposal for instruction, because, in the words of Akhil Amar, it "would have completely undermined the Madisonian system of deliberation among refined representatives."[41]

Congress did not accept all of Madison's proposals, including one that would have protected freedom of speech, freedom of the press, religious freedom, and the right to a trial by jury free from *state* interference. Today, most of the rights in the Bill of Rights apply to the states as well as the federal government. How that happened is an important part of constitutional law, one we will address shortly.

Congress also rejected Madison's proposed format for the Bill of Rights. Madison had drafted the amendments as insertions into the text of the Constitution, but Congress ultimately recommended the bill as an intact supplement to the document. This decision was not without significance. First, as a distinct and easily identifiable body of rights, the amendments achieved a collective status they likely would never have had if they had merely been scattered throughout the document. Also, by not being associated with specific portions of the Constitution, the amendments were free to be given a broader interpretation without limiting contexts that might have provided for narrower readings.

Madison saw the greatest danger to the future of liberty as coming not from "either the executive or legislative departments of government, but in the body of the people, operating by the majority against the minority."[42] Madison's fears for the power of an unrestrained majority anticipate important twentieth-century concerns. Madison looked to the Bill of Rights as a way of educating the people about the very rights he most feared they might violate: "It may be thought all paper barriers against the power of the community are too weak to be worthy of attention . . . yet, as they have a tendency to impress some degree of respect for them, to establish the public opinion in their favor, and rouse the attention of the whole community, it may be one means to control the majority from those acts to which they might be otherwise inclined."[43]

Two amendments recommended by Congress to the states were not ratified. One of these amendments was supposed to address the desire of the Anti-Federalists to guarantee a greater number of representatives in the House of Representatives. Anti-Federalists wanted representatives to be bound closely to the people, an outcome they felt would be more likely to occur if there were fewer persons per representative. The proposed amendment would have put a maximum size on congressional districts, at least for a period of time. The amendment failed (by only one state), possibly because of technical deficiencies in its wording. With a national population of more than 300 million people, the modern House of Representatives could have 10,000 representatives without violating the Constitution.[44] Some would argue that the current number is quite enough.

The ratification of the Bill of Rights was not automatic. The Anti-Federalists opposed ratification in many states, as they had in the Congress, because, as Madison had realized, it would mean the end of their effort to secure a second Constitutional Convention. When Vermont became a state in 1790, it meant that eleven states would need to approve the amendments. For various reasons, Connecticut, Georgia, and Massachusetts were not in a position to provide the crucial eleventh vote. Ironically, the issue came down to Virginia where ratification moved easily through the Assembly but was blocked in the Senate where Anti-Federalists still held a majority. Not all Anti-Federalists in the Senate were against the Bill—George Mason, who originally had regarded it with a jaundiced eye, finally supported it. Jefferson lobbied strongly for passage. In the end, the Anti-Federalists realized that they were playing a losing card and even endangering their reputation for honesty—they had, after all, originally argued for a Bill of Rights—and on December 15, 1791, Virginia provided the crucial final approval. It wasn't until 1939 that Massachusetts, Georgia, and Connecticut ratified the amendments as part of the celebration of the 150th anniversary of the Constitution's ratification.

A Brief Summary of the Bill of Rights

The first ten amendments are now collectively referred to as the Bill of Rights. When Madison drafted the Bill of Rights, he had much material to draw from. The ratification conventions themselves had proposed more than seventy-five amendments for consideration, many involving protection of individual rights. In his excellent volume *Origins of the Bill of Rights*,[45] Leonard Levy shows how virtually all of the amendments in the Bill of Rights appear in one or more state constitutions. The garden from which these rights grew was the English common law and such pivotal moments in English history as the Magna Charta, the Petition of Right of 1628, the Habeas Corpus Act of 1679, the Bill of Rights of 1689 and the Toleration Act of 1689. Additionally, there was the experience of the colonies themselves. The Third Amendment, for example, forbidding the quartering of troops in private homes in times of peace, except with the consent of the owner, was a direct outgrowth of British forced quartering during the pre-Revolutionary War period.

The Bill of Rights acts in two general ways to protect the person: it restrains the government from acting arbitrarily in depriving a person of his or her freedom, and it seeks to make sure that a lawfully arrested person has a fair trial. Protection against arbitrary arrest is provided by the Fourth Amendment's guaranty of the rights of the people to be secure in their persons against unreasonable seizures and by the requirement that warrants providing for the seizure of persons be based upon probable cause. Further protection to the person is provided by the Fifth Amendment's requirement of a grand jury indictment before one can be held for a capital "or otherwise infamous crime" (meaning a felony) and by the Eighth Amendment's prohibition of "excessive bail." The grand jury provision was viewed as highly important in the early Republic because it was seen as society's check against a potentially arbitrary government.

The basic principles for a fair trial are set out in the Fifth and Sixth Amendments. The Fifth Amendment provides in part that no person in a criminal case can be compelled to testify as a witness against himself (the right against self-incrimination) and then, suddenly speaks in much more general terms, stating that no person "shall be deprived of life, liberty, or property without due process of law." The Sixth Amendment entitles a defendant to a "speedy and public trial" and "an impartial jury." It also requires defendants to be tried in the state and district where the crimes were committed, to be informed of the charges against them, to have the opportunity to confront witnesses against them and "to have compulsory process for obtaining witnesses in [their] favor, and to have the assistance of counsel for [their] defense." The Fifth and Eighth Amendments round out these criminal process protections by providing that, if convicted, defendants will not be subject to cruel or unusual punishment (Eighth Amendment), and if not convicted, they will not be tried again for the same crime (Fifth Amendment).

So far, the protections we have cited in the Bill of Rights are procedural in nature. They guarantee that people cannot be arrested in the middle of the night and hauled off to prison, never to be heard from again. The Bill of Rights also sought to assure that government would not threaten what were regarded as basic liberties. These provisions have nothing to do with economic fairness or civil rights. That is the stuff of politics. Rather, they constitute a specific set of restraints on government itself. The major restraints are found in (i) the First Amendment, which protects freedom of religion, speech, and the press and prohibits laws "respecting the establishment of religion"; (ii) the Fourth Amendment, which declares the right of the people to be secure in their "persons, houses, papers and effects." against "unreasonable searches and seizures"; (iii) the Fifth Amendment, which provides that a person cannot be deprived of ownership of his or her property, even for public use, "without just compensation."; and (iv) the Second Amendment, which was recently found by the Supreme Court to protect an individual right to gun ownership.[46]

Neither the Ninth nor the Tenth Amendment guarantees specific individual rights. They are not without their importance, however, and because they are so different from the other amendments and have played interesting and contrasting roles in our constitutional development, they deserve a separate discussion. We will, of course, be discussing many of the rights guaranteed by the first eight amendments throughout our text. For the moment, however, let us turn to the final two amendments of the Bill of Rights.

The Ninth and Tenth Amendments

The Ninth and Tenth Amendments are arguably about nothing and everything at the same time. In one view, they add nothing and are merely declaratory of the obvious. In another, they provide a critical understanding of the true nature of our governmental structure and the meaning of the Constitution itself. To add to the confusion, the amendments themselves today are cited by different justices for very different purposes.

The Ninth Amendment and Unenumerated Rights

The Ninth Amendment states: "The enumeration in the Constitution of certain rights shall not be construed to deny or disparage others retained by the people."

Until the Supreme Court in 1965 decided *Griswold v. Connecticut*,[47] which invalidated a Connecticut statute forbidding the use of contraceptives, the Ninth Amendment enjoyed a very long hibernation. Unlike the first Eight Amendments, it didn't seem to do anything—certainly nothing specific. In *Griswold*, Justice Goldberg (writing for himself and Justices Warren and Brennan) referred directly to the Ninth Amendment, among other provisions of the Constitution, in finding a constitutionally protected right of privacy, After *Griswold*, a star was born. Within fifteen years, the amendment was invoked in more than twelve hundred state and federal cases "in the most astonishing variety of matters."[48]

For all the excitement, however, the Court has never directly incorporated an unenumerated right into the Constitution based solely on the Ninth Amendment. Conservative jurists would argue that this is a good thing, reasoning that there is no principled way of identifying unenumerated rights and, since the Constitution is a formal legal document, it is not appropriate in any event to search for rights outside its provisions. Even scholars who would be comfortable linking constitutional with natural rights (rights arising out of humankind's natural state) concede that "no evidence exists to prove that the Framers intended the Ninth Amendment to protect any particular natural rights."[49]

A word of caution is in order here. The term *unenumerated rights* is sometimes used to refer to any rights that are not expressly provided for in the constitutional text, including rights implied or implicit in the text. The term, however, in relation to the Ninth Amendment speaks to rights existing without any necessary relation to the text at all.

In a very early (1798) case, *Calder v. Bull*, Justice Chase seemed to open the door to invalidating legislation based upon unenumerated rights when he wrote that justices should overrule "flagrant abuses of legislative power" that "authorize manifest injustice by positive law."[50] Such a view, had it prevailed, might have led to a much different approach to constitutional interpretation, broadening the foundation for restrictions on the use of government power. However, Justice Iredell, in his opinion in *Calder* (in the early days of the Court each Justice issued his own opinion), expressed deep reservations about such an approach: "The ideas of natural justice are regulated by no fixed standard; the ablest and the purest men have differed upon the subject; and all that the Court could properly say in such an event, would be that the Legislature (possessed of an equal right of opinion) had passed an act which, in the opinion of the judges, was inconsistent with the abstract principles of natural justice."[51] Justice Iredell's view has carried the day although whether a natural rights jurisprudence has entered through the back door of the Fourteenth Amendment, which we will discuss shortly, is a much-debated subject.

Scholarly views on the Ninth Amendment range widely. Charles Black saw in it the vehicle for infusing a broader conception of human rights into the Constitution. Black argued that the Declaration of Independence "commits all the governments in our country to 'securing' for its people certain human rights," and the Ninth Amendment "unmistakably rejects the idea that a human right, to be valid in law, must be enumerated (or explicitly named)."[52] Other scholars, for example Michael Paulsen, simply see in the amendment an assurance that the existence of federal constitutional rights did not negate "state law rights possessed against state governments."[53] Whatever their views, its seems that most scholars and even justices see in the Ninth Amendment what they want to see, depending very much on their larger view of the Constitution and the proper scope of judicial review.

The Tenth Amendment and Federalism

The Tenth Amendment, like the Ninth, is a broad, declaratory statement: "The powers not delegated to the United States by the Constitution, nor prohibited by it to the States, are reserved to the States, respectively, or to the people."

Unlike the Ninth Amendment's long period of neglect, the Tenth Amendment was viewed prior to the Civil War as, in the words of Thomas Jefferson, "the foundation of the Constitution."[54] Every state that had recommended a bill of rights during the ratification controversy asked, among other things, for an amendment along the lines of the Tenth Amendment. Most scholars agree that the major aim of the Tenth Amendment was to clarify that the federal government was one of limited powers and that it had no authority to act beyond those powers.

But the Tenth Amendment did not go as far as it might have. While the Articles of Confederation had provided that each state retained "every power, jurisdiction and right" not "*expressly* delegated to the United States" (my emphasis), the Tenth Amendment dropped the word *expressly*. Had the Tenth Amendment retained for the states and the people every power other than those *expressly* delegated to the national government, the concept of implied powers might have been more difficult to defend.

After the Civil War, as the scope of the national government grew in importance, the Court was less and less willing to view the Tenth Amendment as a barrier to broad federal regulatory legislation. Thus, most of the federal legislation enacted during the post–Civil War and Progressive Eras, including the Sherman Act, the Interstate Commerce Act, the Meat Inspection Act, and the Food and Drug Act, withstood constitutional challenges. It came as something of a surprise, then, when the Supreme Court, in 1918, held a federal child labor law unconstitutional, relying in part on the Tenth Amendment.[55] Interestingly, the Court in its decision incorrectly imported the word *expressly* into the Tenth Amendment, when it asserted that "to the [states] and to the people the powers not *expressly* delegated to the National Government are reserved" (my emphasis).[56] In 1941, a unanimous Court overruled its 1918 decision; Justice Harlan Fiske Stone, a Coolidge appointee soon to be elevated to chief justice by Franklin Roosevelt, noted in his opinion for the Court that the Tenth Amendment was nothing "more than declaratory of the relationship between the national and state governments as it had been established by the Constitution before the amendment."[57]

Justice Stone's statement was made at a time when the Supreme Court's embrace of national power was at its apex. Today the scope of national legislative power is once again contested, and the Tenth Amendment is cited by those who wish to limit federal power in a particular instance. Indeed, in the early 1990s, more than fifteen states passed resolutions proclaiming the continued importance and relevance of the Tenth Amendment. However, even Justice Scalia has described the Tenth Amendment as "redundant because it is clear under the original Constitution that the Federal Government is a government of specified powers, and that unless those powers have been affirmatively granted to the Federal Government, they automatically remain with the States."[58]

The Other Seventeen Amendments

Since 1789 we have had 44 presidents and 111 justices of the Supreme Court, but only 17 amendments to the Constitution. Some of the most important strands of American history are interwoven with the history of our constitutional amendments. Most significant are the Reconstruction Period amendments (Thirteen through Fifteen) intended to provide constitutional protection for the newly freed slaves. We will have more to say about these amendments shortly. Another important amendment was the Eleventh. Originally intended simply to overrule a Supreme Court decision, it has become over time an important vehicle for debating the rights of the states versus the federal government. It too will receive closer examination.

Most of the other amendments, while important historically, are clear in their meaning and effect and have produced little constitutional controversy. The success and failure of the temperance movement, for example, is reflected in the Eighteenth (1919) and Twenty-first (1933) Amendments, creating and then ending the national experiment with Prohibition. The story of our income tax structure begins with the Sixteenth Amendment (1913) which effectively overruled an earlier Supreme Court decision that had rendered a progressive income tax a practical impossibility.[59] The Twentieth Amendment (1933), which changed the date of the president's inauguration from early March to mid-January and shortened the lame-duck session of Congress, aimed at preventing governmental paralysis at crucial times. The Twenty-fifth Amendment (1967), which established processes for dealing with presidential disability or resignation, followed the murder of President Kennedy.

If there is one overall theme, however, to many of the twentieth-century amendments, it is the widening reach of popular democracy: the Seventeenth Amendment (1913) provided for the direct election of senators (formerly they had been chosen by the state legislatures); the Nineteenth Amendment (1920) extended the right to vote to women (overturning an earlier Supreme Court decision denying that women had been given the right to vote by the Citizenship and the Privileges and Immunities clauses of the Fourteenth Amendment)[60]; the Twenty-third Amendment (1961) extended the franchise in presidential elections to residents of the District of Columbia; the Twenty-fourth Amendment (1964) prohibited the poll tax; and the Twenty-sixth Amendment (1971) extended the right to vote to persons eighteen years of age or older. Only one amendment, the Twenty-second (1951), takes power from the people since it prevents them from electing the same person for president more than twice.

We conclude this chapter with a discussion of the Eleventh, Thirteenth, and Fifteenth Amendments. Because of its pivotal importance in constitutional law, we will devote a separate chapter to the Fourteenth Amendment.

The Eleventh Amendment and Sovereign Immunity

In its first major case, *Chisholm v. Georgia*,[61] the Supreme Court, in 1793, exercised its original jurisdiction in a manner many found shocking and dangerous, entering a default judgment against the State of Georgia in a suit brought by a citizen of South Carolina. Georgia had refused to appear in the case on the ground that a state could not be sued by the citizen of another state in federal court. In *Chisholm*, both Chief Justice Jay and Justice Wilson expressed real skepticism as to the continuing vitality of the notion of state sovereignty within the new constitutional structure. The case raised all the old anxieties about central government power. Within two years of the decision, the Eleventh Amendment reversing Chisholm and insulating states from such suits was ratified.

The Eleventh Amendment posed a major problem for Chief Justice Marshall, an ardent proponent of national power, after he ascended to the Court in 1801. In the words of John V. Orth, " the Eleventh Amendment, by limiting the jurisdiction of the national courts, inhibited judicial power and thereby endangered the dearest tenets of the Federalist faith. If the Court had no jurisdiction over suits against states, it had no jurisdiction in such cases to decide even questions of constitutionality."[62]

Not surprisingly, Marshall's Court construed the Eleventh Amendment narrowly, so narrowly in fact that only once in Marshall's long tenure did the justices accept a claim of immunity based on the Eleventh Amendment.[63] We will shortly see Marshall's creativity at work in the famous case of

Marbury v. Madison, but *Marbury* wasn't the only case in which Marshall's nationalist impulse was evident. In *Osborn v. United States Bank*,[64] Marshall negotiated the shoals of the Eleventh Amendment, as he saw it, by drawing a distinction between a state officer and the state itself. The state officer, Marshall argued, did not share in the state's immunity because the state could not validly authorize an act contrary to the Constitution, and therefore any unconstitutional act had to be the act of an individual. Marshall also relied on the simple fact that an officer of the state was not the state itself; consequently, so as long as the litigation caption did not include the state as an entity, the Eleventh Amendment, according to Marshall, did not apply. *Osborn* opened the way for suits to enjoin state officials from pursuing various actions on the ground that those actions were unconstitutional because they were either a direct violation of a constitutional provision or the source of the official's authority was an unconstitutional state statute.

After the Civil War, the nation faced a new set of challenges. The Compromise of 1877, which resolved the contested presidential election of 1876, elevated Rutherford B. Hayes, a Republican, to the presidency over Samuel Tilden, the Democrat, in return for the withdrawal of federal troops from the former Confederate states. The compromise set the stage for the restoration of white supremacy in the South. During Reconstruction, many southern states, when in the control of freedmen and their supporters, had issued bonds to support social efforts on behalf of the freed slaves. After 1877, southern state governments, once again controlled by plantation aristocrats, had no intention of paying these bonds. Matters came to a head in *Louisiana ex rel. Elliot v. Jumel*,[65] when an out-of-state bondholder sought a court order requiring the state auditor of Louisiana to pay the interest due on certain Louisiana bonds. Under *Osborn*, the case would have been allowed to proceed but times had changed; the country had reconciled itself to the South's insistence on going its own way. Under these circumstances, it is not surprising that the Court simply ignored its *Osborn* precedent and refused to grant the bondholders relief. Chief Justice Waite laid out what the Court claimed was its real predicament: "The remedy sought, in order to be complete, would require the Court to assume all the executive authority of the State . . . and to supervise the conduct of all persons charged with any official duty in respect to the levy, collection, and disbursement of the tax in question until the bonds . . . were paid in full. . . . *It needs no argument to show that the political power cannot be thus ousted of its jurisdiction and the judiciary set in its place*" (my emphasis).[66] Notice here how the highlighted language presents essentially a structuralist argument, namely, that it is simply not part of the Court's role in the constitutional structure to assume the degree of executive authority that would be needed to redress the plaintiff's alleged injury.

The Eleventh Amendment applies by its terms only to suits by out-of-state citizens against a state in federal court. In other words, it applies only to something called *diversity jurisdiction*, which we will be discussing shortly. A related but very separate question was whether a citizen of a state could sue his or her own state in federal court on a question of federal law. The answer came in 1890 in *Hans v. Louisiana*,[67] yet another bond case; this time a Louisiana resident was suing his state for reneging on interest payments on its bonds. In *Hans*, Justice Bradley writing for a unanimous Court once again held for Louisiana. How did he reach this result in the face of the narrowly drawn language of the Eleventh Amendment? Here we have to introduce a new concept, *sovereign immunity*, into the discussion. Sovereign immunity refers to the inherent right of the sovereign to be free from lawsuits without its consent. It arose from English common law and embodied the idea that, since the courts owed their existence to the sovereign (i.e., the king or queen), the sovereign could not be held to account in them. In *Chisholm*, several justices of the Court had argued that there was no sovereign immunity to which the states were entitled when it came to the exercise of the national judicial power. One hundred years later, Justice Bradley in *Hans* wrote that the decision in *Chisholm* had been wrong and that the Eleventh Amendment would not have been necessary at all if the Court had realized that sovereign immunity did apply to the states, that the states had not given up that immunity when the Constitution was ratified, and that a state therefore could not be sued in federal court without its consent even by its own citizens, not because of the Eleventh Amendment, but because of its inherent right to be free from such suits.

By 1890, the states could take comfort from decisions apparently insulating them from suit in federal court. The old notion, however, of a distinction between the state and its officers had never been repudiated, and not surprisingly, a conservative Supreme Court returned to this idea once again when broader federal jurisdiction appeared in the interest of the business community. As the Progressive era unfolded, many politically conservative justices on the Court were alarmed at some of the state social legislation enacted by reform-minded legislatures. Consequently, the last thing this Court wanted to do was prevent challenges by business to these progressive measures. The Court came full circle in 1908 in *Ex Parte Young*,[68] when it allowed the railroad interests to challenge in federal court a Minnesota statute that had mandated a reduction in railroad rates, with severe penalties for violators. The Court allowed the suit to proceed against the state officer charged with enforcing the Minnesota statute on the ground that such an officer, when seeking to enforce an unconstitutional statute, "is in that case stripped of his official or representative character and is subjected in his person to the consequences of his individual conduct."[69] In this case, the Court issued an injunction enjoining the state officer from enforcing the rate reduction mandated by the new law.

The issue of federal jurisdiction over states has continued to be contested. In 1974, the Supreme Court, in a 5–4 decision, limited the reach of *Ex Parte Young*, when it held that the Eleventh Amendment protected a state against liability for retroactive payments allegedly due under a federal program that the state was administering and had voluntarily participated in.[70] More recently, the Court in *Seminole Tribe of Florida v. Florida*[71] extended the reasoning of *Hans* to prohibit a federal court from hearing a federal *statutory* claim (*Hans* had dealt with a constitutional claim) against a state without its consent, and then in *Alden v. Maine*[72] to prohibit a *state court* from hearing a federal statutory claim against a state.

Interestingly, both *Alden* and *Seminole Tribe* were decided 5–4, with the so-called liberal bloc of Souter, Ginsburg, Stevens, and Breyer in dissent each time. Though no longer the kind of issue galvanizing public attention, questions of federal jurisdiction and state sovereignty have clearly retained their ideological character. With the Constitution providing no textual guidance as to how these cases are to be resolved and history, in the words of William Marshall, "sufficiently ambiguous to support numerous theories of state immunity,"[73] we see in these recent cases the subtle ways in which political and legal convictions converge. Not every issue that supposedly divides liberals and conservatives in the political world finds an analogue in the constitutional sphere, but it is generally fair to say that justices classified as liberal tend to support national power over states' rights and, perhaps paradoxically, individual rights over assertions of community morality or government power, particularly in the area of criminal procedure.

If the story of the Eleventh Amendment tells us nothing else, it shows how the Court's view of the Constitution and its own precedents is inseparable from the perceived needs and perspectives of its own time.

The Thirteenth and Fifteenth Amendments

In the wake of the Civil War, three amendments to the Constitution were proposed by Congress and then ratified, each at slightly different times, each the outcome of very different political dynamics. Given its immense importance, our primary focus will be on the Fourteenth Amendment, which we will discuss in the next chapter, but we should not completely neglect the other two amendments.

The Thirteenth Amendment

The Thirteenth Amendment (1865) declares that neither slavery nor involuntary servitude shall exist in the United States. It made the Emancipation Proclamation a constitutional reality for the entire nation, not just the Confederate states to which the Proclamation had, by its terms, applied. First considered by Congress in 1864, it was not formally recommended to the states until the Republican majorities in Congress were increased following the election of 1864. The Thirteenth Amendment also gave Congress the power, as did all the post–Civil War amendments, to "enforce this article by appropriate legislation."

Congress wasted little time in exercising that enforcement power, enacting the Civil Rights Act of 1866. A key provision of the act proclaimed that all citizens of the United States had the same rights as white citizens to "inherit, purchase, lease, sell, hold and convey real and personal property." In 1968, in *Jones v. Alfred H. Mayer Co.*,[74] the Supreme Court determined that "appropriate" legislation authorized under the Thirteenth Amendment included legislation prohibiting all racial discrimination, private or public, in the sale or rental of housing. The Court was, in effect, reversing an 1883 decision of the Court known as the Civil Rights Cases, which held that a provision of the Civil Rights Act of 1875 barring racial discrimination in public accommodations was unconstitutional because the Thirteenth Amendment did not authorize Congress to prohibit private acts of racial discrimination. In the Civil Rights Cases, the Supreme Court, reflecting the spirit of the times, held that private racial discrimination was not a badge of slavery or involuntary servitude and therefore Congress had no authority to prohibit it pursuant to its enforcement powers under the Thirteenth Amendment.[75] As already noted, by 1883, much of the country had lost interest in protecting the rights of Southern blacks. Parenthetically, the final gesture to the South, if one was needed, came with the 1888 appointment of

L. Q. C. Lamar to the Supreme Court by Grover Cleveland. Lamar, born into plantation aristocracy in 1825, had drafted the Mississippi Ordinance of Secession and served in the Confederate army; he was confirmed in a close Senate vote.

By the late 1960s, a much different atmosphere prevailed. Millions of people had been energized over the struggle for civil rights. It was inevitable in this new climate that an attempt would be made to revisit the Court's earlier decision limiting the reach of the Thirteenth Amendment. The lawsuit in *Jones v. Mayer* was brought by an interested homebuyer alleging that a white owner's refusal to sell his home to him because he was black violated the Civil Rights Act of 1866. In upholding the black homebuyer's position that the 1866 Act was "appropriate" enforcement legislation, Justice Stewart's majority opinion took a much different view of the Thirteenth Amendment than had the 1883 Court: "And when racial discrimination herds men into ghettos and makes their ability to buy property turn on the color of their skin, then it too is a relic of slavery. . . . At the very least, the freedom that Congress is empowered to secure under the 13th Amendment includes the freedom to buy whatever a white man can buy, the right to live wherever a white man can live."[76]

Again, as with the Eleventh Amendment, we can see different times bringing forth very different responses from the Court.

The Fifteenth Amendment

The Fifteenth Amendment (1870) outlaws racial discrimination by both the states and the federal government against all citizens exercising their right to vote. It was intended to extend the right to vote to the newly emancipated slaves. Once, however, national support for enforcement of this right waned, discriminatory practices and outright intimidation became the norm. By the turn of the century, few blacks were able to vote in Southern states. The Supreme Court made no effort to reverse these practices, and in *Giles v. Harris*,[77] it implicitly declared the Fifteenth Amendment unenforceable. The concluding passage of the Court's opinion, written by Justice Holmes, is remarkable for its admission that given the extent of white hostility, the amendment simply could not be enforced in the South: "Unless we are prepared to supervise the voting in that State by officers of the court, it seems to us that all that plaintiff could get from equity would be an empty form. Apart from damages to the individual, relief from a great political wrong, if done, as alleged, by the people of a State and the State itself, must be given by them or by the legislative and political department of the government of the United States."[78]

You may have noted in this quote a reference to *equity* jurisdiction. Equity refers to the kind of relief where a court orders something be done, or refrain from being done, as distinct from simply awarding money damages. Holmes, of course, is stating in this passage that whatever the Court might order, the political reality was that blacks would not be allowed to vote unless the Court supervised all the voting in the state, something it was not prepared to do. Ultimately, of course, it was only when the political branches enacted the Voting Rights Act of 1965, with its tough enforcement and registration provisions, that blacks became able to vote in large numbers in the South.

In the pre–Civil War South, you risked your life if you advocated the abolition of slavery or wrote anything that could create discontent among slaves. You were also violating the law since most Southern states prohibited this kind of speech. Southern states even passed laws "requiring postmasters to rifle the mail" in search of antislavery material.[79] These laws were not unconstitutional because in 1833 in *Barron v. Baltimore*,[80] Chief Justice Marshall, writing for a unanimous Court, had held that the first eight amendments to the Bill of Rights applied to federal actions but not to actions of the states. For Marshall the historical evidence was clear: the Bill of Rights addressed fears of central government power, not state power. Most scholars have concluded that Marshall's reading was correct.[81]

Today, most rights set forth in the Bill of Rights now also bind the states. What happened to cause this change? What happened was the Civil War, the emancipation of the slaves, and the enactment of the Fourteenth Amendment, the subject to which we now turn.

3. The Fourteenth Amendment

The Text

The first sentence of the Fourteenth Amendment provides that "All persons born or naturalized in the United States and subject to the jurisdiction thereof, are citizens of the United States and the State wherein they reside." It nullified the infamous *Dred Scott* decision, which had held that blacks could never be citizens under the Constitution. It is also the basis of what is often referred to as "birthright" citizenship since, as a result of the Supreme Court's decision in *U.S. v. Wong Kim Ark*,[1] any child born in this country, including a child born to undocumented immigrants, is automatically a United States citizen.

As important as the first sentence of Section 1 may be, it is the second sentence, prohibiting the abridgement of privileges and immunities of citizenship and promising due process and the equal protection of the law, which has dominated the constitutional landscape for almost a century and a half. It reads: "No State shall make or enforce any law which shall abridge *the privileges or immunities* of citizens of the United States; nor shall any State deprive any person of life, liberty or property, without *due process of law*; nor deny to any person within its jurisdiction the *equal protection of the laws*" (my emphasis). The highlighted concepts have been the battleground for our most deeply held convictions about the Constitution and its practical meaning for our everyday lives. The same guarantee of liberty in the Due Process clause, for example, that once was found by the Supreme Court to prevent a state from enacting a law limiting the number of hours a baker could work[2] now is seen as protecting against state regulation of private sexual conduct.[3]

Ironically, the guarantee of due process in the Fourteenth Amendment, so important today, drew little attention in the congressional debates over the amendment. As one member declared, it was "so just that no member of this House can seriously object to it."[4] Perhaps even more surprisingly, the former Confederate states did not object to it and, instead, were much more focused on Sections 2 and 3 of the amendment that, in the case of Section 2, would reduce the size of the congressional representation of any state that denied males over the age of twenty-one the right to vote, and in the case of Section 3, excluded high Confederate officials who had previously served in Congress or the U.S. military from subsequently holding state or federal office. These provisions were regarded, among other things, as insults to Southern honor and helped lead to the initial rejection of the amendment by the unreconstructed Southern state governments. In one sense, the South need not have worried, for the provision reducing a state's congressional representation if it denied blacks the vote was simply never enforced. It serves as a good reminder that words, even in a constitution, can mean nothing if the political realities dictate ignoring them.

Proposal and Ratification

Like the Bill of Rights, enactment of the Fourteenth Amendment was very much part of the political strategy of the dominant party at the time. Andrew Johnson, a pro-Southern Democrat with little feeling for the plight of the freed slaves, was now in the White House following Lincoln's assassination, and the congressional elections of 1866 would be crucial to the future success of the Republican Party as well as the future course of Reconstruction. The final draft of the amendment, crafted in the shadow of that election, was a compromise worked out in a Republican Senate caucus. In the words of one historian, "Faced by the practical reality of a political struggle for survival in the congressional elections of 1866, the Republicans had closed ranks and agreed on what they considered to be a platform on which they could all stand in that test of political strength."[5]

The need for an amendment seemed clear once the Southern states began passing so-called black codes aimed at restoring white supremacy. Under the Mississippi code, for example, any black who left his job before his labor contract expired was subject to arrest by any white citizen. In South Carolina, a black could not pursue any occupation other than farming or service, except by paying an annual tax. In some states, judges could bind a black child to a white employer if the child's parents were deemed unable to support him or her.[6] In the words of Eric Foner: "Arrested by white sheriffs, tried before white judges and juries, blacks understandably had little confidence in the courts of Presidential Reconstruction."[7]

Passing the Fourteenth Amendment was crucial for the Republicans because, unlike congressional legislation that can subsequently be repealed by a majority vote of Congress, repeal of a constitutional amendment, as you may recall, would require the approval of two-thirds of the House and Senate and three-quarters of the states. And at that time, Southern states were poised to gain power in Congress as a direct result of the freeing of the slaves, since each of them would now count as a full person—not three-fifths of one—in calculating a state's population for representation purposes in the House of Representatives.

The Fourteenth Amendment did not guarantee black voting rights. While Northern sentiment reacted strongly against the black codes, the overall sentiment in the country was not in favor of insisting on black political rights. Even in the North, blacks could vote in only a few New England states, and when it appeared in early 1866 that Congress might be prepared to grant blacks the vote in the District of Columbia, the local city council held a referendum on the idea—the vote was 6,591 against, to 35 in favor of the proposal.[8]

The Republican strategy worked. As a result of the 1866 congressional election, the Republicans dominated both the House and the Senate, controlling 39 of 50 Senate seats and 145 of 191 House seats,[9] but they still had a thorny problem. While the Southern delegations had not been readmitted to Congress, theoretically the Southern states had never left the Union since the Union was not dissolvable, so arguably the votes of the former Confederate States were needed for ratification to occur. Congress solved this problem by making passage of the Fourteenth Amendment a condition for readmission of the Southern representatives into Congress.

While the amendment must be seen as a political response to the needs of its times, its broad phrases—"privileges and immunities" "due process of law" and "equal protection of laws"—speak to ideals that go beyond the immediate problems of race. "This broad language opened the door for future Congresses and the federal courts to breathe broader meaning into the guarantee of legal equality, a process that has occupied the courts for much of the twentieth century."[10]

With its huge majorities, the Republican Congress passed the Reconstruction Acts of 1867, which divided the South into five military districts. Each district was commanded by a major general with extraordinary powers. The reconstructed state governments, elected with the support of blacks now participating in the political process, ratified the Fourteenth Amendment by comfortable margins.

You might be wondering how the Fifteenth Amendment outlawing racial discrimination in voting passed just a few years later when a guarantee of black voting rights couldn't even be written into the Fourteenth Amendment. The answer again is politics. The Fifteenth Amendment was intended to assure continued Republican hegemony in the South and also to help Republicans in some of the Northern states where black support could be crucial in close elections. Grant's election to the presidency in 1868 as a Republican had been close, particularly in the popular vote in key states; the Republican majority hoped to solidify its hold by virtue of the amendment. The Republicans had just enough support to assure ratification notwithstanding that the Democratic Party stood firmly against it.

Let us now focus on the Fourteenth Amendment's key provisions.

The Privileges and Immunities Clause

We begin with the portion of Section 1 that prohibits states from abridging the "privileges or immunities of citizens of the United States." If constitutional provisions could speak, undoubtedly this one would say, "I could've been a contender." And it would be right, for the Privileges and Immunities clause had destiny written all over it. The historical evidence seems clear that the drafters of the Fourteenth Amendment thought that this provision, perhaps more than any other portion of the Fourteenth Amendment, would secure fundamental rights to all citizens of the United States.

The reason that the drafters made this assumption arose in part from the fact that the term *privileges and immunities* had already been interpreted broadly. Article IV of the Constitution also contains a privileges and immunities clause ("The Citizens of each State shall be entitled to all Privileges and Immunities of the citizens of the several states") which prior to the Civil War had been interpreted by one Supreme Court justice, Bushrod Washington (George Washington's nephew), to encompass, as a matter of right, "Protection by the government; the enjoyment of life and liberty, with the right to acquire and possess property of every kind, and to pursue and obtain happiness and safety; subject nevertheless to such restraints as the government may justly prescribe for the general good of the whole."[11] The drafters of the Fourteenth Amendment were aware of this interpretation, for it was referred to often during the debates on the amendment. For Senator Howard, the floor manager of the bill in the Senate, the privileges and immunities guaranteed by the amendment were so broad in scope that "they are not and cannot be fully defined in their entire extent and precise nature"[12]—and included not only the Article IV privileges and immunities but all of the rights contained in the Bill of Rights as well.

The Privileges and Immunities clause, despite its potential, was immediately enfeebled by a Supreme Court decision defining privileges and immunities so narrowly as to make the guarantee of their protection practically meaningless.[13] The decision, known as the *Slaughterhouse Cases*,[14] involved a claim by the white butchers of New Orleans that their right to earn a livelihood had been violated by a municipal ordinance that required all butchering to be done at one central location by a specially chartered corporation that enjoyed monopoly status. Justice Samuel Miller, a Lincoln appointee, writing for the majority in a 5–4 decision, asserted that recognizing the right to earn a livelihood as a privilege protected by the amendment would "constitute this court a perpetual censor upon all legislation of the states, on the civil rights of their own citizens."[15] Justice Miller asserted that privileges and immunities in the clause referred only to the rights of national citizenship, thus limiting their scope to things like access to the federal capital and protection on the high seas. In a famous dissent, Justice Stephen Field, also a Lincoln appointee, argued that the Fourteenth Amendment had intentionally obliterated the distinction between state and national citizenship and therefore Justice Miller's fear that the national judiciary would become the "censor" of all state legislation affecting civil rights was in some sense the very object of the amendment.

The *Slaughterhouse Cases* were followed just a couple of years later by a second decision that left no doubt that the concept of national citizenship had effectively rendered the Privileges and Immunities clause useless as a source of black rights. *United States v. Cruikshank*[16] arose from the infamous 1873 Colfax Massacre when black freedmen unsuccessfully attempted to defend Colfax, Louisiana, a rural county seat, against seizure by a white militia. Their failure and the mass slaughter that followed, including the massacre of more than fifty blacks who had lain down their arms under a flag of surrender, is a low point in American history. Three white men indicted in the lynching of two blacks were eventually charged under federal law for conspiring to deny blacks their constitutional right to peacefully assemble. Remarkably, Chief Justice Waite, writing for a unanimous Court, held that, while the indictment might have been sufficient had it alleged that the lynched blacks were assembling to petition Congress for a redress of grievances since that was a right of national citizenship, the indictment was flawed because it simply alleged violation of the right to peacefully assemble. The result was the outright dismissal of the indictments on the ground that the charges did not allege violations of federal rights. Without the protection of the federal courts, meaningful enforcement of black rights was stillborn. For those seeking to assemble a list of ten worst Supreme Court decisions, this case would rank high on any number of counts.

The Equal Protection Clause

The Equal Protection clause forbids any state from denying to any person within its jurisdiction the equal protection of the laws, but what precisely does that mean? After all, most laws discriminate in one way or another. Lines must be drawn. Sixteen-year-olds may have to go to school, but not seventeen-year-olds; lawyers and doctors must be licensed, but not cashiers; some goods are subject to import tax, others are not; a business with 50 employees may be subject to a regulation that is not imposed on a business with 5 employees. The list is literally endless. A statute that treats sixteen-year-olds differently than seventeen-year-olds is said to have created a classification based on age; licensing statutes create classifications based on occupation. And so on.

Over the years, the Supreme Court has developed a framework for evaluating Equal Protection cases. Most classifications are subject to what is called the rational basis test. Under this test, if the legislation in question is *rationally related to a legitimate governmental objective*, it passes the test and is constitutional. Some classifications, however, most importantly those based on race, are called "suspect" and are subject to strict scrutiny. Under the strict scrutiny test, a classification will only be deemed constitutional if it is based upon a *compelling governmental objective and is drawn as narrowly as possible to meet that objective.* Laws impairing fundamental rights are also subject to strict scrutiny. The strict scrutiny test is difficult but not impossible to meet. We will see the test in action in Chapter 11 when we discuss a major affirmative action case. In recent years, an intermediate standard, somewhere between rational basis and strict scrutiny, has developed for certain classifications, most notably classifications based on gender. *A law that treats men and women differently must be for an important (i.e., less than compelling but more than legitimate) interest and must be crafted narrowly (but not necessarily as narrowly as possible) to meet its objective.*

We should note here that legislation, even under the rational basis standard, is vulnerable when it simply reflects animus against a disfavored group. This is the teaching of *Romer v. Evans*[17] in which the Supreme Court overturned a Colorado law, enacted by referendum, which would have prohibited the passage of future legislation (and automatically repealed existing ordinances) protecting gays against discrimination. The Court found that the legislation had no justification other than dislike of gay persons. Earlier, in *United States Department of Agriculture v. Moreno*,[18] the Court had found that an amendment to the federal food stamp program that would have made ineligible any household in which a nonrelative lived was also irrational since it would affect only those persons so desperately in need of aid that they could not alter their living arrangements so as to retain their eligibility. The legislation had in fact been aimed at discouraging the creation of communes and reflected a dislike of hippie culture.

While scholars debate the appropriateness of levels of scrutiny, they seem to make basic sense. In the words of Justice Brennan, "The use of different levels of scrutiny proclaims that on some occasions official power must justify itself in a way that otherwise it need not."[19]

How the Equal Protection clause has been interpreted by the Court over time is a complex and fascinating subject. There is little doubt, however, as to its initial purpose. In the words of Michael Klarman, "the dominant intention of the Fourteenth Amendment's drafters" was "to protect blacks in the exercise of fundamental rights, rather than to wholly proscribe race-conscious governmental decision making (or even more narrowly, to forbid purposeful racial discrimination)."[20]

The fact that the language of the Equal Protection clause is broader than its historical objective has created a clear ideological division in the modern Court. It is between those, like Justice Scalia, to whom all racial classifications are constitutionally impermissible, and others, like his good friend Justice Ginsburg, to whom the amendment's historical focus means that sometimes, and within appropriate limitations, blacks may be constitutionally favored over whites. We will defer the rest of our discussion to Chapter 11 when we see the Justices at work debating this issue. There is, however, one additional aspect of the Equal Protection clause (also applicable to the Due Process clause) that requires our attention and also marks an important chapter in the development of constitutional law.

The Fourteenth Amendment declares that "no State" shall deny the equal protection of laws. On its face, therefore, it does not apply to the action of private individuals, nor does it apply by its terms to the federal government, though the Court has interpreted it to apply to the federal government as well.[21]

The Court's very strict reading of this provision had serious consequences for the enforcement of black rights following the Civil War and ultimately helped pave the way for the emergence of a segregated South that would not be dismantled for another 100 years. Two cases in particular dealing with the state action requirement mark the abandonment of black rights by the Court.

As previously mentioned, in 1883, the Court, in the Civil Rights Cases,[22] struck down the Civil Rights Act of 1875 prohibiting racial discrimination in places of public accommodation. The basis of the Court's 8–1 decision was that the Fourteenth Amendment did not give Congress the power to prohibit purely private discrimination. Among the unintentionally ironic assertions Justice Bradley made in his majority opinion was that "there must be some stage in his [a former slave's] elevation when he takes the rank of a mere citizen, and ceases to be the special favorite of the laws." Given the violence and fear to which he was continually subjected, it must have come as quite a shock to the southern black man of 1883 to learn that he was the "special favorite of the laws." The first Justice Harlan's lone dissent condemned the Court for ignoring the realities of state involvement: "In every material sense applicable to the practical enforcement of the 14th Amendment, railroad corporations, keepers of inns, and managers of places of public amusement are agents or instrumentalities of the State, because they are charged with duties to the public, and are amenable with respect of their duties and functions, to governmental regulation."[23] Parenthetically, I would note that after Congress in 1964 passed the Public Accommodations Act aimed at the same discriminatory conduct as the 1875 law, the act was unanimously upheld by the Court, not on the basis of the Fourteenth Amendment, but on the basis of Congress's power over interstate commerce.[24] The second case underscoring the Court's retreat on black rights was *United States v. Harris*,[25] where the Court in 1883 held unconstitutional certain provisions of the Civil Rights Act of 1871 (the Ku Klux Klan Act) criminalizing private acts of violence. A group of white Tennesseans had attacked and killed a black man while he was held in the custody of the sheriff, but the Court again found the federal act beyond the scope of the Fourteenth Amendment because it addressed private, not state-sponsored, acts.

Just as these cases narrowly defining state action marked the Supreme Court's tacit acceptance of segregation and the denial of black rights, so too did a later series of voting rights decisions broadening the view of state action under the Fifteenth Amendment prefigure the Court's growing discomfort with the South's suppression of black rights. This series of cases culminated in 1953 in *Terry v. Adams*. For 50 years, a county political association known as the Jaybird Democratic Association had endorsed candidates for county office through what was essentially a straw vote. Blacks were excluded from the association and therefore played no part in the straw vote. Selection in the Jaybird straw vote was tantamount to selection in the primary and general election, but there was no direct involvement by the state in the straw vote. Nevertheless, the Court refused to accept what was clearly a process designed to deny blacks the right to participate in the electoral process. Justice Clark, in an opinion joined by Chief Justice Vinson, Justice Reed, and Justice Jackson, wrote: "When a State structures its electoral process in a form which devolves upon a political organization the uncontested choice of public officials, that organization itself, in whatever disguise, takes on those attributes of government which draw the Constitution's safeguards into play." The Court's more aggressive attitude respecting black rights was also clearly evident in the case of *Shelley v. Kraemer*,[26] in which the Court held that judicial enforcement of racially restrictive covenants itself constituted state action sufficient to trigger a violation of the Equal Protection clause.

It is not always easy to determine when the nexus between state involvement and private discrimination is sufficient to create a Fourteenth Amendment violation. The issue can arise in many contexts. Electric utility companies, for example, are closely regulated by governmental authorities, in part because the electrical services they supply are so important to homes and businesses and in part because they have been granted in many instances partial monopolies. Does that mean that the public utility is engaging in state action when it terminates electrical service? In *Jackson v. Metropolitan Edison Co.*,[27] the Court said no, but the cases in this area are characterized by a degree of confusion that suggests just how difficult these determinations can be. Justice Tom Clark—a Truman appointee who resigned from the Court to avoid the appearance of a conflict of interest when his son, Ramsey, was appointed Attorney General by Lyndon Johnson—acknowledged this difficulty when he wrote in *Burton v. Wilmington Parking Authority*[28] that "to fashion and apply a precise formula for recognition of state responsibility . . . [is] an impossible task. . . . Only by sifting facts and weighing circumstances can the non-obvious involvement of the State in private conduct be attributed its true significance."[29]

I would not want to leave this subject without quoting the words of Laurence Tribe, which capture both the tragedy of the Fourteenth

Amendment's history in the area of race relations and the case for a broader reading of the state-action requirement: "particularly where ostensibly 'private' power is the primary source of the coercion and violence that oppressed individuals and groups experience, it is hard to accept with equanimity a rigid legal distinction between state and society. The pervasive system of racial apartheid which existed in the South for a century after the Civil War, for example, only thrived because of the 'resonance of society and politics . . . the close fit between private terror, public discrimination, and political exclusion.'"[30]

No series of cases underscores more emphatically this link between state and society than the trials and convictions of the Scottsboro boys, a group of black teenage boys unjustly accused of raping two white women in northern Alabama in 1931. Tried in an atmosphere of outright intimidation created by angry mobs surrounding the courthouse, the jurors themselves might have been lynched had they returned anything but guilty verdicts, not that there was any danger of such a verdict being rendered by the all-white jury. The story of the Scottsboro Boys has been dramatically retold by historian James Goodman in *Stories of Scottsboro*, one of the books recommended in Suggestions for Further Reading.

Procedural Due Process

Unlike substantive due process, which we will discuss in a moment, no one doubts that the Fourteenth Amendment guarantees a person procedural due process. The amendment, after all, speaks only in procedural terms, providing that a person may not be deprived of "life, liberty, or property without due process of law." The essentials of procedural due process are well established—proper notice and, if a hearing or trial is involved, an unbiased decision-maker unafraid to render whatever decision is properly called for and a hearing that adequately allows for the gathering, full and fair presentation, and questioning of the evidence by both sides.

It is one thing to outline the prerequisites of due process; it is another to fill in the details. The requirement of notice, for example, is hardly the stuff of newspaper headlines, but notice is extremely important, for how can somebody take action to protect oneself against an action one doesn't know about? On the other hand, persons sometimes know that they are about to be sued and deliberately avoid being personally served with the appropriate papers. Consequently, legislatures and courts must wrestle with what constitutes adequate substitute notice when persons deliberately avoid, or are simply unavailable, to be served. In criminal law, notice takes on a different but equally important sense, for criminal laws that are not clearly written may not put a person on adequate notice that his or her actions violate the law. Thus, sometimes criminal laws are held to be "void for vagueness."

Another important aspect of due process is the right to an unbiased decision-maker. This requirement did recently become a focus of public interest when a state supreme court judge refused to disqualify himself from hearing a case in which one of the persons directly interested in the litigation had provided the judge with huge campaign contributions. His refusal was challenged, and the case made it all the way to the Supreme Court. In a 5–4 split, the Supreme Court, in *Caperton v. A. T. Massey Coal Co.*,[31] decided that the amounts involved had been so huge, in the context of the campaign, that the justice, as a matter of the federally guaranteed right to due process, was required to disqualify himself. The Court was also heavily influenced by the fact that "it was reasonably foreseeable, when the campaign contributions were made, that the pending case would be heard before the newly elected Justice."[32] These "extreme facts" led the Court to conclude that "the probability of actual bias rises to an unconstitutional level."[33] The dissenting justices expressed fears about creating a constitutional right that may lead to a whole new field of litigation; they also worried about a possible chilling effect on one's First Amendment right to support the candidate of one's choice financially. The case is a good illustration of the many factors that the Court must evaluate in deciding constitutional issues and how the Court inevitably acts as a policy maker in applying the broad principles of procedural due process.

Procedural due process cases can have political overtones, particularly when the political process itself is aimed at vulnerable or unpopular groups. In 1951, for example, the Court held that three groups (the Joint Anti-Fascist Refugee Committee, the National Council of American-Soviet Friendship, and the International Workers Order), which had been placed on a list of allegedly subversive organizations maintained by the attorney general, were entitled to a hearing under the Fourteenth Amendment.[34] The groups had protested their appearance on the list, which had been created pursuant to a 1948 Executive Order issued by President Truman.

Procedural due process issues, outside the criminal law context, arise today primarily when the government acts to deprive a person of a benefit that the state itself originally conferred. This aspect of modern procedural due process jurisprudence began in 1970 in *Goldberg v. Kelly*[35] when the Court held that a welfare recipient was entitled to a hearing with an opportunity to present or cross-examine witnesses before termination of benefits. Goldberg broke new constitutional ground in linking an entitlement with the "Property" interest protected by the Due Process clause. Subsequent cases extended the reasoning of Goldberg to other categories of persons, including drivers, students, and public employees.

It is hard to generalize about procedural due process cases, but whether one is entitled to a hearing depends in large measure on whether the interest being taken rises to the level of a property interest or liberty interest protected by the Constitution. This, in turn usually involves a weighing of what state law provides and what the Court regards as the legitimate expectations of the claimant. For example, in *Board of Regents v. Roth*[36] the Court decided that a teacher, hired under a one-year contract that the school failed to renew without explanation, was not entitled to a hearing since he had had no legitimate expectation of continued employment. On the other hand, on the same day that Roth was decided, the Court in *Perry v. Sindermann*[37] held that a nontenured college teacher who had been teaching for a number of years was entitled to a hearing. The difference was that in *Sindermann*, informal understandings had evolved into an unofficial tenure program that gave Sindermann a reasonable expectation that he would be rehired.

Substantive Due Process: The Incorporation Debate

Procedural due process requires that the process by which someone is deprived of a benefit or right be fair; substantive due process prevents Congress or a state legislature from depriving persons of certain rights altogether. How can a phrase that refers to process protect substantive rights? As a literal matter, it cannot, but defenders of substantive due process point out that the phrase *due process of law* implies that the laws themselves must be constitutional, for how could a process implementing an invalid law ever be fair?

The battle over substantive due process has been fought out essentially on two fronts: the first battle, often called the incorporation debate, has involved defining what provisions of the Bill of Rights should also bind the states; the second battle has been over defining what other rights *not* expressed or implied in the Bill of Rights fall within the liberty interest protected by the Due Process clause.

Incorporation, as it is called, of the Bill of Rights into the due process protection of the Fourteenth Amendment has a long history. Recall that in 1833 in *Barron v. Baltimore*, the Supreme Court declared that the Bill of Rights did not apply to the States. Beginning in 1897 with the Fifth Amendment's guarantee that private property not be taken without just compensation[38] and then in 1931 with the First Amendment's guarantee of freedom of speech,[39] the Court has gradually made most of the rights contained in the first Eight Amendments binding on the states.

One might well ask how the Court has identified what rights to incorporate. In 1937 in *Palko v. Connecticut*,[40] the Court addressed the question whether the Fifth Amendment protection against double jeopardy (being tried twice for the same crime) deserved incorporation. The case arose when a Connecticut man was tried for first degree murder but found guilty by a jury only of second degree murder. The state, pursuant to a Connecticut statute that allowed the prosecution to appeal criminal convictions in certain instances, appealed the conviction and won. The defendant was retried and then found guilty of first degree murder. Was this double jeopardy and did the prohibition against double jeopardy apply to the states? Justice Cardozo, speaking for an 8–1 majority, stated that only rights that represent "the very essence of ordered liberty"[41] standing for "principles of justice so rooted in the traditions and conscience of our people as to be ranked fundamental" should be held to bind the states.[42] The Court declined to incorporate the double jeopardy protection and found that Palko's conviction did not otherwise merit reversal.

Defining *ordered liberty* has not been easy, and the Court has reversed itself more than once. For example, *Palko* itself was subsequently reversed by the Warren Court so the protection against double jeopardy now applies to state criminal proceedings.[43] In *Malloy v. Hogan*,[44] the Court also reversed an earlier decision, *Adamson v. California*,[45] and applied the privilege against self-incrimination to the states. In *Adamson*, a state prosecutor had called attention to the fact that the defendant had refused to testify and the question was whether the prosecutor's statements violated the privilege against self-incrimination.

Both *Malloy* and *Adamson* were 5–4 decisions. Interestingly, only four justices in *Malloy* believed that the privilege against self-incrimination was the essence of ordered liberty. Where did the fifth vote come from? It came from Justice Hugo Black, and his position is important. Justice Black did not believe that a concept as amorphous as ordered liberty could be the basis for applying the Bill of Rights to the states. His reading, however, of the history of the Privileges and Immunities clause of the Fourteenth Amendment led him to conclude that the clause was intended to make *all* of the first eight amendments of the Bill of Rights binding on the states. In the earlier *Adamson* case, Black explained his rejection of the ordered liberty concept: "the natural law formula which the Court uses to reach its conclusion in this case should be abandoned as an incongruous excrescence on our Constitution. [I] fear to see the consequences of the Court's practice of substituting its own concepts of decency and fundamental justice for the language of the Bill of Rights as its point of departure in interpreting and enforcing the Bill of Rights."[46]

In *Adamson*, Black failed by just one vote to persuade the Court to accept the full incorporation doctrine. Selective incorporation, as a practical matter, has worked to achieve almost the same results as full incorporation would have done given that the First, Second, Fourth, Fifth (with the exception of the right to be indicted by a grand jury), Sixth, and Eighth (with the possible exception of the excessive bail provisions) Amendments are now fully binding on the states.

The Meaning of Liberty in the Due Process Clause

While Justice Black felt strongly that the Fourteenth Amendment incorporated the entire Bill of Rights, he felt equally strongly that it went no further. Thus, he was not willing to locate in the Fourteenth Amendment any rights that were not specified in the Bill of Rights itself. Indeed, he completely rejected the notion of substantive due process just as Justice Scalia does today when he calls it an "oxymoron" and nothing more than "each Justice's subjective assessment of what is fair and just."[47] This view, however, was rejected even by a justice as conservative and sensitive to states' rights as the second Justice Harlan. His view was expressed in his dissent in *Poe v. Ullman*: "If the supply of content to this Constitutional concept [substantive due process] has of necessity been a rational process, it certainly has not been one where judges have felt free to roam where unguided speculation might take them. The balance of which I speak is the balance struck by this country, having regard to what history teaches are the traditions from which it developed as well as the traditions from which it broke."[48]

Harlan's view of substantive due process was not at all grudging or narrow. Indeed, it led him to find a right of privacy in the due process clause well before the majority of the Court. I quote again from his *Poe* dissent:

> [I] believe that a statute making it a criminal offense for *married couples* to use contraceptives is an intolerable and unjustifiable invasion of privacy in the conduct of the most intimate concerns of an individual's personal life. . . . The full scope of the liberty guaranteed by the Due Process Clause cannot be found in or limited by the precise terms of the specific guarantees elsewhere provided in the Constitution. This liberty is not a series of isolated points. . . . It is a rational continuum which, broadly speaking, includes a freedom from all substantial arbitrary impositions and purposeless restraints.[49]

Substantive due process has had two incarnations: a modern one, still very much alive, and a rejected one focusing mainly on economic and social legislation. A right of privacy defines the modern version, something called Liberty of Contract the earlier one.

Roe v. Wade[50] a decision we will focus on in Chapter 11, is a *modern* substantive due process case because it limited the power of state legislatures to prohibit a woman from choosing an abortion based on a right of privacy that the Court has concluded is inherent in the Liberty interest of the Due Process clause. Modern substantive due process, however, did not begin with *Roe v. Wade*. The constitutional ground for *Roe* (and the contraceptive rights cases of the 1960s) was seeded by two opinions handed down in the 1920s written, ironically, by a most conservative (and probably the Court's most personally disagreeable) justice—James McReynolds.[51]

In *Meyer v. Nebraska*,[52] the Court overturned a Nebraska statute that had prohibited the teaching of any modern foreign language until after the eighth grade. It also prohibited the teaching of any subject in public or private school, except in English. This restriction had "a special impact on Lutheran parochial schools, which used German extensively in their teaching program."[53] The Court found that the law interfered with the rights of students to acquire knowledge and with the power of parents to control the education of their children. In his opinion for the Court, Justice McReynolds took an expansive view of the liberty protected by the Due Process clause, arguing that it denoted "not merely freedom from bodily restraint but also the right of the individual to contract, to engage in any of the common occupations of life, to acquire useful knowledge, to marry, establish a home and bring up children, to worship God according to the dictates of his own conscience, and generally to enjoy those privileges long recognized at common law as essential to the orderly pursuit of happiness by free men."[54] In *Pierce v. Society of Sisters*,[55] decided just a couple of years later, the Court unanimously invalidated an Oregon law requiring all children to attend public school. Again, Justice McReynolds emphasized the liberty interest of parents to direct the education of their children as they thought appropriate without interference from the state. "The child is not the mere creature of the State; those who nurture him and direct his destiny have the right, coupled with the high duty, to recognize and prepare him for additional obligations."[56]

We trace *Roe*'s lineage back to *Meyer* and *Pierce* because these were the first cases that connected the liberty interest in the Due Process clause with the autonomy of individuals and families to make their own decisions about matters that deeply affect their personal lives. *Meyer* and *Pierce* were not, however, the first substantive due process cases. Rather, they were a new branch of a tree that had been growing for decades as the Court from the late 1800s onwards invalidated one piece of progressive economic and social legislation after another, on the basis of a "liberty of contract" that, according to the Court, prevented the state from, among other things, enacting most minimum wage and maximum hour laws. During this era, *liberty of contract* meant the right of employers and employees to be free of government regulation in entering into individual contracts with each other. Of course, in reality, these decisions preserved the power of employers to exploit workers who enjoyed very little legal protection. Between 1920 and 1930, the Court struck down 140 state laws, more often than not on substantive due process grounds.[57]

The leading case on Liberty of Contract was *Lochner v. New York*[58]; it deserves a closer look. In 1895, both houses of the New York legislature had unanimously passed legislation limiting the number of hours bakers could work per week and per day. Some bakers at the time were working more than 100 hours a week, usually in the cellars of tenement houses, where most bakeries were located. The New York legislature concluded that breathing in flour dust 100 hours a week was not particularly healthful and that the overall dampness and extremes of temperature only aggravated the situation. Additionally, the legislature justified the Act on the ground that overworked bakers would be less clean and therefore more likely to produce bread dangerous to the public. Notwithstanding this record, the Supreme Court voided the statute in a 5–4 decision. Interestingly, Justice Peckham, writing for the majority, first cited a case where the Court had upheld a Utah law limiting the employment of workers in underground mines to eight hours a day, citing the dangerous conditions under which miners worked.[59] So how did the Court distinguish the Utah case from the New York legislation and, more importantly, how would it treat similar cases in the future? Justice Peckham's answer set the stage for another two and a half decades of business-protective substantive due process. In each case, wrote Peckham, the Court would ask: "Is this a fair, reasonable, and appropriate exercise of [the police power] or is it an unreasonable, unnecessary, and arbitrary interference with the right of the individual to his personal liberty or to enter into those contracts in relation to labor which may seem to him appropriate or necessary for the support of himself and his family? Of course the liberty of contract relating to labor includes both parties to it. The one has as much right to purchase as the other to sell labor."[60]

Notice the breadth of discretion that the Court had reserved to itself to determine what was "unreasonable, unnecessary and arbitrary," and recall also Justice Iredell's rejection of Justice Chase's assertion of a constitutional basis for rejecting legislation deemed arbitrary by the Court. Had the Court come full circle and arrogated to itself a power that modern conservatives pointedly reject? Not surprisingly, given its probusiness outlook, the Court was, among other things, more than willing to void labor legislation it deemed inconsistent with its notions of Liberty of Contract. In *Coppage v. Kansas*,[61] for example, the Court struck down a Kansas law outlawing "yellow dog contracts." These were contracts in which employees had to agree not to join a union as a condition of employment and had become a standard way for employers to prevent unionization, a tactic that the Kansas legislature had wanted to stop.

Liberty of Contract as a barrier to progressive economic regulation only ceased with the famous decision of the Court in *West Coast Hotel v. Parrish*,[62] upholding a Washington minimum wage law for women; the decision overruled an earlier case that had invoked Liberty of Contract to strike down a similar law. *West Coast Hotel* marked the beginning of the end of the cases outlawing economic legislation on Liberty of Contract grounds, not because Liberty of Contract is not a right protected by due process but because it is not an absolute right that completely preempts reasonable economic and social legislation.

Perhaps because of its checkered past, even justices comfortable with the modern notion of substantive due process understand the wisdom of not rushing too quickly into contested areas. This was well illustrated by *Washington v. Glucksberg*,[63] a case that unanimously upheld the State of Washington's prohibition against causing or aiding a suicide against a facial challenge that it violated the Due Process clause of the Fourteenth Amendment. Chief Justice Rehnquist's majority opinion stated the conservative view of substantive due process, arguing that there was no fundamental right to assisted suicide because a legal right to suicide had never been an accepted part of our traditions. However, only four other justices (Scalia, Thomas, Kennedy, and O'Connor) joined Rehnquist's opinion. The other justices were not comfortable with Rehnquist's emphasis on tradition, feeling that it placed too limiting a boundary on the potential reach of substantive due process. Justice Souter, an appointee of the elder President Bush, asserted that the issue was still too new for a definitive constitutional decision and that the Court for the moment should "stay its hand to allow reasonable legislative consideration." Similar themes ran through the opinions of the other Justices.[64] Even Chief Justice Rehnquist noted, "Throughout the Nation, Americans are engaged in an earnest and profound debate about the morality, legality and practicality of physician assisted suicide. Our holding permits this debate to continue, as it should in a democratic society."[65]

If *Washington v. Glucksberg* shows how a cautious Supreme Court can decide to proceed, *Lawrence v. Texas*[66] shows what a determined Court, even a deeply divided Court, can do when it is prepared for a bold declaration. In *Lawrence*, the Court, reversing a decision (*Bowers v. Hardwick*)[67] rendered less than twenty years earlier, voided a Texas statute that made it a crime for two persons of the same sex to engage in intimate sexual conduct. *Lawrence* is remarkable because it effectively offers a constitutional definition of personhood: "Liberty," wrote Justice Kennedy for the Court, "presumes an autonomy of self that includes freedom of thought, belief, expression and certain intimate conduct"[68] and means that "the petitioners are entitled to respect for their private lives," such that "The State cannot demean their existence or control their destiny by making their private sexual conduct a crime."[69] When the Court overruled *Bowers*, it did so with a cadence that reflected a deliberate though carefully controlled emotional tone: "Bowers was not correct when it was decided, and it is not correct today. It ought not to remain binding precedent. Bowers should be and is now overruled."[70]

That is about as direct an admission of failure as the Court is likely to make. The subtext was unmistakable: we treated some of our citizens unfairly and we were wrong. If the majority, however, was apologetic, the minority was almost apoplectic, for in dissent Justice Scalia (whose opinion was joined by Justices Rehnquist and Thomas) seemed to read the collapse of Western civilization into the Court's decision, not only taking the majority to task for exceeding the Court's proper role, but also foreseeing the possible end of laws against polygamy, and even incest, among others.

Until the Court comprises a majority of justices sharing the views of Justice Scalia, it will continue to hear cases based on the assumption that the Due Process clause has a substantive component. For the moment, the so-called liberal and conservative wings of the Court and their scholarly adherents divide most importantly on the elasticity of the Due Process clause as a source of substantive rights. Conservatives see substantive due process as protecting only those norms and values deeply rooted in our historical and cultural traditions. That is why they oppose the rights protected (they would say "invented") by *Roe v. Wade* and *Lawrence v. Texas* which, they argue, stand outside these traditions. Liberal justices find the conservative view too confining. They see in the Due Process clause an affirmation of values that evolve and express themselves differently in different eras.

Substantive Due Process and Federalism

Vindication of individual rights comes at the expense of government power, state as well as national. Thus, federalism has always been an issue when constitutional rights under the federal constitution are raised. The second Justice John Marshall Harlan, nominated by President Eisenhower in November 1954 and confirmed in March 1955 (the first, as noted before, was Harlan's grandfather after whom he was named), believed strongly in federalism and for that reason hesitated to interpret national constitutional rights too broadly. In one case, for example, *Duncan v. Louisiana*,[71] Harlan, in dissent, wrote: "The States have always borne primary responsibility for operating the machinery of criminal justice within their borders, and adapting it to their particular circumstances. The Due Process clause of the Fourteenth Amendment requires that those procedures be fundamentally fair in all respects. It does not, in my view, impose or encourage nationwide uniformity for its own sake."[72] For Harlan, federalism itself was an instrument for the preservation of individual rights, which, if ignored, could ultimately prove dangerous: "Constitutionally principled adjudication, high in the process of which is due recognition of the just demands of federalism, leaves ample room for the protection of individual rights. A constitutional democracy which in order to cope with seeming needs of the moment is willing to temporize with its basic distribution and limitation of governmental powers will sooner or later find itself in trouble."[73] I should add here that Harlan's belief in federalism was not doctrinaire. For example, he voted in the majority and always defended the Supreme Court's decisions barring prayer in the public schools (also to be discussed later). Harlan replaced Robert Jackson. They are two of the most distinguished justices to ever serve on the Court.

While the debate over substantive due process is complex, one point in favor of restraint is that a decision not to find a constitutional violation leaves states and the public just as much in charge as they were before the decision. Sometimes the public seems to forget this basic fact. In *Kelo v. New London, Connecticut*,[74] for example, the Court held that the City of New London could take private property for an economic development project intended to revitalize the downtown area without violating the Fifth or Fourteenth Amendments. The persons being displaced by the New London project understandably aroused great sympathy. One complainant had been born in her house in 1918 and lived there her entire life, including 60 years of married life with her husband, also a complainant. There was no contention that any of the properties being condemned were blighted or otherwise in poor condition: "they were condemned only because they happen to be located in the development area."[75] Editorial reaction to the Court's decision upholding the condemnation was highly unfavorable.

The public reaction, however, seemed to lose sight of one point, for the Court's decision left the final decision on whether the New London project should go forward in the hands of the legislature and, therefore, indirectly the public. *Connecticut was still free to revise its eminent domain laws to prevent condemnation for economic development purposes in the future, perhaps even to keep the New London project from going forward.* From a constitutional law viewpoint, a national constitutional rule prohibiting the use of eminent domain in economic development projects would have been a much more radical decision, one that would have likely occasioned many lawsuits needed to flesh out the scope of the Court's decision. Instead, public anger over the decision in many states produced new legislation making it more difficult (but certainly not impossible) to pursue through eminent domain the kind of economic development project at issue in *Kelo*.[76]

Enforcing the Fourteenth Amendment

As previously mentioned, all three Reconstruction era amendments, including the Fourteenth Amendment, authorize Congress to "enforce" its terms by "appropriate" legislation. On its surface, this language would not appear likely to raise much controversy, but in fact it has produced a number of recent cases in which the Court has wrestled with defining exactly what "appropriate" means. Most of these decisions have been reached on a vote of 5–4 and show how even technical areas of the law can run along ideological fault lines.

Not surprisingly, the enforcement language of the Civil War amendments was new. It was not needed for the Bill of Rights since it would hardly have made sense to authorize Congress to enforce amendments designed to keep Congress from acting in the first place. The Reconstruction Amendments were different, for they were designed to rein in state power.

"Appropriate" legislation as interpreted by the Court has meant that (1) the legislation must bear a reasonable relation ("congruence and proportionality" is the operative language) between the injury to be remedied by the legislation and the means adopted to remedy it,[77] and (2) there must be a clear record of the necessity for the legislation.[78] The first rule is intended to prevent Congress from rewriting the Fourteenth Amendment under the guise of merely enforcing it, the second to require an actual constitutional violation by the states that needs remedying.

Congressional legislation has been voided for failure to meet these standards. In *Board of Trustees of the University of Alabama v. Garrett*,[79] for example, the Court, in a 5–4 decision, found that a provision of the Americans with Disabilities Act of 1990 that prohibited states as employers from discriminating against the disabled in the terms, conditions, and privileges of employment was not an appropriate exercise of Congress's enforcement powers. The Court concluded that the disabled were not a suspect classification requiring strict scrutiny of state legislation and no record of widespread discrimination against the disabled by the states had been established. Since the law was not appropriate under the Fourteenth Amendment, the Eleventh Amendment was held to bar plaintiff's suit. Interestingly, however, just a few years later, in 2004, the Court, in *Tennessee v. Lane*,[80] another 5–4 decision, upheld a different section of the act as applied to a claim arising out of the failure of the State of Tennessee and some of its counties to provide wheelchair access to its courts. In this case, the Court decided that failure to provide physical access to the courts worked a deprivation of due process and allowed the lawsuit to remedy the situation to go forward.

For our purposes, it is important to recognize how the Court in these enforcement cases is actually determining the scope of the Fourteenth Amendment itself since the enforcement provision can only be triggered by a deprivation of a constitutional right. In effect, the Court in *Tennessee v. Lane* had, quite reasonably, found a due process right to physical access to court buildings but was unwilling to infer a broad right in *Garrett* for the disabled not to be discriminated against in terms of employment.

The Fourteenth Amendment, more than any other amendment, has dramatized the very different views justices hold respecting the appropriate role of the Supreme Court in the constitutional structure, an important subject to which we now turn.

4. The Supreme Court in the Constitutional Structure

Debating the Judiciary at the Constitutional Convention

Article III of the Constitution, dealing with the national judicial power, is so brief as to seem almost an afterthought. The only court actually provided for is the Supreme Court and, as we shall see in a moment, it was left to Congress to flesh out the structure of the rest of the federal judicial system. Only two issues dealing with the judiciary were seriously debated at the convention: (1) whether there should be a system of inferior federal courts and (2) who would appoint Supreme Court justices. These debates were themselves part of larger issues.

The argument over inferior federal courts was simply one dimension of the convention's struggle to achieve a balance between national and state power. Those advocating state power did not want a federal judiciary, other than a Supreme Court, at all. "The people will not bear such innovations" claimed one Southern delegate: "The States will revolt at such encroachments."[1] More national-minded delegates, however, were not willing to trust state courts to administer federal law. In the end, Madison proposed a compromise, giving Congress the power, but not the duty, to create inferior federal Courts, thus leaving the issue of the structure of the federal judicial system to another day and another forum. Madison's suggestion passed overwhelmingly. Football might still be a century away but punting was already a political art form. Given Federalist control of the first Congress, it is not surprising that the creation of an inferior federal court system was the very first order of business for the new Congress, resulting in the Judiciary Act of 1789.

The struggle over the appointment power was part of a larger struggle to define the respective roles of the Congress and the president. Initially, the convention opted to place the appointment power in the Senate alone. This was troubling to Madison who felt that selection by the Senate could mean that justices "alone might be appointed by a minority of the people, tho' by a majority, of the States."[2] One hears in these words both Madison's distrust of the Senate and the faint rumblings of "one person, one vote." In the end, the convention accepted an earlier proposal by Madison that the president would appoint Supreme Court justices with the advice and consent of the Senate.

The creation of a separate judiciary in the Constitution is not something that flowed naturally from the colonial experience. During the Seventeenth Century, English political theory recognized only two kinds of government power: the executive and the legislative.[3] The judicial power in England had developed as a means of enforcing royal authority and of creating a uniform law—the common law—throughout the realm. Thus, enforcing the law was viewed to a considerable extent as an executive function.

It was Montesquieu and his idea of separate departments of government, each confined to its own proper sphere, which laid the groundwork for the separate judiciary. This concept fit well with a colonial history in which both the legislative and judicial powers had, in the eyes of the colonists, been abused and manipulated by executive authority. Not that the judicial power and legislative power were viewed identically. Thomas Jefferson probably reflected the views of many at the outset of the Revolution when he exalted legislative over both executive and judicial power. For Jefferson, legislative power represented the people and therefore could be counted on to make laws impartially while the executive and judicial power would be more subject to the impulses of designing men.

Two other decisions at the convention should be noted. First, as mentioned, the Virginia Plan itself contained a proposal for a Council of Revision. The council would have involved Supreme Court justices joining with the executive branch in considering whether legislation enacted by Congress should become law. It was defeated in part out of a feeling expressed by Rufus King that "the Judges ought to be able to expound the law as it should come before them, free from the bias of having participated in its formation."[4] Had the Council of Revision come to pass, the Court could have easily assumed a larger role in the day-to-day governance of the country and perhaps lost the sense of remoteness and mystery, not to mention impartiality, that are the foundation of the Court's prestige. Second, the Virginia Plan also provided that the legislative branch could nullify acts of state legislatures deemed inconsistent with the Constitution. Had that plan been adhered to, certainly both the concept of dual sovereignty on which federalism is based and the Supreme Court's role as the final arbiter of constitutional meaning, would have been deeply affected. Instead, however, the way was open for the Supreme Court to take on the role that Madison had originally envisioned for the Congress.

Article III: Defining the National Judicial Power

Just as Article I of the Constitution vests "All legislative powers herein granted" to Congress and Article II vests "the executive Power" in a president, Article III vests the "judicial Power of the United States . . . in one Supreme Court, and in such inferior Courts as the Congress may from time to time ordain and establish."

The scope of national judicial power is described in the first paragraph of section 2 of Article III. I have divided the paragraph into three parts with the most important language italicized:

> (PART 1) *The judicial Power shall extend to all Cases, in Law and Equity, arising under*
> (PART 2) *this Constitution, the laws of the United States, and Treaties made, or which shall be made under their Authority;* to all Cases affecting Ambassadors, other public Ministers and Consuls;—to all Cases of admiralty and maritime Jurisdiction;—
> (PART 3) *to Controversies* to which the United States shall be a party;—to Controversies between two or more States;—between a State and Citizens of another State;—*between citizens of different States;*—between Citizens of the same State claiming Lands under grants of different States, and between a State or the Citizens thereof, and foreign States, Citizens, or Subjects.

The Cases and Controversies Limitation

The first thing to notice about this paragraph is that it limits the judicial power to "Cases" and "Controversies." This is an important limitation. It means that the Supreme Court can't just dial up (or text message) the president or congressional leaders and announce that this bill or law is unconstitutional. The case or controversy limitation also means that the Court is a reactive, not an agenda-setting body. This statement, however, needs one important qualification. As we shall see in Chapter 8, the Court receives thousands of petitions each year to hear cases, accepting only a few. Since the Court is now free to accept whatever cases it chooses, it does determine its own docket, in a sense its agenda, but only out of the body of cases asking for Supreme Court review.

Standing

The Court assures adherence to the case or controversy limitation through its standing requirement. If anyone could bring a constitutional claim raising any issue they wanted, the case or controversy requirement would not be much of a limitation. To limit this possibility, a case or controversy can only be brought by a person with "standing," meaning not that he or she is an upright citizen, but that he or she is alleging a personal injury to him or herself, traceable to the action complained of and which will be redressed by the relief sought. A vivid illustration of the standing requirement at work occurred when six congressmen who had voted against the Presidential Line Item Veto Act immediately sued to have it declared unconstitutional as a violation of the Separation of Powers shortly after it was signed into law by President Clinton. The Supreme Court, however, dismissed the case, holding that the injury alleged by the representatives was not sufficiently concrete with respect to them as to meet the standing requirement.[5] When President Clinton, however, exercised his line item veto respecting certain budget items, plaintiffs who were actually injured by the loss of funding were found by the Court to have standing; the Court ultimately found the act to be unconstitutional.[6]

Generally, a taxpayer lacks standing to complain that a particular appropriation by Congress is beyond its power. The rationale was expressed by Justice Alito in *Hein v. Freedom from Religion Foundation, Inc.*[7]: "If every federal taxpayer could sue to challenge any Government expenditure, the federal courts would cease to function as courts of law, and would be cast in the role of general complaint bureaus."[8] One longstanding exception to this rule has allowed taxpayer suits asserting violations of the First Amendment's prohibition against laws favoring the establishment of religion.[9] *Hein* called the breadth, if not the viability, of that exception into question when it held that taxpayers did not have standing to contest executive branch expenditures made for the purpose of encouraging faith-based initiatives from funds appropriated for the executive's general and administrative expenses.

The standing requirement is one that sometimes divides justices along liberal and conservative lines, the more conservative justices tending to be less welcoming to novel constitutional claims and more willing to erect standing as a bar to the pursuance of a claim. The *Hein* case discussed above, for example, split the Court 5–4 along ideological lines, as it did in a 2011 case, *Arizona Tuition School Organization v. Winn*,[10] when the Court held that plaintiff taxpayer lacked standing to challenge an Arizona statute that granted tax credits to taxpayers for funds contributed to tuition organizations that used the funds to pay for scholarships, often to religious schools. The Court drew a distinction between a suit regarding expenditure of tax revenues (for which standing presumably would have been allowed) and a system of tax credits. In a strong dissent marking her as a force to be reckoned with in the future, Justice Kagan argued that the Court's formalistic distinction utterly ignored the fact that there was no practical difference between the two forms of support and threatened to eliminate any taxpayer standing to contest the government's monetary support of religion.

Broad Grant of Power

Another important thing to notice about the national judicial power is its breadth. There is nothing narrow or nuanced about it. It applies to all cases in law and equity arising under the Constitution and federal law (subject matter jurisdiction) as well as to cases arising between certain categories of parties (diversity jurisdiction). This broad grant of authority gains added stature when read in conjunction with the Supremacy clause previously discussed. The grant of equity jurisdiction is also important because it means the Court can hear cases requesting injunctive relief (meaning relief involving an order that something be done or stop being done) as opposed to simply hearing cases where money damages are at issue. Civil rights cases, for example, often involve a request for injunctive relief as do many other cases involving claims of individual rights.

The Political Question Doctrine

Notwithstanding this broad grant of authority, there are certain kinds of cases that the Court avoids on principle because they involve "political questions." The doctrine can be traced back to Marshall's opinion in *Marbury v. Madison,* in which he wrote, "Questions in their nature political, or which are, by the Constitution and laws, submitted to the executive, can never be made to this Court."[11]

In *Baker v. Carr,*[12] the Court described six classes of cases that fall within this doctrine, including a case where there is "a lack of judicially discoverable and manageable standards for resolving it."[13] This can be an important limitation. The inability of the justices, for example, to agree on the applicable standard for determining when partisan gerrymandering of legislative and congressional districts has gone further than constitutionally permitted has prevented the Court from curbing or regulating this practice. In a recent case, several justices suggested that the Court should simply give up the effort and treat partisan gerrymandering as a political question, but the Court has yet to go that far.[14]

In *Baker v. Carr,* the Court also characterized as political questions cases involving "an unusual need for unquestioning adherence to a political decision already made" or "the potentiality of embarrassment" if more than one department pronounced on a question.[15] Both of these aspects of the doctrine can be seen at work in Justice Black's reasoning for refusing to consider the question of the constitutionality of the Vietnam War. President Johnson's reliance on the Gulf of Tonkin Resolution for prosecuting the Vietnam War had been attacked on constitutional grounds in a number of cases, including one in Massachusetts. Justice Black thought the issue inappropriate for the Court to consider: "Black wanted no part of the Massachusetts case. Whether one believed that Congress had meant to authorize the Vietnam War, or whether the President was conducting it on his own authority—either way in Black's view, the decision was a 'political decision' to be made by another co-equal branch of government. . . . If the war were to be attacked, Black said, it should be by Congress, not by the Court." [16]

One way of encapsulating the doctrine is to say simply that it is usually applied to avoid deciding a sensitive issue, often with strong political overtones, for reasons having to do with the Court's relationship to one of the political branches.

In some cases, application of the political question doctrine means that certain provisions of the Constitution are off limits for judicial consideration—for example, the Court very early on made clear that it will not consider claims that the national government has failed to fulfill its obligation under Article IV, Section 4 to guarantee "to each State a Republican Form of Government."[17] Application of the political question doctrine is not always neutral in its effects. For example, the Court's general unwillingness to take cases challenging presidential decisions regarding the deployment of troops or even whether treaties have lapsed,[18] has helped by default to contribute to the growth of presidential power in the area of foreign affairs. By way of illustration, the Court refused to rule on the constitutionality of President Carter's unilateral decision to withdraw from our mutual defense pact with Taiwan without congressional authorization.[19]

Diversity Jurisdiction

The Court's diversity jurisdiction means that if a citizen of New Jersey and a citizen of New York have a significant legal dispute, they can go to the presumably unbiased federal court to have the case heard, rather than the possibly biased state court of one of the litigants. Notice that diversity jurisdiction exists even when no question of federal law is at stake. The framers did not provide diversity jurisdiction simply as an exercise in good government, for many state courts in the 1780s had begun to favor in-state debtors against out-of-state and foreign (particularly English) creditors, some states going so far as to deny British creditors access to their courts. This was a violation of the Treaty of Paris ending the American Revolution and had given the British an excuse not to withdraw from certain forts in the then Northwest. Diversity jurisdiction, combined with the congressional power to create inferior courts, would solve this problem.

You might be wondering what law applies when, let's say, a citizen of New York sues a citizen of New Jersey over a breach of contract. The Judiciary Act of 1789 provided some guidance by instructing federal courts to apply state law in diversity cases. Recall, however, from chapter 1 that there are two kinds of law (other than constitutional law): statutory law, meaning laws enacted by bodies like Congress and state legislatures with lawmaking power, and common law, meaning law created by the decisions of judges. Judges will apply a statute to a dispute when it is applicable and common law in the absence of a relevant statute.

The critical question which the Judiciary Act did not answer was whether the instruction to apply state law included state common law as well as state statutory law. In 1842, in the famous case of *Swift v. Tyson*,[20] the Court held that "state law" as used in the Judiciary Act meant only state statutory law, not state common law. This decision freed the federal courts to develop their own federal common law in diversity cases. Unfortunately, when federal common law differed from state common law, someone could have a right to sue a fellow citizen of his state under state common law but no right to sue in an identical dispute with a citizen of another state under federal common law. It took nearly a hundred years but the Supreme Court finally rectified this problem in *Erie v. Tompkins*,[21] reversing *Swift v. Tyson* and holding that federal courts should apply state common law in diversity cases. If you ever want to shorten a conversation with a lawyer, ask whether he or she thinks that Erie was correctly decided. Have smelling salts available as memories of law exams past descend upon your victim. (There is an entire body of law called Conflicts of Law which in part determines the law of which state applies in diversity cases.)

Political Controls on the "Independent" Judiciary

In *Federalist* No. 78 Alexander Hamilton called the federal judiciary "the least dangerous branch,"[22] a theme he elaborated on in *Federalist* No. 81 when he noted the Court's "total incapacity" to engage in "usurpations by force."[23]

While the Framers were committed to an independent judiciary, they did give Congress and the president enormous power to structure the Court to its liking. Even something as basic as the number of Supreme Court justices is simply left to Congress to decide. In the Judiciary Act of 1789, Congress set the number of justices at five. That number changed six times during the first 80 years of the Republic, sometimes based upon Congress's view of the Court's work load as new states were added and other times on naked politics. The Judiciary Act of 1801, passed in the last days of John Adams's administration, reduced the number of Supreme Court justices by one to avoid giving Jefferson an appointment, and the Radical Republicans did the same thing to Andrew Johnson. The number of Supreme Court justices has been fixed at nine since 1869.

In addition to giving Congress the responsibility for structuring the entire federal judiciary below the Supreme Court, Article III also gives to Congress the power to define the Supreme Court's appellate jurisdiction. The extent of this power is unclear, but introducing bills to strip that jurisdiction has become one well-worn way for members of Congress to vent their displeasure over particular Supreme Court opinions. A number of bills, for example, were introduced to deprive the Court of its power to hear cases involving school prayer after the Court's decisions banning prayer in public schools, and more recently there have been proposals to strip the Court of its ability to decide cases relating to abortion and even the Pledge of Allegiance. These efforts have failed.

A few efforts to regulate the judiciary's freedom of action, if not its jurisdiction, have succeeded, most notably the Norris-LaGuardia Act, enacted in 1932, which stripped the federal judiciary of the power to issue injunctions against strikes by labor unions. This act was a direct response to what Congress regarded as a misinterpretation by the judiciary of the Clayton Act and is an example of a rare instance in which Congress asserted its authority to curb the Court's remedial powers. A more recent example of

Congress's power is provided by the Illegal Immigration Reform and Immigrant Responsibility Act of 1996, which limits judicial review of certain administrative actions affecting immigrants.

Another reason that Hamilton thought of the Court as the least dangerous branch was its dependence on the executive to carry out its orders. When a president fails to do so, there is little the Court can do. In the early 1830s, President Jackson refused to accept the Court's decision in *Worcester v. Georgia*[24] voiding a Georgia law that asserted control over Cherokee lands. The result was one of the most shameful episodes in American history, the forced expulsion of the Cherokee from their ancestral lands in clear violation of treaty agreements between the Cherokee, as a sovereign nation, and the United States.

President Jackson is not the only president who has ignored the Court. At the start of the Civil War, the nation's capital was in danger of being completely isolated militarily if Union troops could not travel through Maryland to help defend it. Sympathy for the Confederates was strong there; a riot in Baltimore had caused Union troops to avoid the city altogether on their march south. If Maryland seceded, the Union cause could be lost at the outset. With great reluctance, Lincoln suspended the writ of habeas corpus, meaning that the military could arrest civilians and not have to produce them in Court to justify their arrest. Suspension was deemed vital since it was feared that otherwise those aiding the Confederate cause would simply be released by sympathetic federal judges. The chief justice of the Supreme Court, Roger Taney, took the view that only Congress could suspend the writ under the Constitution and therefore, notwithstanding Lincoln's suspension, Taney issued the writ in response to the petition of one John Merryman, the son of one of Justice Taney's oldest friends. Merryman was believed by the military to be actively aiding the rebel cause. When the military refused to produce Merryman, as ordered by Taney, Taney issued a strongly worded opinion denouncing the suspension. Taney's opinion created a sensation in the country. Scholars debate whether, as a legal matter, Taney was correct. Lincoln himself, in a subsequent message to Congress, posed an even larger question when he asked, even assuming that he had technically violated the law, "are all the laws, but one, to go unexecuted, and the government itself go to pieces, lest that one be violated?"[25] Taney might have been responsible for upholding the Constitution, but Lincoln was responsible for the nation; for our purposes, it is simply important to see how powerless Taney was to contest Lincoln's disregard of his order.

Outright defiance is obviously an extreme measure and is certainly not the only tool in the president's toolbox. Nothing, for example, prevents a president, or Congress for that matter, from interpreting Supreme Court decisions as narrowly as possible to preserve their own freedom of action.

There is no guarantee that a major constitutional clash between the president and the Court might not occur in the future, and we have been somewhat lucky in avoiding them in the past. In the 1930s, most notably, a crisis was averted only when, by a 5–4 vote, the Court, in the *Gold Clause Cases*,[26] upheld President Roosevelt's decision to go off the gold standard. It is clear that Roosevelt was prepared to defy the Court on this issue had it attempted to void his actions, a defiance that would have created a major dilemma for lower courts whether to follow the Court or the president when enforcement of gold clauses in private contracts was sought.

The political branches are, of course, also free to attack Court decisions and use the Court to their political advantage. Supreme Court decisions are frequent fodder for campaign appeals. Republican candidates in the 1960s and 1970s rebuilt the party's fortunes by running as the party of neighborhood schools, law and order, and states' rights, issues that gained traction in part as a reaction against numerous decisions of the Warren Court related to busing and the rights of criminal defendants. The need to preserve or overturn *Roe v. Wade* is a consistent theme respectively of Democratic and Republican candidates. Again, the Court as an institution is at an extreme disadvantage in defending itself. Any attempt to answer critics in a sustained way so as to influence public opinion directly would be deemed highly improper. Supreme Court opinions must stand and fall on their own without further explanation or defense from the Court.

A Cautious but Not Cowardly Court

It is important not to overstate the Court's sense of vulnerability to the president and Congress. When necessary, it will confront the political branches. Among other things, the Court has nullified Congress's refusal to seat a duly elected congressman (Adam Clayton Powell);[27] rolled back President Truman's seizure of the steel mills;[28] required President Nixon to turn over the Watergate tapes that ultimately forced his resignation;[29] allowed the publication of the Pentagon Papers in the face of a claim that publication would endanger national security;[30] invalidated the reporting provisions in the Balanced Budget and Emergency Deficit Control Act (also known as the Gramm-Rudman Act);[31] declared unconstitutional the line item veto;[32] and declared unconstitutional the legislative veto, invalidating in one decision the provisions of over 200 laws that had in one form or another empowered the executive to act subject to the right of either the House or Senate to disapprove the action.[33]

Perhaps the most dramatic example of the Court's willingness to stand up to the political branches, particularly the president, occurred on what New Deal proponents came to call Black Monday, May 27, 1935. On that day, the Court in three separate decisions, each one unanimous, held unconstitutional the National Industrial Recovery Act, the Frazier Lemke Farm Mortgage Act of 1934 discussed below, and President Roosevelt's removal of a Federal Trade Commissioner. While there was some hesitation about delivering all three opinions on the same day, "Justice Brandeis considered by some to be an unofficial representative of the New Deal on the Court, said he saw no reason to postpone any decisions 'on that account' and urged that the proceedings be carried through."[34]

Judicial Independence and the Impeachment of Justice Chase

Under Article III, federal judges hold their offices during good behavior and cannot have their compensation diminished. At the Constitutional Convention, the Framers clearly came down on the side of an independent judiciary not only in the tenure of office and salary provisions but also by overwhelmingly rejecting a proposal that would have allowed judges to be removed by a vote of the Senate and House of Representatives. Judicial independence was not a hallmark of state governments of the time, which in many cases provided for annual elections of judges; even in states where judges held their office during good behavior, there were relatively easy procedures for removing judges from the bench and lowering judicial salaries.

The essence of judicial independence is that judges will not be removed for decisions that the political branches do not like. This outcome was not inevitable for the Supreme Court and was established only after a political struggle that culminated in the impeachment trial of Supreme Court Justice Samuel Chase in 1805.

There is no question that Chase, a Federalist Supreme Court justice, had acted in a highly partisan manner in conducting trials under the Alien and Sedition Acts, enacted in 1798 as a way of stifling dissent over Adams's foreign policies. The Sedition Act resulted in a number of convictions of prominent Republicans for voicing their political views but was never tested by the Court because the Republicans let it expire by its terms when they came to power in 1801. The articles of impeachment against Chase, as proposed in the House of Representatives, had initially been limited to charges of criminal behavior but were revised to include two counts alleging simply that Chase had made erroneous decisions. Had Chase been convicted on either of these counts, precedent for a much looser interpretation of good behavior would have been established. Since the Senate was controlled by the Republicans 25 to 9, the party had the necessary two-thirds majority to convict Chase on a purely partisan vote though a defection of only 3 Republicans would result in acquittal. As it turned out, 6 Republicans along with all the Federalists voted for acquittal on every count. In the view of Keith Whittington, the Chase impeachment, while it preserved the concept of an independent judiciary, also stood as a "warning" to future judges that acting in a partisan fashion should be deemed "inappropriate, exceptional, and requiring justification."[35]

We alluded earlier to the fact that the Constitution does not explicitly give the Supreme Court the power to invalidate either federal or state statutes on constitutional grounds. The Court asserted these powers fairly early in our history, and it is to these developments that we now turn.

Marbury v. Madison and the Start of Judicial Review

Scholars sometimes speculate what the presidency might have been like had the Framers not known that the office's first occupant would be George Washington. Similarly, one might ask what the Supreme Court would have become without John Marshall, its chief justice for 35 years, from 1801 to 1835. Parenthetically, between 1801 and 1864, the country had fourteen presidents but only two chief justices of the Supreme Court, Marshall and Roger Taney. The first crisis Marshall faced as chief justice arose from an omission he had made when he was secretary of state, and it led directly to the famous case of *Marbury v. Madison.*[36] Had he not handled that case as astutely as he did, perhaps a much weaker, more timid Court would have resulted.

The problem Marshall faced in *Marbury* had been brought about by the more extreme members of his own Federalist party. These Federalists (sometimes known as the High Federalists) had sought to invoke the original (trial) jurisdiction of the Supreme Court, as authorized by the Judiciary Act of 1789, to force James Madison, Jefferson's secretary of state, by issuance of a writ of mandamus, to deliver commissions to four justices of the peace in the District of Columbia appointed by Adams in the last days of his administration so that they could begin their work. Ironically, it was Marshall himself who, as secretary of state under Adams, had failed to deliver the commissions, a circumstance that today would have prevented Marshall from even taking part in the case.

The suit was part of a much larger picture. The Federalists had been beaten badly in the election of 1800, losing control of both Congress and the presidency. In desperation, they sought to entrench themselves in the judiciary. In February of 1801, just a few weeks before Jefferson's inauguration, the Senate confirmed John Marshall's appointment as chief justice and Congress passed the Judiciary Act of 1801 reorganizing the federal judiciary. Among other things, the act enabled Adams to appoint sixteen new Federalist judges, the famous "Midnight" judges. The act also excused the then-sitting Supreme Court justices from riding circuit, an onerous obligation requiring the justices to travel extensively for part of the year and to participate, as individual justices, in cases being heard in the geographic area (the circuit) for which they were responsible. (Being a Supreme Court justice in the 1790s did not have quite the cachet it does today. In fact, John Rutledge left the Court to become chief justice of the South Carolina Supreme Court, and John Jay left to become governor of New York.)

While the historical record is mixed, it appears that Jefferson might have been willing to accept the new Judiciary Act, much to the disappointment of the more Anti-Federalist wing of his own party, who would have preferred an assault on the whole idea of an independent judiciary. The Federalist's suit to force the Republicans to deliver the commissions, however, forced Jefferson's hand, and in 1802 Congress repealed the Judiciary Act of 1801, returning, among other things, Supreme Court justices to the task of riding circuit.

Confronting *Marbury v. Madison*, Marshall knew that if the Court issued a decision requiring delivery of the commissions it was likely to be ignored. This would have led directly to a constitutional crisis, particularly if it emboldened the more extreme Republicans to attack the appellate jurisdiction of the Court or to seek to eliminate the inferior federal court system. Marshall's opinion was politically masterful. While he found that the four justices of the peace were entitled to their commissions, he also wrote that the Constitution, not Congress, defined the Supreme Court's original jurisdiction. Since that original jurisdiction, according to Marshall, did not include the power to issue writs of mandamus, Marshall concluded that the Court had no power to order the issuance of the commissions. In one brilliant stroke, Marshall had (1) acted with great judicial modesty in declining a grant of power from

Congress, (2) declared a provision of federal law unconstitutional, an act of great judicial self-assertion wrapped in modesty's cloak, and (3) avoided a potential constitutional crisis since he had given the Republicans a victory and there was no order for Jefferson to ignore.

In *Stuart v. Laird*,[37] Marshall also upheld the repeal of the Judiciary Act of 1801. Though High Federalists had wanted to precipitate another crisis by having the justices refuse to return to riding circuit, Marshall disagreed, and a crisis was averted.

I should note here the work of a distinguished constitutional historian, Bruce Ackerman, who believes that history has badly distorted the relative significance of *Marbury* and *Stuart*, that "it is wrong to treat *Marbury* as the main event and *Stuart* as an historical curiosity. *Marbury* is better viewed as a footnote to *Stuart*."[38] For Ackerman, *Stuart v. Laird*, decided a week after *Marbury*, represented "an utter capitulation"[39] in which the Supreme Court justices served "as Jefferson's willing collaborators in ousting the midnight judges and dispensing federal justice on Jefferson's terms."[40] Ackerman is not completely critical of this "strategic retreat,"[41] arguing that it brought the federal judiciary valuable time to buy good-will so that "when the moment of truth came at the Senate Impeachment trial [of Justice Chase in 1805], enough Republican Senators joined the Federalist minority to acquit Chase."[42]

In any event, a few things are undisputed. Marshall and Jefferson, both from Virginia, disliked each other intensely. Both were great partisans but more in the center of their parties. Together, their actions and refusals to act helped legitimize the federal judiciary at a very fragile time in its history. The irony, of course, is that Marshall's judicial nationalism found the perfect complement in Jefferson's purchase of the Louisiana Territory from France, an act that Jefferson thought unconstitutional but an opportunity he was not prepared to forego.

Martin v. Hunter's Lessee and the Supremacy Clause

Justice Holmes believed that our constitutional structure would survive even if the national judiciary lost its power to declare federal legislation unconstitutional but would not survive if it lost its power to declare state acts unconstitutional. The power of the Supreme Court to invalidate state laws and actions if they conflict with the U.S. Constitution is not specifically set forth in the Constitution but is arguably implicit in the Supremacy Clause. Congress certainly thought so when it enacted section 25 of the Judiciary

Act of 1789 providing for Supreme Court review of state statutes and state supreme court decisions that rejected claims under federal law. This provision was to be tested in the landmark case of *Martin v. Hunter's Lessee*.[43]

To appreciate fully the significance of this case, some historical background is in order. When Congress enacted the Judiciary Act of 1789 and created federal courts below the Supreme Court, it did not give the federal courts general jurisdiction over cases involving questions arising under federal law. Thus, the state courts were primarily responsible for hearing cases involving federal questions. This situation did not change until the passage of the Judiciary Act of 1875, which finally conferred general federal question jurisdiction on the federal courts.

Martin v. Hunter's Lessee presented a challenge by the highest court of the state of Virginia to the right of the U.S. Supreme Court to invalidate state legislation it deemed in conflict with superior federal law. It was a battle of wills, anticipating in its own way the violent conflict that ensued four decades later. The case came about when the Virginia Court of Appeals (Virginia's highest court) refused to recognize the validity of a U.S. Supreme Court decision (*Fairfax's Devisee v. Hunter's Lessee*).[44] The decision had held that a Virginia state statute expropriating property from Loyalists was inconsistent with the Treaty of Paris ending the Revolutionary War and Jay's Treaty, both of which protected Loyalist property. The Virginia Court of Appeals refused to enter judgment in compliance with the Supreme Court's decision, arguing that the Constitution was a compact between the states and that section 25 of the Judiciary Act was itself unconstitutional. The Virginia court's position led to a second case, *Martin v. Hunter's Lessee*, in which Justice Story, writing for a unanimous Supreme Court, upheld section 25. Story's opinion is noteworthy for the vigor with which he argues that the States "are expressly bound to obedience by the letter"[45] of the Constitution with respect to the powers granted to the United States. While there are technical aspects to the case, the basic issue, at least for Story, was clear. The Constitution gave to the national judiciary, not to the states, the ultimate authority to decide questions involving federal power, and no state court decision deemed by the federal judiciary to be inconsistent with federal law should be allowed to stand.

Although not a direct challenge to the structural relationship between the federal and state court systems, it is worth noting and briefly describing Southern resistance to *Brown v. Board of Education*,[46] the 1954 Supreme Court decision outlawing the South's system of segregated public schools, because it too ultimately involved the issue of federal versus state authority. The resistance was encouraged by a protest (the Southern Manifesto) signed by 101 members of Congress, including all but three southern U.S. Senators, which called the decision "a clear abuse of judicial power" with "no legal basis." In 1958, President Eisenhower was forced to send the National Guard into Little Rock, Arkansas, to restore order and allow black students to attend the previously segregated high school. Interestingly, at the end of the school year, Little Rock school officials asked for and received a federal district court order postponing further desegregation for a period of two and a half years. The National Association for the Advancement of Colored People appealed the order, and the Supreme Court in *Cooper v. Aaron*,[47] in an opinion individually signed by all nine justices, a highly unusual move intended to underscore the Court's resolve in the face of Southern resistance, reversed the postponement. In so doing, the Court, perhaps with the Southern Manifesto in mind, declared that state governors and legislatures were bound to follow the Constitution and that the federal judiciary "is supreme in its exposition of the law of the Constitution."[48] This is perhaps the most definitive assertion of judicial supremacy ever made by the Court.

From Judicial Review to Judicial Supremacy

Judicial review, for our purposes, refers to the authority of the Supreme Court to void legislative acts it deems unconstitutional. Some scholars, including liberal scholars, question the historical basis for judicial review. For example, Larry Kramer, a former law clerk of Justice Brennan, argues that "the status of judicial review on the eve of the Federal Convention was . . . uncertain at best" [49] and that "the Founders expected constitutional limits to be enforced through politics and by the people rather than in courts."[50] He adds, "If judicial review was to occur, it would [be] . . . as a political-legal act, a substitute for popular resistance, required by the people's command to ignore laws that were ultra vires—though only when the unconstitutionality of a law was clearly beyond dispute."[51]

There is, of course, considerable evidence to the contrary. Hamilton, for example, in *Federalist* No. 78, wrote that it is the "duty [of judges] . . . to declare all acts contrary to the manifest tenor of the Constitution void. . . . Without this, all the reservations of particular rights or privileges would amount to nothing."[52] Less well known is John Marshall's argument at the Virginia ratifying convention that federal justices could be relied upon to strike down laws that exceeded Congress's delegated powers. Such laws, said Marshall, "would be considered by the judges as an infringement of the Constitution which they are to guard. They would not consider such a law as coming under their jurisdiction. They would declare it void."[53]

Putting history aside, there is a strong practical case for judicial review. Presumably, somebody must be in a position to void unconstitutional acts, otherwise the Constitution loses its legal force. Arguably this authority should rest with the judiciary, not only because of its superior knowledge of the law, but also because the political branches by their very nature cannot be depended upon to protect individual and minority rights, dependent as those branches are upon the very political majorities whose impulses might tempt them into unconstitutional actions in the first place. Also, structurally, who but the Court can impartially decide constitutional disputes between the president and Congress?

In discussing judicial review, we should not forget that the president actually has the first say in determining the constitutionality of federal legislation since the president has complete discretion to veto a bill he or she deems unconstitutional. This has been true since the beginning of the Republic. The first major piece of federal economic legislation (creating a national bank) was preceded by a vigorous debate about its constitutionality both on the floor of Congress and within Washington's cabinet. Washington not only received a memorandum from his attorney general, Edmund Randolph, on the subject but also highly conflicting papers from Jefferson and Hamilton, one of the first real indications of the depth of the differences between them.[54] Had either Congress or the president concluded that the Bank Bill was unconstitutional, it would simply never have come before the Court as an issue at all. Presidents Madison and Monroe, for example, both believed that a federal system of internal improvements was unconstitutional and vetoed bills that would have provided funds for those purposes. President Jackson vetoed a renewal of the Second National Bank for the same reason; in his veto message, he asserted the right of both the president and Congress to independently assess issues of constitutionality in discharging their legislative responsibilities.

That basic dynamic is still part of our governmental structure. When the president vetoes an act because he thinks it unconstitutional, he is, of course, simply exercising a power clearly given him under the Constitution. The Court will not review that decision just as it will not review any presidential decision that is discretionary in nature, whether or not that discretion is derived from a statute or the Constitution.[55]

In recent times, judicial review has not only been conceded but even defended by the political branches. President Eisenhower, for example, was hardly sympathetic to left wing causes. Nevertheless, his attorney general, William Rogers, vigorously opposed a bill to deprive the Supreme Court of its power to decide First Amendment issues relating to the rights of communists and their supporters (*fellow travelers* in the phraseology of the time) after Court rulings in their favor. The bill actually passed the House of Representatives but failed in the Senate.

If today the power of judicial review is acknowledged, real differences exist as to how free the Court should feel to exercise it. For some scholars, judicial review is a distasteful necessity at best. In *The Least Dangerous Branch*, Alexander Bickel called it "a deviant institution in the American democracy"[56] and "a counter-majoritarian force in our system," which, when it declares a legislative act unconstitutional, "thwarts the will of the representatives of the actual people of the here and now."[57] For observers like Bickel, judicial review is undemocratic because justices are not elected while legislators are, so legislatures derive their power from the will of the people while judges do not. This in turn means that the Court should exercise its power of judicial review only in the clearest of cases, and justices "should confine themselves to enforcing norms that are stated or clearly implicit in the written Constitution."[58]

Other scholars, however, are not so troubled by the idea of judicial review. In a seminal article written in 1957, Robert Dahl attacked the most basic assumption of the counter-majoritarian perspective, arguing that it was overly simplistic to even describe the political culture in majority/minority terms. "Few of the Court's policy decisions," he wrote, "can be interpreted sensibly in terms of a 'majority' versus a 'minority.' Generally speaking, policy at the national level is the outcome of conflict, bargaining and agreement among minorities; the process is neither minority rule nor majority rule but what might better be called *minorities* rule, where one aggregation of minorities achieves policies opposed by another aggregation."[59] In light of his position, it is not surprising that Dahl also concluded that "it is probably impossible to demonstrate that any particular Court decisions have or have not been at odds with the preferences of a 'national majority.'"[60] Dahl makes a number of other points that space does not allow us to describe but both the strengths and weaknesses of his perspective make this important essay worth further reading. In his work, *Constitutional Self-Government*, Christopher Eisgruber also questions the premises of the counter-majoritarian difficulty, namely that judicial review is antidemocratic. He points out that Supreme Court justices are "political appointees, nominated and confirmed by elected officials" and adds, "The familiar hand-wringing about the 'counter-majoritarian' character of the federal judiciary obscures the respects in which judges owe their positions to electoral choices."[61] Eisgruber also offers an additional argument. For him, the independence of justices (life tenure) and their lack of personal ambition (they are already at the "apex" of their profession) assure that judges will decide "deeply contested moral judgments" on the basis of "principled judgment—a judgment . . . about what is good from a moral perspective, rather than a judgment about what is good for their careers or their pocketbooks."[62]

The amount of ink, not to say passion, expended on the subject of judicial review is immeasurable. Perhaps it is time for a moratorium. At least that is the implicit suggestion of one prominent scholar. Every year the Harvard Law Review asks a well-respected scholar to review the prior term of the Court, a very prestigious assignment often used to discuss some interesting aspect of constitutional law. In his review of the 2005 term, Frederick Schauer, a professor at the Kennedy School of Government, presented data showing, among other things, that the Court rarely deals with the issues that most concern the public.[63] In June 2006, for example, those issues, according to a Harris poll, were the Iraq War, immigration, the economy, health care, gas/oil prices, education, employment/jobs, Social Security, federal budget, taxes, terrorism, poverty programs, energy, military/defense, and the environment. Schauer concluded that the Court's "essentially low-salience existence" with its "docket of low-salience issues" "calls into question much of the contemporary and not-so-contemporary angst about the countermajoritarian or antidemocratic behavior of the Court."[64] Schauer was not minimizing the importance of judicial review but simply pointing out the irony of condemning its undemocratic character when the issues it was deciding ranked so low on the people's priorities.

When Congress has doubts about the constitutionality of legislation it is enacting, it will occasionally provide in the legislation itself for an expedited review process by the judiciary. This would have disturbed James Thayer, a leading legal scholar of the late nineteenth and early twentieth centuries, who saw Congress as an important partner in the creation of constitutional meaning. In the words of Robert Post of Yale Law School, "Thayer conceptualized constitutional law as in part made up of the judgments of Congress," and "for that reason, Thayer argued, the Court should think long and hard before constructing constitutional law in ways that override the constitutional beliefs of Congress."[65] Thayer's hopes have not been realized and few would argue today that the Court should refrain from voiding laws because their constitutionality has already been carefully considered by Congress. Justice Scalia has expressed particular frustration at Congress's unconcern for issues of constitutionality.

Judicial review does not mean that the Court should necessarily be the last word on the subject of constitutionality. It is one thing for the Court to let its opinion on constitutionality determine an individual case—after all, nobody would contest the right of the judicial branch to decide cases before it—it is quite another to say that the Court's opinion should bind the political branches. Nevertheless, judicial supremacy—meaning the recognition by the president, the Congress, the states, and the people of the binding authority of the Supreme Court to review and declare state and federal laws and actions unconstitutional—seems well established, in part, because, in the words of Keith Whittington, "As it has become evident that judicial supremacy is more often a help than a hindrance to political leaders, judicial supremacy has become more prominent and secure."[66]

The Court likely owes its success in establishing judicial supremacy in part to its own sensitivity to public opinion. Jeffrey Rosen, a law professor at George Washington University, for example, has emphasized how the Court has served the country "by reflecting and enforcing the constitutional views of the American people."[67] Certainly, a Court constantly at odds with public opinion would have reduced the incentive of political actors to embrace the idea of judicial supremacy.

I suspect, however, that judicial supremacy needs to be explained on a deeper level. It may have something to do with a diverse and immigrant nation instinctively embracing the stability that a single source of constitutional meaning provides. Our democracy is, after all, unique in the way its system of federalism, separation of powers, and checks and balances build conflict into the very heart of the system. These built-in conflicts, plus the fact that our most basic rights have been committed to writing in a formal legal text, suggest a deep need in the architecture of our democracy for a neutral, trusted arbiter of constitutional meaning. It is natural that the least political branch operating within the professional traditions of the law would best fill that need.

The Isolated Branch

Chief Justice Warren described his first day at the Supreme Court as the loneliest one of his life. After a long career in politics, he was shocked to arrive at his office to be greeted by the prior chief justice's secretary, three law clerks, and two old messengers. "And that was my staff, that's all there was."[68] Years earlier, Justice Douglas could not get over how the phone simply stopped ringing once he went to the Court, a far cry from his life as chairman of the Securities and Exchange Commission amid his continuing battles with Wall Street.[69] Harold Burton, a Truman appointee who went from the U.S. Senate to the Court, said that it felt like going from a circus to a monastery.[70]

The roles of the president and Congress require that they either work together or confront each other. Presidents have legislative programs and propose budgets, both of which require the assent of Congress in its lawmaking capacity. Congress enacts laws that the president can veto but which Congress can override with a two-thirds majority. By virtue of their assigned powers under the Constitution, the president and Congress have collaborative roles when it comes to key appointments, including Supreme Court appointments, the making of treaties, and the funding of wars. The Court operates outside this process. It renders its decisions without consulting the other branches, and it would be highly improper for individual justices of the Court to reach out for the views of others in arriving at their decisions.

This isolation is partly due to the Court's own sensitivity to the ideal of separation of powers at a very early stage in its history. At the beginning of Washington's first term, Thomas Jefferson, then secretary of state, wrote to the justices on behalf of the president, requesting the Court's interpretation of certain existing treaties. The justices, citing the need for a distinct separation of powers, declined the offer and established the critical precedent that the Court does not give advisory opinions. At roughly the same time, Congress enacted legislation giving the justices a role in the review of pension claims of Revolutionary soldiers. The justices made clear that they thought this practice inappropriate, and Congress repealed the legislation in the following session.

Interestingly, the Framers really didn't consider the many ways in which the political branches could isolate the judiciary just by exercising their ordinary powers. Congress's power over the purse strings, for example, gives it leverage over the Court that it has never really used but also underscores the Court's institutional weakness. The fact is that the Court depends on the Congress to pay for supplies and heat the building as much as any other entity of the federal government. In the words of Charles Geyh, author of an excellent study of the struggle between Congress and the federal courts, the Framers "apparently gave no thought to the judiciary's dependence on Congress for non-remunerative resources, such as building, clerical, and circuit-riding expenses, which Congress could manipulate to the same effect as salaries. Nor did they appear to consider the possibility that congressional control over court structure, size, practice, procedure, or administration might be exploited to compromise the judiciary's institutional integrity."[71] While the Congress has not abused these powers, it did vote, shortly after the Court had ruled against prayer in the public schools, to increase the salaries of lower court federal judges by $7,500 but Supreme Court justice salaries by only $4,500,[72] not exactly a frontal attack but a clear message nonetheless.

The Court is not insensitive to the need to present its best face to Congress in pursuing its own financial needs. Chief Justice Warren, for example, made it a practice to send Justice Clark to "sweet talk Congress into looking favorably upon the Court's budget request" because of his excellent relations with powerful congressional southerners.[73]

Choosing Supreme Court Justices

The most powerful way in which Congress and the president influence the direction of the Supreme Court is by deciding who does and does not sit on it. That process has changed enormously over the years and, in the eyes of many, not necessarily for the good.

When Earl Warren became chief justice in 1953, neither he nor the other eight justices he joined, save one (Sherman Minton), had ever served on the U.S. Circuit Court of Appeals. All of them, however, had held important positions in public service—three had been U.S. senators (Black, Burton and Minton). The others included a former chairman of the Securities and Exchange Commission (Douglas); a distinguished academic who had also served as an assistant to the secretary of war and chairman of the War Labor Policies Board during World War I (Frankfurter); a former state legislator and former general counsel to important government agencies, including the Reconstruction Finance Corporation (Reed); a former governor of California and vice presidential candidate (Warren); a career prosecutor and Justice Department lawyer (Clark); and a former general counsel to the Internal Revenue Service, solicitor general. and, for a brief period before his appointment, attorney general (Jackson).[74]

In contrast, today, every justice on the Court has also served as a judge on the Circuit Court of Appeals,[75] except the newly appointed Justice Kagan, and none of them has ever held an elective position. The reason for this change is not a great mystery. Because the Court has become a focus for ideological factions of both parties, as well as for major public interest groups along the political spectrum, the selection process has a dimension that is actually quite new.[76] The first open confirmation hearing did not occur until 1916 with Justice Brandeis who, interestingly, did not appear as a witness.[77] Today that would be unthinkable as confirmation hearings have become a political circus that simply would have no reason for being without the star attraction.

Because nominations, until the past few decades, were based on many factors and were not part of an ongoing ideological battle in which the public itself was heavily invested, the choices and their subsequent careers as justices were sometimes unpredictable. "Although a nominee of President Wilson, a Democrat, Justice McReynolds was among the most consistently conservative justices during his tenure while two of President Hoover's appointments (Justices Stone and Cardozo) were among those who, with Justice Brandeis, tended to support liberal positions on New Deal and Civil Liberties cases."[78] In the absence of ideological litmus tests, presidents even felt free to use Supreme Court appointments as a way of garnering opposition party support. President Eisenhower, for example, nominated William Brennan, a New Jersey Democrat, to the Court two months before the election of 1956 as a way of appealing to Irish Catholic Democrats.

This is not to say that Congress has historically rubber-stamped presidential nominees. Quite the contrary, roughly one-third of the presidents' nominees failed to make it to the Court during the nineteenth century. For the most part, however, these rejections were motivated by purely partisan considerations or as a means to getting at the president personally for past transgressions, rather than out of concern for how the rejected nominee might actually perform on the Court.

Today, the last thing a president wants to do is offend the activist faction of his own party. For this reason, presidents want a nominee with a proven track record, and certainly service on the circuit court can supply that record. The second President Bush didn't fully appreciate the need for this assurance when he nominated his counsel, Harriet Miers, an error that he quickly corrected when he withdrew her name and nominated Judge Alito after an outcry from his conservative base.

Has the politicization of Supreme Court appointments become inevitable? Certainly, the identity of future justices will be of great interest to the public so long as issues like abortion, affirmative action, gun control, the scope of federal power, gay marriage, campaign finance, and the proper place of religion in public affairs are constitutionally contested. And no one knows what other issues might emerge in the future. Given the stakes, it is likely that future Supreme Court appointments will continue to be significant political events. That is not necessarily regrettable and simply reflects the dynamics of our democratic process. Over the long run, however, the danger of ideological appointments is twofold. First, there are undoubtedly many fine potential justices who do not necessarily have such a fixed set of views as to comfort the ideological wing of whichever party might be in power. This means that we are likely even now to be overlooking potential justices whose lack of predictability might actually be a virtue but who will simply not be considered in the current atmosphere.

Second, the danger of choosing justices geared to assuring certain predictable votes is that we implicitly denigrate more important personal qualities that we should ask of any justice—intelligence, open-mindedness, a sense of fairness, respect for precedent, a degree of moderation, some feeling for the consequences of the Court's decisions, particularly as they affect the less powerful elements in society, and, above all, judicial temperament—a justice who listens carefully to both sides, even if his or her own philosophy is likely to point in a particular constitutional direction.

It has been suggested that future hearings for Supreme Court nominees should scrutinize for these kinds of qualities, as well as a justice's overall judicial philosophy and understanding of the function of judicial review.[79] This focus would give the hearings a real purpose instead of the scattershot charade they have become when nominees avoid the few legitimate questions asked and politicians are more concerned about their political audience than arriving at independent assessments of the nominee.

The one saving grace is that these hearings, in their present state of disrepair, do not happen too often. Since justices serve for life and most of them seem to like the job, turnover is slow, and it is unusual for presidents to make more than a couple of appointments: President Obama has had two appointments in his first term; the two Presidents Bush, both the father and the son, and President Clinton each had two appointments; President Reagan had three and President Carter none. This relative infrequency helps assure some degree of diversity on the Court but it can also create some problems when the Court and the political branches are completely out of sync. This occurred most notably during Franklin D. Roosevelt's first term. As mentioned earlier, a conservative Old Guard led the Court in striking down certain key New Deal legislation, including the National Industrial Recovery Act and the Agricultural Adjustment Act, both of which had been regarded by Roosevelt as keys to economic recovery.[80] The Court also voided thirty state laws, most all of them regulating economic matters, during this period. These decisions led directly to Roosevelt's famous plan to pack the Court by giving him the right to appoint a new justice for every justice over the age of seventy then on the Court, thereby instantly creating a new majority for New Deal legislation. A crisis was averted when the Court began to vote to uphold critical New Deal statutes, including the National Labor Relations Act[81] and the Social Security Act[82] and Roosevelt began to appoint justices as a result of deaths and retirements. During his second term Roosevelt was able to appoint five justices, including Hugo Black, Felix Frankfurter, Robert Jackson and William Douglas.

As a matter of historical interest, I should note that, before the Civil War, geographical balance was an important element in the selection of Supreme Court justices. This partly reflected sectional rivalries but was also due to the feeling that justices should know the laws of the states in which they rode circuit. The circuits were constituted in such a way that this practice assisted the South in retaining a dominant influence on the Court during the Antebellum period, particularly in the decade immediately prior to the War.[83] Even as late as the New Deal, geographical considerations were not unimportant. In the infighting that led to his selection, William Douglas worked hard to establish his credentials as a Westerner to meet the perceived political desirability of having at least one justice from that region on the Court.

Should Supreme Court Justices Have Life Tenure?

Independent justices do not have to be lifetime justices. A Supreme Court justice appointed for a single twenty-year term would be as independent as a lifetime justice since he or she would have no prospect of reappointment and presumably would be devoid of other political ambitions. With presidents tending to choose younger and younger justices and people living longer and longer, thirty or forty years on the bench could easily become the norm. Is this a cause for concern? Perhaps not, if wisdom increases with age. Yet, there is something disquieting about the possibility of a Court filled with justices deciding constitutional cases bubbling up from a world from which they are four decades removed. Constitutional law is inseparable from the times in which it is made since its raw material is the very controversies and clashes those times produce. The very remoteness from the hurly burly of everyday politics that allows us to place a certain faith in the integrity of the Court may, in the case of justices entering their fifth decade of service, become a liability leading to a majority incapable of reacting to or even understanding a changing society. Moreover, while perhaps still a decade or two away, it is likely that, if the trend to younger and younger justices persists, we may have a series of presidents with very little opportunity to appoint Supreme Court justices. That would not be good for either our politics or the Court. We are already suffering from this new mathematics in a different way, for in today's politics, there is an actuarial table for Supreme Court nominees that eliminates almost any sixty-five year old, no matter how distinguished, from consideration. This is the kind of loss whose impact is impossible to gauge as is the possibility that very bright, very able persons are being brought on to the Court at an age when they might well have benefited from a little more seasoning in the "real" world.

How the Court and Congress Talk to Each Other

One aspect of the Court's relationship to Congress deserves special attention, for the Court and Congress are in a continuing dialogue over both statutory and constitutional meaning. The vast majority of the Court's work involves statutory, not constitutional, interpretation. It falls to the judicial system to fill in gaps and address ambiguities when litigants clash over a statute's meaning. Sometimes the Court gets it wrong. In the late 1980s, for example, the Court issued a series of decisions making it more difficult to sue for acts of racial discrimination under existing federal law. These decisions led to the Civil Rights Restoration Act of 1991, enacted by a Democratic Congress and signed by a Republican president. More recently, Congress reversed a much-criticized decision of the Court that had interpreted the Equal Pay Act in a way that precluded a woman from pressing a discrimination claim unless she had learned about it very early in her employment.[84]

When it comes to determining the meaning of statutes, Congress and the president can have the last word. For this reason, statutory review is not as serious in its implications for the system of checks and balances as is judicial review for constitutionality. When the Court declares legislation unconstitutional, then only a reversal by a future Court or a constitutional amendment will undo the Court's decision. That does not mean, however, that matters are at an end, for it is not at all unusual for Congress to attempt to fix constitutional problems and try again. As noted, at the height of the controversy over the Court in 1935, the Court invalidated the Frazier-Lemke Farm Mortgage Act of 1934 intended to give relief to small farmers and save them from foreclosure. The hastily drafted act, however, had gone too far in the eyes of a unanimous Court in favoring the debtor over the mortgage holder and amounted, wrote Justice Brandeis, to taking property without just compensation in violation of the Fifth Amendment. Congress then recast the act to provide more protection for the mortgagee, and the Court upheld the revised act.

Sometimes the Court decides an issue of federalism that then forces the Congress to act. For example, in 1886, the Court decided that the Interstate Commerce clause (to be discussed more fully shortly) precluded the states from regulating rates of interstate railroads within their borders.[85] This meant, of course, that unless Congress took action, there would be no regulation of railroad rates at all. To fill this new void, Congress promptly enacted the Interstate Commerce Act of 1887, which provided for the regulation of railroad rates by the newly created Interstate Commerce Commission.

The dynamic between Congress and the Court is a complex one, well illustrated by a series of cases and statutes that has had an important impact on First Amendment law. It began in 1991 when the Court in *Employment Division, Department of Human Resources of Oregon v. Smith*[86] effected a major change in First Amendment law. An Oregon statute had denied unemployment benefits to an individual fired because he had engaged in criminal activity: he had smoked peyote (an illegal drug) as part of a religious ritual. The employee brought suit claiming that denial of benefits for smoking peyote as part of his religious worship violated the First Amendment. Under then prevailing constitutional doctrine, the employee would probably have prevailed since the application of the Oregon law would have been subject to strict scrutiny requiring a compelling governmental interest for denying the benefits. In *Smith*, however, the Supreme Court in a 5–4 opinion upheld the denial of benefits to the plaintiff, ruling that acts of general applicability not aimed at religion did not have to meet the strict scrutiny standard, even when their natural application limited a person's religious rights.

Congress thought that *Smith* was wrongly decided and in the Religious Freedom Restoration Act of 1993 (RFRA) restored the strict scrutiny standard in free exercise cases. A few years later, a Catholic archbishop relied on the RFRA to argue that the refusal of municipal authorities to issue a building permit for an expansion of its church without a compelling reason was improper.

The case went to the Supreme Court, which in *City of Boerne v. Flores*[87] held the RFRA unconstitutional. In so holding, the Court made clear that Congress's power to enforce the Fourteenth Amendment did not include the power to define First Amendment rights, which was the job of the judiciary. *Boerne* can be viewed—in my opinion is properly viewed—as a case in which the Court acted precipitously. Congress was, after all, expanding the vision of a constitutional right, arguably at its own expense. The Court's position in *Boerne* is also surprising since sometimes the Court will invite Congress to take action to expand rights. In 1978, for example, the Court, in upholding a warrant to search a campus newspaper office for photographs of students who had attacked police during a student demonstration,[88] reminded Congress that "the Fourth Amendment does not prevent or advise against legislative or executive efforts to establish non-constitutional protections against possible abuses of the search warrant procedure."[89]

The dialogue between Congress and the president did not end with the *Boerne* decision. Following *Boerne*, Congress enacted more limited legislation providing in part that inmates confined in a state prison receiving federal funds could not be deprived of their right to worship in their own way without a compelling justification from the State, reviving the RFRA but in a much narrower context. This new statute had been carefully crafted to meet concerns expressed by the Court in *Boerne*. Following passage of the legislation, inmates in an Ohio prison invoked the statute when they were prohibited from performing certain special services. The State argued that the new federal statute was unconstitutional but the Court in a unanimous decision upheld it.[90]

Over the course of a decade and a half, the Court had rendered a decision that Congress did not like; Congress had attempted to challenge the Court's decision; the Court had reasserted its sole authority to determine how a constitutional right is to be determined; Congress listened and tested the contours of the Court's rulings with a narrower statute and the Court approved the narrower statute.

5. What the Court Does: The Stuff of Judicial Review

Overseeing the Constitutional Structure

The Supreme Court, in implementing the Constitution, performs two major functions: it decides cases dealing with the constitutional structure and it decides cases establishing the scope and nature of our individual rights. The Court's main structural tasks are to define the scope of national lawmaking power, manage controversies arising over the relationship between the federal and state governments, and oversee the system of checks and balances and separation of powers within the national government.

Defining the Scope of the National Lawmaking Power

The Constitution created a national government of strictly enumerated powers written for a nation of farmers at a time when it could take a week to go from Boston to Philadelphia by land. Very soon, however, the nation began its rapid expansion both geographically and commercially. It fell to the Supreme Court to assure that the constitutional structure did not impede these developments. We have already encountered John Marshall, the judicial politician who navigated the Court through the dangerous days of Jefferson's first term. It was, however, Marshall the ardent nationalist for whom posterity has reserved its greatest praise and accords him recognition as one of the greatest, if not the greatest, of the Court's justices.

As mentioned, John Marshall was chief justice of the Supreme Court from 1801 to 1835. The Marshall Court encouraged the promotion of national power and a market economy by, among other things, (1) broadly construing congressional power (*McCulloch v. Maryland*); (2) prohibiting exercises of state power that interfered with federal power (*Gibbons v. Ogden*); and (3) protecting settled expectations of property owners and creditors (*Fletcher v. Peck* and *Sturges v. Crowninshield*). The Court did not create our national economy nor provide its dynamism. It did, however, through these major cases, and others as well, help shape a legal environment that, at a minimum, did not interfere with these developments and perhaps, to some small degree, allowed these forces to take hold.

In *McCulloch v. Maryland* (1819),[1] Chief Justice Marshall, writing for a unanimous Court, approved Congress's creation and incorporation of a national bank. Marshall relied in part on Congress's authority to "make all Laws which shall be necessary and proper for carrying into Execution" its enumerated powers: in this case, incorporation of a bank was deemed in furtherance of Congress's enumerated power to borrow money. Marshall also asserted, as a separate argument, that the right to incorporate a national bank was inherent in the very purposes of the Constitution itself. In one of his most important expressions on the subject of the national government's power, Marshall wrote: "Let the end be legitimate, let it be within the scope of the Constitution, and all means which are appropriate, which are plainly adapted to that end, which are not prohibited, but consistent with the letter and spirit of the constitution, are constitutional."[2] In *McCulloch*, the Court also held that the state of Maryland could not tax the National Bank, thus establishing the principle that, when the national government exercises its powers, its interests prevail over those of the state, when they conflict.

In *Gibbons v. Ogden* (1824),[3] the Court held that a New York state law that had granted a monopoly to Robert Fulton to operate steamboats on the Hudson River was preempted by a federal law granting a federal coastal license for steamboat operation. The case established the supremacy of federal law over state law in areas covered by Congress's enumerated powers and clearly was aimed at limiting the potential for destructive rivalries between the states that might disrupt the commercial development of the nation as a whole. Shortly after the Court's decision, the New York legislature repealed the law that had authorized the granting of monopoly status to Fulton.

In *Fletcher v. Peck* (1810),[4] the Court protected the interests of property owners, upholding their claim of title to land, notwithstanding that the initial land grant to which they had succeeded had been conveyed in exchange for bribes given to a corrupt Georgia legislature. A later session of the legislature had attempted to rescind the original, tainted grants, but the Supreme Court held in *Fletcher* that such repeal was ineffective since it violated the provision of the Constitution prohibiting states from passing any law violating the obligation of contracts (the "Contracts Clause"). The decision had the effect of protecting the finality of property transactions.

In *Sturges v. Crowninshield* (1819),[5] the Court also protected property rights by applying the Contracts clause to void a New York insolvency law that discharged a debtor's obligations once he surrendered property securing the debt.

Interestingly, fifteen years after *Sturges*, in a case where contract rights arguably stood in the way of further economic development, the Court opted for development. The case, *Charles River Bridge v. Proprietors of Warren Bridge*,[6] came to the Court during Chief Justice Taney's first term. Taney served as chief justice almost as long as Marshall, 1836 to 1864. The case arose because the state of Massachusetts had effectively wiped out the investment of the owners of the Charles River Bridge, a toll bridge connecting Cambridge and Boston built in 1785 whose construction the state had authorized by charter. In 1828 Massachusetts authorized a second neighboring bridge that would become free to the public six years after its construction, clearly an impossible situation for the competing toll bridge. The charter of the Charles River Bridge owners did not end until 1856, and the owners were in effect asking the Court to imply an exclusive right to operate a toll bridge, at least in that immediate vicinity, until the expiration of the charter. The Supreme Court, however, in a 4–3 decision, allowed the second bridge to go forward. Chief Justice Taney wrote the majority opinion holding that charters involving the public interest should be narrowly construed. Justice Story, in dissent, argued that the charter was a valuable contract on which the state was reneging. Both men undoubtedly thought that theirs was the more progressive view, Story because it would allow business to rely on legitimate expectations in their dealings with the state, Taney because it meant that long-ago commitments would not shackle the present unless those commitments had been made absolutely clear.

The dark side of judicial nationalism in this era was the Court's determination to uphold and enforce fugitive slave laws, even when it meant, for example, returning a black woman and her children, who had lived their entire lives in freedom, to slavery, as the Court did in the famous case of *Prigg v. Pennsylvania*.[7]

As the post–Civil War era began, the Court had to consider whether the federal government could constitutionally require that the paper currency called "greenbacks," issued by the Union to help finance the war, be accepted as legal tender for the payment of all taxes and debts. In a decision with important economic implications, the Court, in *Hepburn v. Griswold*,[8] said no, holding that greenbacks could not be made legal tender for debts entered into prior to enactment of the law authorizing the greenbacks. The problem was that the decision threatened to cause great confusion in the national economy since a major form of currency was now subject to a severe limitation, making it something less than full legal tender. Immediately after *Hepburn* was decided, President Grant had the opportunity to fill two vacancies on the Court. The Court quickly set two new cases for argument and overruled *Hepburn* in what is known as the Legal Tender Cases, upholding the act and its retroactive application as within Congress's authority in dealing with an extreme emergency. In language that would resonate sixty years later when the Court was considering Franklin Roosevelt's action in taking the United States off the gold standard, the Court noted, "The degree of the necessity for any congressional enactment, or the relative degree of its appropriateness, is for consideration in Congress, not here."[9] The Court would not be so deferential in the future.

After the Civil War, an industrializing economy, unified both physically and psychologically by the growth of the railroads, needed a source of authority that would allow for Congressional regulation of a wide variety of activities. The clause empowering Congress to regulate interstate commerce (the Commerce clause) seemed the perfect vehicle for assuring the government the tools it needed to meet a new age. Relying on the clause, the Court, among other laws, approved the Interstate Commerce Act of 1887 creating the Interstate Commerce Commission, the Sherman Anti-Trust Act attempting to assure competition in the marketplace, and Progressive era legislation such as the Meat Inspection Act of 1906 and the Food and Drug Act. The Court even approved federal legislation prohibiting the interstate movement of lottery tickets, legislation clearly motivated more by moral than economic considerations.[10]

The Court's Commerce clause jurisprudence during this period is a fascinating subject and worth a little extra attention, for it shows a Court struggling to reconcile its own view of the Constitution with the needs of a rapidly industrializing and growing nation.

In 1895, the Court seemed to have put the Sherman Act in a strait jacket when, in *United States v. E. C. Knight Co.*,[11] it held that Congress lacked authority to regulate manufacturing since that was a local activity. Reasoning from this premise, the Court ruled that the act did not authorize the U.S. Government to seek to prevent the American Sugar Refining Company from acquiring four other sugar refineries, even though the result would be American's ownership of 98 percent of American sugar refining capacity. The Court in *Knight*, as it had in the *Slaughterhouse* and the Civil Rights Cases, resisted a conclusion that it felt would greatly expand national power.

Writing for the Court in an 8–1 majority opinion (the first Justice Harlan dissenting), Chief Justice Fuller wrote: "Slight reflection will show that if the national power extends to all contracts and combinations in manufacture, agriculture, mining, and other productive industries, whose ultimate result may affect external commerce, comparatively little of business operations and affairs would be left for state control."[12]

Over time, however, the Court retreated from its formalistic distinction in *Knight* by allowing for national regulation of what might have been considered impermissible matters under *Knight*. Thus, an injunction under the Sherman Act against meat dealers who had entered into a price fixing arrangement was unanimously sustained by the Court in *Swift & Co. v. United States*.[13] Justice Holmes, writing for the Court, implicitly rejected the more formalistic approach to the Commerce clause announced in *Knight*, when he noted, "Commerce among the states is not a technical legal conception, but a practical one, drawn from the course of business."[14] While the *Knight* case continued to have vitality until the 1930s, the Court, as early as 1904, in the famous *Northern Securities* case,[15] approved the application of the Sherman Act to prevent corporate consolidation activities deemed harmful to competition. The *Northern Securities* case dealt with a consolidation of railroads, not manufacturers, but the case dealt with ownership and therefore, under a strict reading of *Knight*, might have been deemed outside the Commerce clause.

There was one point during this period on which the Court did not waver. When it came to labor relations, the Court had no interest in breathing life into the Commerce clause. Most famously, the Court, in 1918, concluded in *Hammer v. Dagenhart*,[16] another 5–4 decision, that Congress did not have the power to prohibit the interstate transportation of goods produced by child labor. A Supreme Court that just fifteen years earlier had approved prohibiting the distribution of lottery tickets in interstate commerce justified this decision on the theory that cotton goods produced by children were not inherently harmful, as were items like liquor and lottery tickets and even loose women. Justice Holmes, in dissent, asserted that "It is enough that in the opinion of Congress, the transportation encourages the evil."[17]

As previously noted, the basic pro-business bias of the Court continued throughout the first term of Franklin Roosevelt resulting in the Court's declaring major pieces of New Deal legislation unconstitutional. In March 1936 the Court invalidated an act aimed at fixing working conditions in the coal industry.[18] It would be the last hurrah of the anti–New Deal Court.

In November 1936 Roosevelt was reelected by a huge landslide and shortly thereafter Justice Owen Roberts, a Hoover appointee after Hoover's initial nominee (John J. Parker of North Carolina) failed to win Senate confirmation, began voting to approve legislation passed during what historians refer to as the Second New Deal, including the Social Security Act of 1935 and the National Labor Relations Act of 1935 (popularly known as the Wagner Act). The case approving the Wagner Act, *NLRB v. Jones and Laughlin Steel Corp.*,[19] was particularly important in characterizing the right to engage in collective bargaining as a fundamental right and making clear that the Commerce clause embraced a general authority to regulate manufacturing industries to further the goal of industrial peace.

In 1942 in *Wickard v. Filburn*,[20] the Court seemed to place no economic activity beyond Congress's reach when it held that a farmer's production of wheat on his own land for his own consumption could be regulated on the theory that the farmer's consumption enabled him to avoid the need to purchase wheat produced for interstate commerce.

With *Wickard*, the triumph of a broad reading of the Commerce clause seemed complete. However, as you may by now be beginning to suspect, little is absolutely final in constitutional law. Chief Justice Rehnquist had never been enamored of the Court's Commerce clause jurisprudence and in 1995, after 60 years of complete deference to Congress, the Court found in *Lopez v. United States*[21] that a law making it a federal offense to possess a firearm in a school zone was beyond the reach of the Commerce clause and therefore unconstitutional. In 2000, in *United States v. Morrison*,[22] the Court held that a federal law providing a civil remedy for gender-motivated violence was also beyond the reach of the Commerce clause. In both these cases, the Court focused on the fact that Congress was intruding into areas traditionally reserved for state regulation—education and citizen protection—which had only the remotest relation to interstate commerce.

If these decisions portended a possible federalism revolution, it has not yet come to pass. One scholar has noted that the actual statutes involved in the *Lopez* and *Morrison* cases had "little practical importance,"[23] meaning not that the subjects were unimportant but that states and local communities were in many cases addressing these subjects themselves. It is unclear what the future holds. Chief Justice Rehnquist is no longer on the Court, and in the same year that it invalidated the Violence against Women Act, the Court also upheld Congress's authority to prohibit the states from selling information in their Department of Motor Vehicles databanks, a decision actually written by the late Chief Justice Rehnquist himself.[24] Most significantly, in *Gonzalez v. Raich*,[25] the Court, in a much different context, reaffirmed the breadth of the Commerce clause. Two seriously ill California women used marijuana to control their pain. The use was perfectly legal under California's Compassionate Use Act of 1996. One of the women actually grew the marijuana herself. However, possession (as well as manufacture and distribution) of marijuana is a violation of the federal Controlled Substances Act. Notwithstanding the highly personal nature of the use of marijuana in this case and the fact that the California legislature had made such use legal, the Court by a 6–3 vote held that the federal act preempted California's Compassionate Care statute.

It is too early to bury the federalism revolution, but it is hard to disagree with one scholar's assessment that "Scholars of real revolutions would be amused by the Rehnquist Court's federalism revolution" given that "not a single central feature of the New Deal's regulatory regime" has been overturned nor any of "the central elements of the Great Society's programs displaced."[26] This, however, is a story that may not be over. In November 2011, the Supreme Court agreed to hear a case involving the constitutionality of the recently enacted federal health care law, a decision that may well have major implications for the federalism revolution.

While many people are aware of the significance of the Commerce clause in expanding the reach of national power, the importance of the spending power seems to be much less well known by the general public. Yet it provides the constitutional underpinning for our limited form of welfare capitalism. The welfare part of the description refers, of course, to the vast array of entitlement programs, including Medicaid, Medicare, Social Security, and welfare programs enacted by the federal government, often in cooperation with the states. None of these programs is authorized by a specific grant of congressional power, but Congress does have the power "To lay and collect Taxes, Duties, Imposts and Excises, to pay the Debts and provide for the common Defense and general Welfare of the United States." We have to do a little parsing here. This provision might be read to lodge a general power in Congress to legislate for the general welfare, but such an interpretation would arguably give Congress the power to enact any regulatory legislation which it thought would advance the general welfare and effectively eliminate the autonomy of the states in the federal system. The Supreme Court in *United States v. Butler*[27] rejected this view and held that the reference to the general welfare was a qualification on the power to tax, not an independent grant of authority. At the same time, however, Justice Owen Roberts also noted that "the power of Congress to authorize the expenditure of public moneys for public purposes is not limited by the direct grants of legislative power found in the Constitution." This sounds like a pretty broad interpretation of the taxing power, and it is. As noted, it has allowed for the development of our social welfare system. The problem comes, constitutionally, when the federal government attaches conditions to its programs so that the states, for example, must change their laws in order to receive federal funds. This was precisely the issue in *South Dakota v. Dole*[28] where the federal government conditioned grants of a portion of highway funds to the states on the state's not establishing a drinking age lower than twenty-one. The Court held that this was a permissible condition but stressed that the amount of highway funds that would be lost by a state with a lower drinking age would only be 5 percent of funds otherwise obtainable. There are not as many cases on this subject as one might expect, one reason undoubtedly being the standing requirement discussed in the last chapter, which, you may recall, generally bars taxpayer suits questioning the constitutionality of federal spending programs. One scholar has written, correctly, in my view, that "The spending power is probably the most important federal power in terms of its impact on the daily lives of Americans."[29]

Managing the Federal/State Relationship

A separate aspect of the Court's structural role has to do with managing the relationship between the federal government and the states. The Court becomes involved in several ways.

For one thing, while it is clear under the Supremacy clause that state governments cannot regulate federal activities, the Constitution does not address the extent to which the federal government can regulate state activities. One problem is defining when federal laws of general applicability may not apply to state activities because they impinge too heavily on state sovereignty. For most of its history, the Court denied state efforts to avoid the impact of general federal legislation that simply affected some state activities, allowing for example the application of a federal tax on the sale of bottled water from state-owned springs.[30] The Court, however, in 1976 in *National League of Cities v. Usery*,[31] under the influence of a newly invigorated conservative wing, held that concerns for state autonomy precluded application of maximum hour and minimum wage provisions in the federal Fair Labor Standards Act to the states as employers. This portended a possible revolution in federal/state relationships, but within less than a decade the Court, in *Garcia v. San Antonio Metropolitan Transit Authority*,[32] reversed itself. Justice Blackmun, who had been with the majority in *National League of Cities*, had grown frustrated with the difficulty of trying to protect state autonomy in a principled way. Blackmun changed sides partly because he became convinced that the states were adequately protected from undue regulation by the structure of the federal system itself, particularly the equal representation of states in the U.S. Senate. Blackmun did not rule out the possibility that the Court might find a breakdown in the political process which would require judicial intervention to protect the states. As a general matter, however, he had become convinced that "The political process insures that laws that unduly burden the states will not be promulgated."[33]

Blackmun's logic has not been extended to other situations where it arguably could also apply. For example, after President Reagan was shot in 1981, Congress, in passing the Brady Bill, mandated that the states assist in making background checks for gun purchases. (The bill was named after President Reagan's press secretary who was badly wounded in the incident.) This time the Court, in *Printz v. United States*,[34] sided with the states, invalidating the mandate as an impermissible infringement on state sovereignty. The case is an important one since it indicates that there are serious constitutional limits on the authority of Congress to utilize the machinery of state government to effectuate national policies. Similarly, the Court in *New York v. United States*,[35] found that Congress had gone beyond its powers when it required states to take title to low level radioactive waste by a certain date if it had not already taken appropriate steps for its disposal.

The Court also influences the state/federal relationship when it decides whether state law has unconstitutionally intruded into areas which Congress has chosen to regulate. Preemption cases don't generally engage the passions but they are not unimportant. *Prigg v. Pennsylvania*, previously alluded to, was essentially a preemption case in which Justice Story effectively nullified state Personal Liberty laws. These laws had provided some measure of due process protection for seized blacks. Story held that those laws were preempted under the Constitution, and only Congress could enact laws addressing the fugitive slave issue.

If Congress has clearly expressed a desire to preempt state law, then under the Supremacy clause, states may not also legislate on that subject. Where, however, Congress's intent is not clear or it has not occupied a field, the judiciary must decide whether a given state law or regulation is preempted.

Preemption can be of great benefit in a liability context to big companies if it protects them from suits based on alleged violations of state law and regulations. The stakes can be very high for both companies and aggrieved plaintiffs. For example, in 2006, the Second Circuit Court of Appeals held that a group of Michigan residents could sue Warner-Lambert (now part of Pfizer) for damages caused by use of the diabetes treatment drug Rezulin. This drug had been approved for use by the Food and Drug Administration (FDA). Under Michigan law, pharmaceutical companies are shielded from liability for damages caused by FDA-approved drugs, with an important exception. Michigan law allows a suit if approval of the drug is based on the company's fraud or misrepresentation. Warner Lambert claimed that this exception was preempted because it would allow state courts to second-guess the integrity of the FDA's approval process. Plaintiffs countered that the exception simply allowed for a traditional area of state tort liability and did not threaten the federal regulatory scheme. Interestingly, the Supreme Court divided 4–4 on the issue (Chief Justice Roberts not taking part in the case). A tie results in an affirmance of the decision of the Court below. In this case, the result was a victory for the plaintiffs.[36] For our purposes, the key point is that even subjects as esoteric as federal preemption can have enormous practical consequences. Unless Congress has made its intentions absolutely clear, the judiciary must decide when a national regulatory scheme is undermined by state law.

One aspect of the federal state relationship has a special history and deserves separate attention. The so-called Dormant Commerce clause doctrine was first enunciated in 1852 in *Cooley v. Board of Wardens of the Port of Philadelphia*.[37] Cooley answered an important question, namely, whether the authority confided to Congress by the Commerce clause was exclusive, barring state action even when Congress had not acted. The answer the Court gave was that it was exclusive only if by the nature of the subject matter it had to be exclusive. The case arose out of a Pennsylvania law that allowed the Port of Philadelphia to impose a financial penalty if a ship came or left the port without using local pilots. Two ships had left the port without using local pilots and the Board of Wardens sued to recover the penalty. The Court upheld the state statute on the ground that there were some subjects that did not require a uniform national rule and, in fact, were particularly fitted for local treatment: "Now the power to regulate Commerce, embraces a vast field, containing not only many, but exceedingly various objects, quite unlike in their nature; some imperatively demanding a single uniform rule, operating equally on the commerce of the United States in every port; and some like the subject now in question, as imperatively demanding that diversity, which alone can meet the local necessities of navigation."[38]

The Dormant Commerce clause is a species of preemption, but it is a preemption created not by federal statutory law but by the Supreme Court's view of what the Commerce clause allows. Under current doctrine, the Court essentially engages in a test which seeks to balance the strength of the local interest against the law's effect on interstate commerce. For example, where the local law seeks legitimately to protect health and safety with only a minimal impact on interstate commerce it will be upheld. Such was the case when the state of Maine barred the importation of baitfish into its borders for what the Court found to be genuine environmental concerns.[39] On the other hand, state laws imposing physical requirements on trains and trucks have been held unconstitutional given their obvious potential impact on the interstate movement of goods.[40]

Overseeing the System of Checks and Balances and Separation of Powers

The importance of this aspect of the Court's work is not fully appreciated, perhaps because it involves for the most part overseeing the political working of the government. There are moments, of course, when it has put the Court very much in the public eye, as for example, when the Court disapproved President Truman's seizure of the steel mills because of a lack of congressional authorization and when it required President Nixon to turn over the Watergate Tapes in the face of his claim of executive privilege. The real significance, however, of the Court's work in this area involves its long range impact on the workings of government.

One important area has dealt with the question of delegation of congressional power. Since the New Deal, the scope of the federal government has grown enormously, penetrating every aspect of American life. This expansion has led to the creation of scores of independent regulatory agencies, such as the Federal Trade Commission, the Federal Communications Commission, the National Labor Relations Board, the Securities and Exchange Commission, the Environmental Protection Agency, and the Federal Aviation Administration, to name just a few. These agencies, in contrast to the heads of executive branch departments such as the Department of Agriculture, exercise enormous discretionary authority. Constitutional issues arise because the legislative power resides with Congress and there are, therefore, constitutional limits on the scope of discretion which can be given to these independent agencies. For the most part, the Court has allowed for the creation of strong, effective agencies while policing the boundaries of appropriate delegation. The basic test is whether the delegation provides an intelligible principle to which the delegated authority must conform its actions; if it does, the delegation is constitutional.

Another important area in which the Court has made its presence felt is in defining the president's power of removal. In a case that has had enormous ramifications for the growth of quasi-legislative, quasi-judicial agencies, the Court in *Humphrey's Executor v. the United States*,[41] held that President Franklin Roosevelt did not have the authority to remove a Federal Trade Commissioner before the end of his seven year term. The president had argued that removal was an inherent part of his executive power; the Court, however, disagreed, finding that the Federal Trade Commission was not a purely executive agency but rather an entity performing quasi-judicial and quasi-legislative functions. As a result of this decision, the determinations and policies of administrative agencies like the Federal Communications Commission and the National Labor Relations Board are beyond the power of the president to direct, at least by the threatened exercise of his removal power.

It is not always the president's power of removal that is at issue. The comptroller general of the United States, though nominated by the president and confirmed by the Senate, is removable by statute only at the initiative of Congress and then only for certain specified reasons, including neglect of duty and malfeasance. A Separation of Powers issue arose when, in 1985, Congress passed the Gramm-Rudman Act aimed at controlling the federal deficit. The act entrusted the comptroller general with certain responsibilities. Once the Supreme Court determined that these responsibilities were executive in nature, it is not surprising that the Court found that the duties delegated to the comptroller general violated the concept of separation of powers. In the words of the Court: "To permit an officer controlled by Congress to execute the laws would be, in essence, to permit a congressional veto. Congress could simply remove, or threaten to remove, an officer for executing the laws in any fashion found to be unsatisfactory to Congress. This . . . is constitutionally impermissible."[42]

Separation of powers issues come in many forms. The Court has, among many other things, allowed a civil suit to go forward against the president of the United States while in office[43]; approved a federal statute creating an independent counsel to investigate executive wrongdoing[44]; disapproved a federal statute giving the president a line item veto[45]; and disapproved the legislative veto. The legislative veto had been a staple of federal legislation for more than fifty years, appearing in more than 200 pieces of legislation, when it was struck down in 1983 in *Immigration and Naturalization Service v. Chadha*.[46] It had allowed Congress to delegate certain power to the executive while retaining the right of one or both houses of Congress to veto the executive's decisions. It had become particularly important in allowing Congress to have the ultimate say when administrative agencies exercised their rule-making authority. The Court determined that the legislative veto impermissibly short circuited the carefully designed plan for consideration of legislative matters set out in the Constitution.

One recent case involving separation of powers deserves special attention because it highlights how important constitutional and public policy issues can intersect. In *Boumediene v. Bush*,[47] both sides in a 5–4 vote claimed to be upholding the separation of powers principle. *Boumediene* is one of a string of cases in which the Court has wrestled with the constitutional rights of the prisoners held at Guantanamo Bay. In *Boumediene*, the majority held that the prisoners were entitled to the privilege of habeas corpus and Congress's attempt to strip the federal judiciary of habeas corpus jurisdiction respecting these prisoners was unconstitutional. Justice Kennedy, writing for the Court, argued that the judiciary has a special responsibility in the constitutional structure to safeguard the right of habeas corpus, noting that "few exercises of judicial power are as legitimate or as necessary as the responsibility to hear challenges to the authority of the Executive to imprison a person."[48] For Justice Scalia, in dissent, respect for separation of powers required exactly the opposite result. Because Scalia felt that a prior Supreme Court decision had clearly indicated that habeas corpus would not be extended to the enemy aliens at Guantanamo, he accused the majority of engaging in a game of "bait and switch"[49] that "will almost certainly cause more Americans to be killed."[50] "What drives today's decision," concluded Justice Scalia, "is . . . an inflated notion of judicial supremacy."[51] Application of the separation of powers principle is not as straightforward as the simplicity of the principle itself might suggest, as *Boumediene* clearly shows.

The Full Faith and Credit Clause

Section 1, Article IV of the Constitution, known as the Full Faith and Credit clause, attempts to define the deference which the states owe to each other regarding their respective laws and judgments. It reads: "Full Faith and Credit shall be given in each state to the public Acts, Records and judicial Proceedings of every other state. And the Congress may by general Laws prescribe the Manner in which such Acts, Records and Proceedings shall be proved and the effect thereof." This provision of the Constitution marks the terrain on which such issues as the duty of one state to recognize a same-sex marriage in a sister state or a judgment of adoption by a gay couple will be fought.

In 1996, Congress passed the Defense of Marriage Act (DOMA) providing, in part, that no state is required to recognize a same-sex marriage in a sister state. Is DOMA within Congress's authority to enact? The answer is no, if the Full Faith and Credit clause requires valid marriages in one state to be recognized in sister states. But what effect should be accorded the second part of the Full Faith and Credit clause giving Congress the authority to adopt general laws prescribing the effect of state "Acts, Records, and Proceedings"? The general rule, as developed by the Supreme Court over time, is that the Full Faith and Credit clause does not require state A to give effect to the law of sister state B when it is contrary to state A's public policy. State A, however, is generally required to give effect to a judgment in state B regardless of whether that judgment would have been against the public policy of state A. This means, for example, that while state A might not be required to recognize a marriage performed in state B, it might be required to recognize as valid a judgment of adoption by a gay couple in state B even though such a judgment would be against the public policy of state A.

I note here that Section 3 of DOMA defines marriage for federal purposes as solely between a man and a woman, meaning that even a same-sex couple legally married in their state is not recognized as married by the federal government and therefore, for example, cannot file a joint federal tax return or receive spousal social security benefits. Section 3 does not raise an issue under the Full Faith and Credit clause since it does not deal with state recognition of sister state laws and judgments. It does, however, provide that the federal government will not accord recognition to valid state marriage laws. In February 2011, the Obama administration announced that it would no longer defend Section 3 in federal court, where its constitutionality has been challenged. Recalling our discussion of the standard of review under the Equal Protection clause, the administration concluded that Section 3 requires heightened scrutiny because of the history of discrimination against gay persons and fails to survive that scrutiny. This case will very likely be ultimately decided by the Supreme Court.

Recently, the 10th Circuit Court of Appeals (see Chapter 6 for a brief description of the federal court system) held that an Oklahoma statute that refused to recognize out-of-state adoptions was unconstitutional.[52] The State of Oklahoma decided not to appeal the decision. Can Congress, pursuant to the Effects clause, pass legislation authorizing the states not to give effect to out-of-state adoptions by gay couples? Such legislation would test the limits of Congress's authority to define the contours of the Full Faith and Credit clause, as would a case raising the constitutionality of the Defense of Marriage Act.

Full Faith and Credit questions cut simultaneously in several different ways when considered in the broader context of federalism. This is well illustrated by *Nevada v. Hall*,[53] a case in which three important concepts— comity, sovereignty, and sovereign immunity—clashed. An employee (also a resident) of the state of Nevada was involved in an automobile accident in California while on official state business. A California resident sued the state of Nevada in a California court; the Nevada driver was found to have been negligent. By statute, the state of Nevada had waived its sovereign immunity to allow suits against itself in Nevada courts but limited the recovery to $25,000. In the California lawsuit, Nevada raised two arguments: First, it argued that its limited waiver of sovereign immunity in Nevada courts did not preclude it from claiming sovereign immunity in California; Second, it argued that, even if it could be sued in California courts, California was bound under the Full Faith and Credit clause to honor the $25,000 limitation on recovery. In a six to three decision, the Supreme Court rejected both of Nevada's arguments. In essence, the Court found that California was not bound to recognize Nevada's claim of sovereign immunity in its own courts and also found that the Full Faith and Credit clause did not create a requirement of constitutional comity between the states requiring California to apply Nevada's $25,000 limitation. In effect, the Court was valuing California's right to apply its own legal system over Nevada's claim of sovereign immunity. The case is a fascinating one, quite accessible even if somewhat technical. For our purposes, it is significant as a good example of how notions of comity, sovereignty, and sovereign immunity can create difficult questions that in the end must be sorted out by the Supreme Court.

Nevada v. Hall involved the issue of sovereign immunity, but similar difficulties attend the question of enforcement of judgments even when sovereign immunity is not involved. To the extent that state A's judgments must be recognized by state B, the authority of state A within the federal system is enhanced but arguably at the expense of the authority of state B within its own borders. To the extent, on the other hand, that state B can resist judgments of state A, not only is state A's authority within the federal system compromised, but the whole idea of comity among states is endangered.

Protecting Individual Rights

Issues of federalism and constitutional structure do not generally excite great passion in the public at large. Not so for the Court's other major challenge—defining our rights. The Bill of Rights and 14th Amendment are written expansively. As previously noted, they guarantee the "free exercise of religion"; prohibit laws respecting an "establishment of religion" or abridging "the freedom of speech"; assure freedom from "unreasonable searches and seizures" of one's "persons, houses, papers and effects"; forbid deprivation of "life, liberty or property without due process of law"; forbid "cruel and unusual punishment"; and guarantee "the equal protection of the laws." In interpreting these and other critical provisions of the Constitution, the Court has issued its most controversial decisions, including decisions relating to abortion, affirmative action, school prayer, reapportionment, campaign finance, capital punishment, and criminal procedure.

Constitutional rights defy easy categorization, except, as noted in Chapter 1, they are essentially negative in that they constrain the government from acting in certain ways, rather than requiring the government to act to achieve societal goals. The Constitution, at least as interpreted by the Court, including its liberal members, has never been held to guarantee a minimum level of economic opportunity or to mandate the creation of a minimum safety net. Unemployment compensation is a statutory program, not a constitutional entitlement. The closest that the U.S. Supreme Court probably has ever come to mandating a level of equality was in *San Antonio Independent School District v. Rodriguez*,[54] where the Court was asked to declare public school education a fundamental constitutional right. The Court turned down the offer and, accordingly, preserved the Texas system of financing public school education on the basis of the property tax, notwithstanding that it meant that poorer school districts could not afford the same quality of education as richer ones. One can only speculate whether a more expansive view of individual rights might have developed had the Warren Court era lasted a few more years with a President Humphrey (who lost to Richard Nixon in 1968), rather than President Nixon, making four Supreme Court appointments. The fact that *Rodriguez* was a 5–4 decision, with all four of the justices appointed by President Nixon voting to preserve the Texas financing system, suggests that such expansion, at least in the context of education, would have been likely.

You may recall from our earlier discussion that laws that impair the exercise of a fundamental right are subject to strict scrutiny. Whether a fundamental right is involved in a case can, therefore, be very important to its outcome and is often contested. Those arguing, for example, for a federal constitutional right to same-sex marriage assert that the laws prohibiting gays from marrying each other are subject to strict scrutiny since the Court has held that marriage is a fundamental right.[55] Opponents argue that such laws are not subject to strict scrutiny since marriage itself has never been defined in a way that includes marriage between persons of the same sex.

We have already focused on a major source of constitutional rights in our discussion of the Fourteenth Amendment. We will be focusing on these and other rights again in Chapter 11 in our extended discussion of six landmark cases. Because of its supreme importance to our whole democratic process, we will first focus in this subsection on three problem areas addressed by the Court in defining the boundaries of free speech. We will then consider certain aspects of the Court's individual rights jurisprudence intended to provide a fuller picture of the nature of constitutional rights in general and the problems they pose for the Court.

One preliminary observation about freedom of speech needs to be made, namely, that the kind of speech that the First Amendment is designed to protect goes far beyond mere verbal utterances. It protects works of art, literature, and film. It also has been deemed to include the wearing of a vulgar expression on a jacket, the burning of a draft card, picketing, the expenditure of money in connection with political campaigns, and even the display of a motto on a license plate. The license plate case is illustrative of the kinds of definitional problems the Court can face in applying the First Amendment. The state of New Hampshire required all license plates of passenger vehicles to display the state's motto "Live Free or Die." A Jehovah's Witness objected to the motto and sought to cover it up on his license plate. For this action, he was arrested. He claimed a constitutional right not to display the motto. The Supreme Court agreed, concluding that forcing the Witness to display the license amounted to a form of compelled speech since it required him "to participate in the dissemination of an ideological message by displaying it on his private property . . . for the express purpose that it be observed and read by the public."[56] For then Justice Rehnquist and Justice Blackmun, the majority had gotten it all wrong, arguing that the state hadn't required the Witness to say anything but simply required the Witness, along with everyone else, to display a license plate containing the state motto. Was the license plate a form of compelled speech? Obviously, there is something to be said for both positions, underscoring, for our purposes, how difficult constitutional choices can sometimes be.

Free Speech and Obscenity

Almost every law limits individual behavior in one way or another. This is particularly true for laws and practices that involve an expression by the community of the majority's cultural and religious values. The extent to which the community can legitimately impose its notions of decency on the individual is a profound problem of both philosophy and politics, but it also presents problems of a constitutional dimension under the First Amendment.

In this respect, no issue has proved more troublesome for the Court than the question of obscenity, because defining it in a way that distinguishes it from protected speech has proved almost impossible. The Court first explicitly declared obscene materials unprotected in 1957 in *Roth v. United States*.[57] Seven years later, Justice Potter Stewart, an Eisenhower appointee, famously declared in another case that, though he could not define obscenity, "I know it when I see it."[58] The difficulty of defining obscenity, among other considerations, eventually led Justice Brennan to conclude in *Paris Adult Theatre I v. Slaton*[59] that, while there might be a sufficient state interest in protecting juveniles and nonconsenting adults from exposure to sexually oriented materials, the First Amendment should bar in absolute terms any other state regulation of obscenity. His reason was simple: allowing obscenity laws for any other purpose was simply not worth the effort given "the substantial damage to constitutional rights and to this nation's judicial machinery" entailed in such enforcement efforts.[60] Justice Brennan refused to accept the assumption behind most obscenity regulation that commerce in obscene materials leads to antisocial behavior. He also worried that if the state had the right to prevent people from reading certain materials deemed antisocial, it could also insist that citizens read certain books or view certain films for some other presumably laudable goal.

It is important to recognize that a novel may graphically describe sexual acts that most people would regard as indecent, but such descriptions would not make the novel obscene, even under the oldest, now abandoned definition of obscenity as encompassing works without any redeeming social value appealing solely to the prurient interest. The problem, of course, is at the edges where distinguishing between indecency and obscenity is not easy. As noted, Brennan came to believe that even trying to make the distinction could not be done without trampling on the deep commitment of the First Amendment to free expression.

In 1973, the Court held that obscenity itself could be defined differently from community to community. For years the Court had actually reviewed allegedly obscene material in the basement of the Supreme Court building and then issued decisions without opinion either affirming or reversing the court below. In 1973, it abandoned the task, freeing itself from its basement duties. The new standard, still in place, requires that the legislature first define in explicit bodily detail what is forbidden and then requires a judge or jury to determine whether the average person *applying local community standards* would find that the work, taken as a whole, appeals to the prurient interest and lacks serious literary, artistic, political or scientific value. Thus, a work obscene in one state may be perfectly legal in another.

Free Speech and National Security

Constitutional rights are inevitably at risk in time of war or great fear for the national security where the perceived need for unity and conformity are at their height. In what many regard as one of the worst decisions in the history of the Court, *Korematsu v. United States*,[61] the Court, relying to some degree on technicalities relating to the facts of the particular case, refused to address the constitutionality of a military order forcing all persons of Japanese ancestry living on the West Coast into inland relocation centers. Justice Black, writing for a 6–3 majority, simply refused to question the military's judgment that it was impossible to separate loyal from potentially disloyal Japanese Americans. Black denied that the military order was racist, arguing that it was motivated by the demands of national security and, more importantly, was a judgment for the military, not the Court, to make. Black defended this position throughout his life. In dissent, Justice Murphy criticized the Court for not examining more deeply the basis of the military's order, arguing that it was based on "the misinformation, half-truths and insinuations that for years have been directed against Japanese Americans by people with racial and economic prejudices."[62]

Korematsu was not a free speech case, but it showed how a nation's worst fears and prejudices can lead to an act that history and subsequent generations have condemned and apologized for and how a Court, even a Court composed of justices who thought of themselves civil libertarians, will bow to national security concerns.

The right of free expression is often hailed as our most precious and important right—precious because without that right we are individually less than whole and important because its absence would make a mockery of our democratic system, as it does in so many countries where the right to free elections is really a facade. Yet, as Lincoln observed in justifying his suspension of the writ of habeas corpus, the Constitution is not a suicide pact.

In 1917, during World War I, Judge Learned Hand prohibited the federal government from preventing the mailing of a radical publication, *The Masses*, even though the postmaster general had been given the authority under the Espionage Act of 1917 to suppress publications aimed at disrupting the War effort. Hand did not deny that speech in the Masses might hamper the war effort, but he strongly believed that to judge the constitutional acceptability of speech on the basis of predictions of its potential consequences was too vague and could easily allow an overzealous government to stifle legitimate criticism. He proposed instead a simple rule: "If one stops short of urging upon others that it is their duty or their interest to resist the law, it seems to me one should not be held to have attempted to cause its violation."[63] Hand wanted an objective rule that would allow a speaker or writer in effect to know in advance whether his or her speech was protected. This was not, however, the formula that evolved over time. Indeed, Hand's decision was almost immediately reversed by the Second Circuit Court of Appeals. Shortly after Hand's decision, Justice Holmes enunciated the "clear and present danger" test that tied the unconstitutionality of speech to the likelihood of it causing "substantive evils that Congress has a right to prevent," the very speculation that Hand wished to avoid. Holmes and Hand were good friends (Hand, decades younger than Holmes, really idolized him) and engaged in a correspondence on their differences that was recounted in a fascinating 1975 law review article by Gerald Gunther.[64] We see in this exchange all the dilemmas faced and value judgments made in the fashioning of constitutional law. Holmes's views themselves evolved and though he never fully accepted Hand's thinking, he rejected the way in which the clear and present danger test was applied, most famously in his dissent in *Abrams v. United States*.[65] Ultimately, the Court, in 1969 in *Brandenburg v. Ohio*,[66] embraced Hand's position by protecting speech that did not constitute direct incitement and by requiring, in an instance of direct incitement, that the incitement be "likely to incite or produce" "imminent lawless action."[67] In effect, the Court had married the positions of Hand and Holmes to produce an even stronger protection for free speech.

Free Speech, Fighting Words, and Hate Speech

In the previous subsection, we saw the Court grappling with the limits which the First Amendment puts on government efforts to regulate speech that arguably threatened society's interest in law and order and the government's own existence. In recent years, a distinct but related issue has emerged with efforts to regulate speech aimed at individual and group sensibilities, sometimes called hate speech.

Hate speech is closely related to the concept of "fighting words." In 1942, in *Chaplinsky v. New Hampshire*,[68] the Supreme Court upheld the conviction of one Chaplinsky, a Jehovah's Witness, who had called the city marshall of Manchester, New Hampshire, a "God damned racketeer" and "damned Fascist" when the marshall refused to intervene to protect Chaplinsky when he was distributing Witness literature. Chaplinsky had apparently attracted a crowd by denouncing all other religions as a racket. Chaplinsky was convicted under a state law making it a crime to "address any offensive, derisive or annoying word to any other person who is lawfully in any street or other public place" or to call such person "by any offensive or derisive name." The decision stands for the proposition that "fighting words" are outside First Amendment protection and has never been formally overruled. A number of decisions, however, have undermined the vitality of *Chaplinsky*. Among other things, the Supreme Court has reversed the conviction of a young man who wore a jacket emblazoned with the words "F——— the Draft" into a courthouse[69] and found unconstitutional a Georgia statute that made it a misdemeanor for any person to use, "without provocation . . . opprobrious words or abusive language, tending to cause a breach of the peace."[70] The Court noted that the Georgia state courts had consistently interpreted the law in an overly broad way to allow convictions to stand that involved protected speech. Overbreadth (in which a statute attempts to regulate protected as well as unprotected speech or conduct) will usually render a statute unconstitutional.

The main argument for placing fighting words outside the First Amendment is that they do not in any way attempt to communicate an idea. To the extent that their primary aim is to provoke their target, they are also a close cousin to words intended to incite imminent lawless action.

Hate speech and obscenity offer interesting parallels and differences. Like obscenity, hate speech is deemed intrinsically unworthy of constitutional protection by its very nature. Also like obscenity, many worry about the effect of allowing it on the community itself. Unlike obscenity, however, there is often a political dimension to hate speech that makes attempts at regulation particularly problematical since political speech enjoys the highest kind of protection under the First Amendment. Indeed, in the landmark case of *New York Times v. Sullivan*,[71] the Court granted a measure of protection even to libelous statements when made in the context of public debate. In 1941, just a year before *Chaplinsky* was decided, the Court in *Beauharnais v. Illinois*[72] upheld the conviction of the president of the White Circle League for distributing a leaflet which asserted that whites would inevitably have to unite to protect themselves against the "rapes, robberies, knives, guns and marijuana of the negro."[73] Beauharnais was convicted under a "group libel" statute prohibiting speech that portrayed any class of citizens of any race, color, creed, or religion in a way that it held it up to contempt and ridicule "which is productive of a breach of the peace or riots." Like *Chaplinsky*, *Beauharnais* has never been overruled but it too is in some measure a product of another constitutional era, a time before the Court had moved so boldly to protect the vigor of public debate. Today, universities seek to foster a climate of tolerance on their campuses by developing codes of conduct that prohibit stigmatizing individuals on the basis of race or other characteristics. The Supreme Court has not passed directly on these codes, although lower courts have invalidated some for vagueness or overbreadth.[74] In a recent case, however, *Virginia v. Black*,[75] the Court held that even an act as obviously offensive to blacks (and most everyone else for that matter) as cross burning, is a form of expressive conduct[76] and not unconstitutional in and of itself unless accompanied by an attempt to intimidate. The Court also held that evidence of the cross burning was not sufficient to establish an intention to intimidate.

While generalities in this area are dangerous and there is hardly an aspect of these cases that is not contested, it does seem reasonably safe to say that, outside of the university context where the issue is still quite open, any comments aimed at particular groups or individuals, no matter how offensive they might be, are constitutionally protected unless accompanied by some form of prohibited conduct—e.g., an incitement to lawlessness or an attempt to intimidate. At that point, it is arguably the conduct, not the speech, which is being proscribed.

Implied Rights

Implied rights are rights derived from express rights because, without them, the express rights would themselves be less than what they were intended to be. The First Amendment provides a couple of examples. The Court has reasoned that people have a constitutional right to associate together for political purposes since, without such a right, one of the basic purposes of the First Amendment guaranty of free speech—to allow for a functioning democracy—would be fatally undermined. Thus, the First Amendment prevents the party in power from outlawing other parties. It also means that political parties have a right to protect their ideological identities; this was the basis for the Court's invalidation of one primary system that seemed to threaten this right by allowing non–party members to determine the choice of a party's nominee.[77]

Implied rights can themselves imply other rights. The Court, for example, has held that the right of people generally to associate with each other, a right itself implied by the First Amendment, further implies a right to exclude those whom the group finds objectionable or whose presence might interfere with its message. It is on this basis that the Court, in *Boy Scouts of America v. Dale*,[78] ruled that a state civil rights law could not constitutionally require the Boy Scouts to accept a gay scoutmaster. On the other hand, the Court, in *Romer v. Evans*,[79] held unconstitutional, on equal protection grounds, an amendment to the Colorado state constitution that would have prohibited any Colorado government entity from enacting antidiscrimination laws to protect gays. Understandably, many fundamentalist groups applauded the Boy Scout decision and denounced the Colorado decision, and gay rights advocates did the opposite. These cases, however, while reaching inconsistent results from the standpoint of rooting interests in the culture wars, are easily reconcilable constitutionally. The Court, whether correctly or not, found that the right of expressive association would have been undermined had the Boy Scouts been forced to accept gay scoutmasters, given their belief that homosexuality was morally wrong. On the other hand, there was no particular group whose rights were at stake in the Colorado case and the Court found no rational basis for the Colorado law other than pure animus against gays.

Another important implied right involves the right to travel. The Court has held that this right has several components. It protects (1) the right of a citizen of one state to freely enter and leave another state, (2) the right of that citizen to be treated as a welcome visitor in that second state, and (3) the right of travelers who decide to stay permanently in a state to be treated like other citizens of that state. Interestingly, the Court has relied on different provisions of the Constitution in upholding these rights—the Interstate Commerce clause for the actual right to enter and leave other states,[80] the Privileges and Immunities clause for the right to be treated as a welcome visitor,[81] and the Equal Protection clause for the right to reside in a new state of choice on equal terms with its other citizens.[82]

Tensions between Rights

Some of our most basic rights can be in tension with each other. The First Amendment freedom of the press can sometimes clash with the defendant's right to a fair trial. The Court, for example, wrestled with the constitutionality of allowing trials to be televised, fearing that they could lead to sensationalism, but finally deciding, unanimously, that they were permissible with appropriate safeguards.[83] Another notable tension is between the right of privacy and the freedom of the press. Freedom of speech and the press is deemed of enormous importance because of its role in our democratic processes and in creating an informed citizenry. This led the Court in a recent case to allow a radio station to broadcast an illegally taped private conversation between two persons actively engaged (on the same side) in a collective bargaining negotiation. Notwithstanding their clear right to an expectation of privacy, the Court held that since the conversation involved a legitimate subject of public interest, the radio station, which had done nothing to encourage the illegal taping, could broadcast it without exposure to a damage claim otherwise provided under federal law for intercepted private conversations.[84]

A test of our commitment to First Amendment principles occurs most forcibly when the speech it protects offends our deepest sensibilities. In 2011, the Court in *Snyder v. Phelps*,[85] by an 8–1 vote (Alito dissenting), held that the First Amendment protects the right of a small group of anti-gay protestors to picket a soldier's funeral with placards, including one proclaiming "Thank God for dead soldiers." The Court's decision sustained the decision of the Fourth Circuit Court of Appeals overturning a jury award of more than $10 million in favor of the family, which had sued under state law for intentional infliction of emotional distress.

The First Amendment does not always win out when rights clash. The Court faced an interesting dilemma, for example, when a municipal ordinance prohibiting picketing of an individual residence was claimed to violate the First Amendment.[86] Abortion protestors had sought to picket the residence of a physician who performed abortions. Picketing, as a form of expression, is entitled to First Amendment protection. Notwithstanding that abortion is clearly a matter of public concern, meaning that speech relating to abortion is highly valued, and notwithstanding that the picketing was taking place on a public street, a traditional forum for First Amendment activity, the Court in a 6–3 decision held that the ordinance was constitutional since the municipality had a strong interest in protecting residential privacy and because there were alternative channels for the protestors to make their views known. The ideological lineup in the voting was particularly interesting, with the conservative bloc voting to protect the right of privacy, and perhaps more to the point, an interest in property, and Justices Brennan, Marshall, and Stevens dissenting.

Today, perhaps our most notable tension is between the First Amendment's prohibition against laws respecting the establishment of religion and the guarantees in the same amendment of free speech and the free exercise of religion. To illustrate, the Court recently had to decide whether a school district had improperly denied the "Good News Club" the right to use school facilities for after school meetings for elementary age children. The district had made its facilities available to all other community groups but had feared that the club's activities would violate the Establishment clause. There was a reasonable basis for its concern since children at the meeting were invited to pray and to trust the Lord Jesus to save them from sin. The Good News club argued, among other things, that the school's policy involved governmental discrimination against a religious viewpoint in violation of the First Amendment's guarantee of free speech. The Good News Club prevailed by a vote of 5–4.[87] As previously noted, specific facts can be enormously important in these cases. For example, the majority in the Good News case noted that the club meetings did not take place in the elementary school classrooms where the students spent the majority of their school day, and that no teacher served as an instructor, an important point for those justices sensitive to the need for avoiding the appearance that the school was endorsing the religious viewpoint of the Good News Club. On the other hand, four justices felt that any use of school facilities for the purpose of proselytizing was prohibited under the Establishment clause and therefore not a matter of governmental viewpoint discrimination.

Some Degree of Unavoidable Subjectivity

When rights are in tension, the Court often has to resort to balancing tests. Balancing is a metaphor that some justices and scholars are more comfortable with than others. For some, the application of a clear principle is always a preferable way of deciding a case because they believe that a clear set of rules makes the law both more predictable and rational. Other justices are more comfortable with the idea of balancing and do not regard it as an admission of failure. Balancing, however, is concededly more of a subjective enterprise. Certain issues by their nature defy bright line rules. For example, the Court has held that sometimes regulations affecting property ownership can be so burdensome as to amount to a taking and therefore require compensation under the Fifth Amendment's Eminent Domain clause. Such cases, however, depend greatly on a host of individual facts that simply cannot be broken down into a clear framework or set of principles. In such instances, the Court balances the various factors involved and comes to a decision.

Whenever the Court must decide whether a governmental action or jury verdict is reasonable or excessive, it also embarks on what is inherently a highly subjective inquiry. To cite just one example, the Court has recently held that "excessive" state punitive damage awards violate the Fourteenth Amendment. However, determining what is excessive inevitably becomes an "I know it when I see it" sort of judgment. While the Court has resisted a bright line mathematical test, it has indicated that an award of more than four times compensatory damages "might be close to the line of constitutional impropriety."[88] Why four times, as opposed to six or seven times, is a distinction difficult to defend in any principled way but a line must be drawn somewhere once the basic right to be free from excessive state awards is accepted.

No clause calls for more subjective judgments than the Eighth Amendment's prohibition against cruel and unusual punishment. As in the case of punitive damages, the concept of "excess" moves to the front of the constitutional stage. In *Lockyer v. Andrade*,[89] the Court was asked to affirm a sentence of 25 years to life for a third-strike conviction of a man who had stolen five videotapes worth $84.70 from a Kmart store in Ontario, California. Like the third conviction, the defendant's two previous felony convictions were not for violent crimes. Under California's three-strikes law, any felony can constitute the third strike and thus subject a defendant to such a sentence. While there were technical aspects to the case, the Court's decision ultimately came down to whether the sentence was grossly disproportionate to the offense for which it was imposed. The Court in a 5–4 decision followed the California Supreme Court in affirming the sentence. Justice Souter, writing for the four dissenters, noted "If Andrade's sentence is not grossly disproportionate, the principle has no meaning."[90] *Lockyer* illustrates how inevitably subjective are the judgments that justices are sometimes called upon to make. What made the case particularly troubling, from this writer's perspective, is that the trial judge had it within his discretion to reclassify the earlier nonviolent felonies into misdemeanors but declined to do so. In other words, this was not a case where the three strikes law itself did not allow for the use of judicial discretion that would have avoided the automatic application of the three-strikes rule.

Criminal Procedure

Many of the specific guarantees in the Bill of Rights deal with ensuring a fair trial to criminal defendants. Implicit in these guarantees is the right to be free from overreaching conduct by the police. As we have seen, most of these guarantees have been held to apply to the states as well as the federal government, meaning that Supreme Court decisions in this area have enormous consequences for local police and prosecutors. Two of the most important and controversial Court decisions have been *Mapp v. Ohio*,[91] a 5–4 decision in which the Court in 1961 made applicable to the states the federal rule requiring the exclusion from evidence of items seized in violation of the Fourth Amendment; and *Miranda v. Arizona*,[92] also a 5–4 decision, in which the Court in 1966 held that police must issue the now famous Miranda warnings (you have the right to remain silent, anything said can be used in evidence against you, you have the right to counsel and to have one appointed if you are indigent) whenever a person is in police custody and under interrogation. In applying these rulings, the Court has had to construct what amounts to a constitutional code of conduct for police and prosecutors. By way of illustration, the Court in a 2011 case, *J.D.B. v. North Carolina*,[93] had to decide whether the police should take account of a child's age in determining whether or not to give Miranda warnings.

The Court, in a 5–4 vote, held that age was relevant because children were more likely than adults to perceive themselves in custody and therefore not free to leave the interrogation.

Two other important decisions from the Warren Court era deserve brief mention. In *Terry v. Ohio*,[94] the Court held that the common police practice of stopping and frisking someone engaged in suspicious behavior was an activity of constitutional concern under the Fourth Amendment, but the Court approved the practice as long as it met the test of reasonableness based on the factual circumstances. In *United States v. Wade*,[95] the Court held that police line-ups did not violate the Fifth Amendment protection against self-incrimination but also held that a suspect was entitled to have a lawyer present when the line-up was occurring.

Regulating the Democratic Process

Since 1964, the Court has taken on a role that it previously rejected: regulator of the rules of the game for the democratic process. The journey began with the Court's holdings that congressional and state legislative districts must be equal in population, the so-called one person–one vote principle.[96] Since then the Court has had a profound impact on the way our electoral process works. Among other things, it has prevented Congress and the states from limiting the amount of money that can be spent in election campaigns and from regulating corporate and union spending to influence election results[97]; it has invalidated laws in twenty-two states that had imposed term limits on their U.S. senators and representatives, ending one of the most important grass-roots political movements in the nation's political history[98]; it has substantially weakened political party organizations by virtually eliminating the system of political patronage (the spoils system) on First Amendment grounds[99]; it has invalidated congressional districts created primarily for the benefit of a particular race[100]; and, most famously, it ended a presidential election recount.[101] It has also issued important rulings, among other things, respecting ballot access,[102] filing requirements for candidates,[103] partisan gerrymandering,[104] candidate rights to appear in debates,[105] and state restrictions on speech rights of judicial candidates.[106]

The Court most often grounds its democracy-defining decisions on the First Amendment or the Equal Protection clauses. The simple fact, however, is that the Constitution says almost nothing about how the democratic process should work, and these decisions, when carefully examined, often turn on the Court's own assumptions about the political process, though they rarely couch their decisions in those terms. Because the Court is so used to dealing with text-based issues, it does not seem to have a vocabulary for dealing with issues that really are about the health of the political system as a whole.

If one thing is clear, however, it is that the Courts are strong believers in the two-party system and the stability it supposedly brings to both electoral and governmental processes. It thus has no hesitancy about protecting that system, even at the expense of the minor parties.[107] One way to see this is by comparing two decisions of the Court. In a recent decision, *Clingman v. Beaver*,[108] the Court upheld an Oklahoma statute that prohibited registered voters from participating in the primaries of other parties. The decision was helpful to major parties because it prevented minor parties from building their strength by inducing registered voters, perhaps not yet ready to change their major party affiliation, to at least participate in their minor party nominating processes. In an earlier decision, however, the Court had invalidated a Connecticut law that had prohibited the major political parties from opening up their own primaries to independent voters.[109] Both decisions benefited the major parties, allowing them to attract independent voters to their own primaries, if they so chose, while protecting them from third-party competition for their own registered voters.

While limitations of space prevent us from delving too deeply into this fascinating and important area of constitutional law, the case on term limits deserves special mention, in part because it has been of immense practical political importance, but also because it underscores how differing perspectives on the nature of federalism influence these democracy defining cases.[110] The case arose out of a challenge to an amendment to the Arkansas state constitution, adopted by its voters through a ballot initiative, which limited Arkansas's congressional representatives to three terms and its U.S. senators to two terms. All the justices in the case seemed to agree that term limits constituted an additional qualification for office (not having served for the proscribed length of time being the additional qualification). A key issue for the Court, therefore, was whether the age and citizenship qualifications set forth in the Constitution for senators and representatives were meant to be exhaustive. This question in turn evoked radically different visions of what the founding had been all about. For Justice Stevens, who wrote the majority opinion (the case was decided 5–4), it was clear that "the Framers envisioned a uniform national system, rejecting the notion that the Nation was a collection of states, and instead creating a direct link between the National Government and the people of the United States."[111] Understandably, Justice Stevens and the other justices forming the majority were uncomfortable with the idea that different states could have different qualifications for their congressional representatives. Equally understandably, Justice Thomas and his fellow dissenters did not find this prospect troubling. "The notion of popular sovereignty," wrote Justice Thomas, "that undergirds the Constitution does not erase state boundaries, but rather tracks them."[112]

The Court's Place in Our National Life

In 1954, not long before his death, Justice Robert Jackson asked himself what comes first, either "in time or importance, an independent and enlightened judiciary or a free and tolerant society." His answer was that "the attitude of a society and of its organized political forces, rather than its legal machinery, is the controlling force in the character of free institutions."[113] When Justice Jackson wrote these words, the Cold War and McCarthyism were raising fundamental questions as to how a democracy, with its checks and balances and diffusion of power, could protect itself against perceived forces of internal subversion, just as today we are considering similar questions in the context of the threat of international terrorism. While Jackson did not denigrate the role of the judiciary, he was cautioning against too great a reliance on "the legal machinery." In a democracy, he was reminding his audience, it is "organized political forces" that ultimately determine the character of its institutions.

These organized political forces can and do profoundly affect our constitutional direction. The Alien and Sedition Acts, for example, enacted by the Federalists to control political dissent, could have been something other than an important footnote in our history had not Jefferson won the election of 1800 and, of course, we might not be one nation today with one Constitution, had not Lincoln won the election of 1864.

Political forces are organized to achieve results. They will applaud when Courts decide consistent with their desires, even when those results run counter to their ostensible judicial philosophy. I will cite just one example from a much earlier time. In 1859, a newspaper editor in Milwaukee had assisted a slave to escape his slave master while they were in Wisconsin. This was a violation of the federal fugitive slave law and the editor was arrested. The Wisconsin Supreme Court, nevertheless, freed him, finding the federal law unconstitutional. The national government, however, appealed to the United States Supreme Court which held that the Fugitive Slave Law was constitutional and reinstated the conviction. Editorial reaction in the North harshly condemned the decision. According to Robert McClosky: "The decision was violently attacked, the state was urged to resist, the cry that the Court had no power to thus overrule a state was heard, not only in Wisconsin, but throughout the North."[114] Suddenly the North was espousing a constitutional position that it would shortly spend the next four years contesting in the bloodiest war in the nation's history.

A number of modern scholars have questioned the degree to which even the most revered decisions of the Supreme Court have actually resulted in real change. Gerald Rosenberg, in his influential work, *The Hollow Hope*, concludes that even *Brown v. Board of Education* and *Roe v. Wade* produced "mostly disappointing results" measured in terms of significant social reform.[115] He also argues that litigation strategies can be harmful to a movement if they come at the expense of a stronger focus on Congress and legislatures where the real political power resides. Rosenberg asserts that the women's movement, the civil rights movement, and the pro-choice movement all could have mobilized politically much earlier and more effectively if they had not looked first to the Courts as agents of change. Other scholars have echoed Rosenberg's position. Michael Klarman, for example, while conceding that the Court's constitutional decisions can produce "small but real changes in social practices" has written, "Supreme Court decisions rarely matter as much as is conventionally assumed. *Brown v. Board of Education* did not create the civil rights movement. Women in most of the United States almost certainly would enjoy some form of abortion right even had the Court never decided *Roe v. Wade*. *Marbury v. Madison* did not create the judicial review power, and *McCullough v. Maryland* was not responsible for the United States developing into a nation."[116] This is an important perspective, one that unfortunately we do not have the space to examine in depth. I would note, however, that the Constitution itself was not designed to be an instrument of social change; the rights it embodies, as previously discussed, are negative rights, that in the famous words of Justice Brandeis, are "conferred, as against the Government" and embody "the right to be let alone—the most comprehensive of rights, and the right most valued by civilized men."[117]

This does not mean, however, that the Court's decisions do not occupy a significant place in our national life. Determining what the government can and cannot do is enormously important and does affect our everyday life. Was the decision prohibiting prayer in public schools unimportant in our national life? Would a decision abolishing all forms of affirmative action not be significant? Did the fact that the day after *Roe v. Wade* was decided, young women in Idaho or Alabama could contemplate securing legal abortions not involve a major social change that would not likely have occurred but for the Court's decision? Causation is never easy to measure but, even if the struggle to integrate schools has had only limited success, it seems to this writer hard to argue that landmark constitutional law decisions have not had an important psychological dimension well beyond the particular issue involved in the case. To measure the importance of *Brown v. Board of Education* solely by developments in the field of education is too narrow a reading of its social significance. *Plessy v. Ferguson* is justly condemned today because it sanctified the whole regime of apartheid, not just because it meant that blacks had to ride in segregated rail cars. Just as importantly, *Brown v. Board of Education* is revered, not just by legal scholars, because of how it condemned an entire way of life and attitude toward an oppressed race. The white rioters at Little Rock High School understood this dimension better than anyone.

We should also not overlook the immediate consequences that Supreme Court decisions can have in affecting social behavior. Consider for a moment what happened after the Court decided in 1940 that a school district had the power, under the Constitution, to require all children, including Jehovah's Witnesses, to salute the flag, even if it went against their religious convictions. In his fascinating book, *Scorpions*, Noah Feldman writes: "After the *Gobitis* decision, sentiment against Jehovah's Witnesses spread fast. Multiple cities and towns adopted school flag salute ordinances similar to the one at issue in the case. When Witnesses refused to salute, children were expelled. Between June 12 and June 20, 1940, the FBI received reports of hundreds of cases of anti-Witness violence. . . . On June 9, a mob of 2,500 surrounded the Witnesses' Kingdom Hall in Kennebunk, Maine, and burned it to the ground."[118] A few years later, the Court reversed itself and held that requiring the children to salute the flag was a form of "compelled speech" and violated their First Amendment rights. That decision marks an important boundary beyond which government cannot go in rallying the country behind its policies.

Less dramatically, the Court, through its decisions, helps shape a legal environment that profoundly influences day-to-day life. Consider, for example, the internet. Certainly no recent development has more transformed our day-to-day living. In 1997, the Court was faced with the question whether a provision of the Communications Decency Act that made it a crime to transmit "patently offensive material" to children violated the First Amendment. The Court, in a broadly worded opinion, made clear that regulating content on the internet was no more appropriate than regulating it in newspapers or books.[119] A different kind of opinion might have created a much different legal climate for this new technology with unpredictable impact. To cite one more example, zoning laws, now a staple of local governance, were thought by many, earlier in the twentieth century, to constitute uncompensated takings under the Eminent Domain clause. The issue was not resolved until 1926 when, in *Euclid v. Amber Realty Co.*,[120] the Court held (6–3) that zoning laws were an appropriate exercise of governmental police power. A different decision would have made local regulation of property uses much more problematic.

Certainly, many of the Court's landmark opinions were moving in history's direction. How could the nation as a whole continue to endorse segregation after World War II in which so many black lives were given in defense of their country, particularly when, as Randall Kennedy has noted, "The unspeakable brutishness of Nazism's racial laws had cast a dark shadow over ideas that supported the South's peculiar ways."?[121] How long could rural-dominated legislatures be allowed to hold on to power at the expense of huge metropolitan areas?

The Court in its boldest decisions is placing a bet on where the country is and where it wants to go. Sometimes it gets it completely wrong. In the *Dred Scott* decision, Chief Justice Taney thought he was putting an end to the slavery dispute when he actually helped it reach its boiling point.

Let's return for a moment to *Brown v. Board of Education.* The Court knew, of course, that its decision would impose wrenching change on Southern society. What had happened in the period between *Plessy* and *Brown* to make the Court so much braver? Simply, that by 1954, the South was isolated in its defense of legally enforced segregation. This was not true when *Plessy* was decided. In 1909, a decade and a half after *Plessy*, President Theodore Roosevelt—a man not easily cowed—had been so widely condemned, both north and south, for having Booker T. Washington, a renowned black scientist who preached self-reliance to his people, for lunch at the White House that neither Washington nor any other black leader was ever again invited by Roosevelt for a similar occasion.

In reflecting upon *Brown v. Board of Education*, Justice Robert Jackson, stated: "I don't know how to justify the abolition of segregation as a judicial act. Our problem is to make a judicial decision out of a political conclusion."[122] If in fact, one of the most important cases ever decided by the Court rests upon "a political conclusion," then perhaps the most important question for any path-breaking constitutional decision is not so much whether the Court got the Constitution right as whether it got history right—and not the history already written but the history to be written.

The Court is not unaware of the political context in which it operates. As recounted in Jim Newton's biography of Earl Warren,[123] on October 18, 1963, just a month before President Kennedy's assassination, a bare majority of the Court (Justices Black, White, Frankfurter, Clark, and Stewart) had tentatively voted to sustain the trespass convictions of sit-in demonstrators protesting segregated eating counters. Justices Brennan and Warren were extremely anxious to avoid any decision that might complicate passage of the Kennedy civil rights bill then pending before Congress by seeming to side with the opponents of the bill. The four justices in the minority, with the support of Justice Stewart, were able to delay an adverse decision by requesting an amicus brief from the Solicitor General's Office. Meanwhile Justice Brennan began circulating drafts of dissents aimed at winning over at least one justice in the majority. In the end, Justice Brennan was able to convince Clark (a Truman appointee and father of Ramsey Clark) and Justice Stewart (an Eisenhower appointee) to change their votes and the convictions were overturned on narrow grounds in June of 1964. The chief justice's delaying tactics were uncharacteristic of a man known for his fairness, but he was determined that the Court would be on the right side of history. Two weeks after the Court handed down its sit-in decisions, President Johnson signed the Civil Rights bill into law, the Senate having broken a southern filibuster a month earlier.

I should note here that the Court's decision was difficult to justify technically. The problem was that the Equal Protection clause did not apply to a private restaurant owner. The Court's solution was to hold that the trespassing statute under which the students were convicted—the statute clearly being state action—had not given the students fair warning that once they trespassed on the premises, they would have to leave when asked. The dissent pointed out the absurdity that anyone would "have been misled by the language of this statute into believing that it would permit them to stay on the property of another over the owner's protest without being guilty of trespass."[124] This was a case where the Court was determined to be on the right side of history, and it certainly did not want to take an important weapon out of the civil rights movement's arsenal.

The Supreme Court is a political institution in the sense that its decisions, however reasoned and grounded, affect public policy. But the Court's decisions occur within a relatively bounded field. The Court does not decide to go to war. It cannot reverse an irresponsible fiscal policy. It does not set budget priorities or enact health care legislation or create environmental policy. At critical moments, however, it can assist the country by nudging it in a direction consistent with the country's fundamental ideals and history and for which there is a sufficient measure of support, as it did in *Brown v. Board of Education* and *Baker v. Carr*. It also, of course, affects history simply by virtue of its decision-making authority, as it did in *Bush v. Gore* and as it may do if it finds the 2010 federal health care law unconstitutional.

6. The Federal Judicial System

Federal Jurisdiction

Jurisdiction refers to the authority of a court to hear a case. *Original* jurisdiction refers to jurisdiction at the trial court level, *appellate* jurisdiction to appeals from mistakes that may have occurred at the trial. Juries (or judges in the event of a nonjury trial) render verdicts based on the evidence. They determine the facts, often from conflicting testimony, and then apply the facts to the law, as explained to them by the judge presiding at trial. To determine, whether person X committed crime Y, the jury first must establish what X did, a question of fact, and then whether those facts establish that X committed Y.

The distinction between facts and law is crucial because appellate courts generally do not review factual determinations made at trial, in part because their concern is with the law and whether it was properly interpreted and applied and in part because they simply are not in as good a position as the trial court to establish what the facts are. Appellate courts, for example, are not in a position to observe witnesses and draw conclusions about the credibility of different witnesses. The application of the facts to the law is not always easy, and so trial court judges are empowered to instruct juries on how to apply the facts to the law. If the trial judge does that incorrectly and the mistake is serious enough, a conviction or civil verdict may be overturned. Such is also the case if the judge makes a serious mistake during the course of a trial, for example, failing to allow the defendant to introduce relevant evidence or allowing the prosecution to admit improperly obtained evidence.

You might be wondering who reviews factual findings of federal administrative agencies made in the process of quasi-judicial hearings, such as entitlement to social security benefits, immigration status, or workmen's compensation claims among many other types of hearings. Generally, those factual findings are given great deference with one important exception. Where a finding itself is the basis of the agency's jurisdiction or involves the possible deprivation of a constitutional right, the Supreme Court has made it very clear that those facts are subject to a completely independent review by the federal judiciary. These are often referred to as constitutional or jurisdictional facts. To provide just one example, suppose in a deportation hearing the potential deportee claims to be an American citizen. Should he or she appeal an adverse ruling, the judiciary will independently reexamine this question since the Immigration and Naturalization Service would be without any jurisdiction at all if the subject was an American citizen.[1]

Federal jurisdiction can be a very technical subject but, mercifully, its broad outlines are easily described. Except for the specific instances of original jurisdiction provided for in Article III, which *Marbury v. Madison* held Congress could not add to, the Constitution leaves it to Congress to define the jurisdiction of the Supreme Court and such inferior federal courts as Congress chooses to create. As already mentioned, Congress did not empower the federal court system to hear cases arising under the Constitution and federal law until 1875. Only then was the constitutional definition of the national judicial power coextensive with the actual jurisdiction of the federal judiciary.

You may recall that federal jurisdiction falls into two broad categories: *subject matter* jurisdiction involving cases arising under the Constitution or federal statutory law, and *diversity* jurisdiction involving cases involving certain kinds of parties. Today many cases can be initially heard in either state or federal court. In some instances, however, a case brought in state court can be removed at the request of one of the parties to federal court. The removal rights of the parties are governed by federal law. Sometimes Congress provides for exclusive federal court jurisdiction. Cases arising under copyright and patent laws, for example, can be brought only in federal court.

States for the most part define for themselves the jurisdiction of their courts. The Supreme Court, however, did hold in 1878 in *Pennoyer v. Neff*[2] that the Due Process clause of the Fourteenth Amendment does prohibit a state from exercising jurisdiction over people or property outside its own borders. One noted constitutional scholar has pointed out that *Pennoyer* was not only significant in its own right as a procedural due process case but was also "an important first step toward the later position that due process limited the extraterritorial reach of state substantive laws as well."[3] This later position means, for example, that a Texas law respecting contracts cannot be applied to a contract that had no connection with Texas at the time it was made, unless the parties agree by contract to apply Texas law.

In a global economy, the kind of contacts needed for a state to establish jurisdiction over foreign corporations is becoming increasingly important and, as illustrated by *J. McIntyre Machinery, Ltd. v. Nicastro*,[4] a 2011 case, a source of controversy on the Court. It is worth our attention, because it allows us to see the Court wrestling with a changing world where the constitutional text provides little guidance. The case involved a suit against a British manufacturer for bodily injury (loss of four fingers) brought by a resident of New Jersey in New Jersey courts for an industrial accident occurring in New Jersey allegedly caused by the manufacturer's metal cutting machine. The manufacturer had instructed its U.S. distributor to sell its products, including the machine in question, anywhere in the United States. The machine in question was the only one that had been sold in New Jersey; the manufacturer had no physical presence in New Jersey. Four justices of the Court (Scalia, Thomas, Roberts, and Kennedy) asserted that there was no basis for jurisdiction since the manufacturer had no physical presence in the state and had not made any effort to invoke or benefit from its laws. The views of these justices would provide a safe harbor for corporations allowing them to sell products in a state without exposing themselves to liability as long as they operate solely through a separate distributor and don't otherwise have activities in the state. Two justices (Breyer and Alito) were not prepared to announce such an absolute rule but also rejected jurisdiction on the facts of the case given that there was only one isolated sale in the state. Three justices (Ginsburg, Sotomayor, and Kagan) would have found jurisdiction appropriate based on a basic premise that when a manufacturer clearly intends for a product to be sold in a state, it should be liable for damage done in the state. These three opinions reflect a real division on the Court, two sets of justices, lining up as you would expect ideologically, with very clear principled views, and two justices (Alito and Breyer), one generally on the conservative side of ideological issues, the other on the liberal side, cautioning against broad pronouncements although agreeing that there was not enough contact in this particular case.

The Federal Judicial Structure

Today, the federal district courts are the trial-level courts in the federal system, and the circuit courts of appeals the appellate courts. The Supreme Court sits atop the federal system and is primarily responsible for assuring that federal law, including constitutional law, is being properly interpreted and applied. Obviously, when circuit courts disagree, some court is applying federal law incorrectly and so it is not surprising that many times the Supreme Court will take cases to resolve these conflicts.

Remarkably, today's three-tier system of federal courts can be traced all the way back to the Judiciary Act of 1789 when both district and circuit courts were originally established as trial courts, although the circuit courts heard appeals from the district courts as well. The early circuit courts were an interesting institution. While there were circuit courts, there were, strictly speaking, no circuit court judges. Rather, circuit courts were composed of one district court judge and one Supreme Court justice (initially, for a brief period, two Supreme Court justices). Circuit courts had the major trial-level responsibility in the federal system, handling most diversity cases where the amount in controversy exceeded $500 and most major federal crimes.[5]

The required presence on the circuit court of a Supreme Court justice accounted for the justice's circuit-riding responsibilities mentioned earlier. While they might not have liked it, Supreme Court justices were not being singled out for special treatment since circuit riding was an established practice for judges in early America: All the state systems established after independence, with a few exceptions, required the judges of the highest court to ride the circuit, as was the custom also in England.[6]

Today's circuit courts only hear appeals; they do not conduct trials, which are conducted at the district court level. There are currently 94 district courts with 679 federal district judges throughout the country. There are currently 11 numbered circuit courts of appeal covering separately designated regions of the country plus two other circuit courts—the circuit court for the District of Columbia, which hears appeals not only from the D.C. district court but also from actions involving federal regulatory agencies; and (2) the federal circuit court of appeals, which hears cases covering a variety of federal subject areas, including patents and trademarks. Circuit courts generally hear appeals in three-judge panels, although in very important cases the entire circuit court—which ranges in size from 6 judges (First Circuit) to 28 judges (Ninth Circuit)—will hear a case. Sometimes a litigant who has lost with a three-judge panel will ask the entire court to reconsider the case en banc, particularly in cases where the three judges hearing a case are regarded as having an ideological cast different from that of the majority of the judges in that circuit. Understandably, this development has stirred some controversy.

All federal judges are appointed for life (assuming good behavior) by the president with the consent of the Senate. One informal but highly observed form of federalism known as "Senatorial Courtesy" allows a senator from the same political party as the president to submit a list of potential candidates to fill a district court vacancy in his or her state. The president will generally select a candidate from that list since the senator's disapproval of a nominee will kill that nomination.

The Role of the Lower Courts in Constitutional Law

The importance of the district courts and the circuit courts of appeal in the development of constitutional law cannot be emphasized too strongly. It is these courts which flesh out the meaning of Supreme Court decisions by applying them to the many cases arising in the everyday life of the country. The Supreme Court may write the musical score but it is the district courts and circuit courts that get to perform it. The more ambiguous a Supreme Court opinion is, the greater the opportunity for the circuit courts to put their own phrasing on it.

As we will see shortly, Supreme Court precedents can be broadly or narrowly interpreted. The construction of precedents depends in large part on the level of generality that one wishes to impart to a particular decision. If a district or circuit court judge does not like a Supreme Court decision, the judge is likely to confine it as much as possible to the facts of the case, minimizing its overall significance for the development of the law. On the other hand, a judge who sees a Supreme Court precedent moving constitutional law in a direction he or she approves is more likely to give the decision a broad reading. When the lower courts give substance to Supreme Court decisions, they not only administer constitutional law, they also provide an opportunity for the Supreme Court to evaluate its own decisions and perhaps test the waters for future developments. Let me provide one example to show how this can occur.

In 2009, in *Herring v. United States*[7] (a 5–4 decision), the Supreme Court created an exception to the rule adopted in *Mapp v. Ohio*, which requires the suppression of physical evidence at trial if obtained by an illegal search. The defendant in *Herring* had been pulled over, unjustifiably, as it turned out, because a data bank improperly listed his car as being stolen. In the course of searching his car, the police found illegal drugs, and he was arrested. In the words of one advocate for a victims-rights group, the decision "jumped a firewall" setting the stage possibly for the wholesale abandonment of the exclusionary rule by the Court.[8]

As a result of *Herring*, there is now clearly some new play in the exclusionary rule, but how much will be defined by the lower courts. Judge X favorably disposed to the exclusionary rule will emphasize that Herring did not involve any improper conduct on the part of a police officer but was simply the result of incorrect information in a data base that falsely indicated that the defendant was subject to an arrest warrant. Thus, when the next case comes along dealing more directly with conduct involving carelessness by the officer himself, Judge X will distinguish Herring on the ground that Herring did not involve any negligent behavior by the officer. On the other hand, Judge Y, not favorably disposed to the exclusionary rule, will point to Chief Justice Roberts's statement in his majority opinion that "To trigger the exclusionary rule, police conduct must be sufficiently deliberate that exclusion can meaningfully deter it, and sufficiently culpable that such deterrence is worth the price paid by the justice system."[9] This is very loose language and clearly not unintentional. It invites the lower Courts to redirect the exclusionary rule along certain lines. The result will give the Supreme Court the opportunity to see exactly how its new flexible approach plays out in the real world of criminal justice.

Very occasionally, even a district court can have a profound effect on the constitutional debate. In the celebrated Dover School District case (*Kitzmiller v. Dover Area School District*),[10] Judge John E. Jones III found that *intelligent design* was simply another word for creationism, which the Supreme Court had previously ruled could not be constitutionally included in public school science curricula. This was a major victory for the "pro-evolution" forces not because district court opinions are binding precedent (they are not) but because public opinion was focused so closely on the case and because it was a Republican judge appointed by President George W. Bush who, after hearing testimony of numerous experts on both sides, had written a detailed, cogent opinion so completely dismissive of the claims made for intelligent design as an alternative scientific theory. We see here how important constitutional questions can be fought out at any level of the judicial system. The decision was not appealed because a few weeks before its issuance, a slate of candidates opposed to the prior school board's actions, which had started the controversy, triumphed; the new board obviously had no interest in appealing a decision with which it agreed.

Very occasionally, it is clear that the Supreme Court will ultimately have to decide a constitutional issue. A case in point is the provision in the new federal health care law requiring otherwise uncovered individuals to pay a tax or penalty (the case may turn on which characterization is embraced) if they do not purchase health insurance. Four federal district courts and three courts of appeal have already weighed in on this issue. While the Supreme Court will be the final authority, we should note here how the entire federal judicial system participates in a constitutional conversation, a facet not often remarked upon but which can ultimately be very helpful to the Court. District court trials also are important because this is where the factual record is developed that can often decide a case. Parenthetically, I would note that the determination of the Court in the *Citizens United* case, to be discussed shortly, to proceed to address a matter that was not considered at the trial level and for which therefore, there was no factual record, was a very legitimate criticism of the Court's sweeping opinion.

We focus in this text on the Supreme Court since it fixes constitutional doctrine, but we should not forget that the application of constitutional law occurs in the day-to-day administration of justice in the lower courts. The Supreme Court not only recognizes this fact but sometimes seeks to use it to better inform its own future decisions.

7. Life on the Court

The Work Environment

The Court's year begins in October and ends in June. By the start of its year, it has already selected many of the cases that it will hear for the coming term. The 2010 term, for example, began in October 2010. The petitioner (the party seeking reversal of the decision below) is always happy to be before the Court because (1) it represents a second chance at success, and (2) the petitioner is more likely than not to win, since the Court, not surprisingly, reverses more decisions than it affirms. Occasionally both parties want the Supreme Court to take a case because each side was dissatisfied with some aspect of the prior decision.

There is a distinct rhythm to the Court's year, nicely captured by former *New York Times* Supreme Court reporter Linda Greenhouse, describing her first year on the job:

> The nine-month term was a mountain. My job was to climb it. The slope was gentle when the term began, every first Monday in October; the court was busy choosing new cases and hearing arguments, but it was not yet ready to issue decisions. The upward path steepened in January and February, when grants of new cases, arguments and decisions all came at once, competing for attention. Spring brought a breather as the path flattened out again; all the arguments had been heard and the decisions were sporadic. The steepest climb came predictably, every June, with the final outpouring of decisions before the summer recess.[1]

For most of its history, the Supreme Court lacked a home of its own. Its first quarters were above an open-air market in New York, and when the new government moved to Philadelphia in 1791, the Court spent most of the remainder of the decade in Philadelphia City Hall. Then it was on to Washington, D.C., but it took 135 years before the Court was able to free itself from the confines of the Capitol Building, where it was housed for most of that time, and move into a place of its own, a marble structure with imposing Corinthian columns that, like everything else about the Court, has provoked marked differences of opinion, some finding it stately and dignified, others cold and pompous. Chief justice Taft, also our 27th president, deserves the main credit for finally getting the Court its own mailing address. Having had to deal with Congress as president, he likely understood better than most that a government of separate powers should also be one of separate corridors. The imposing Court building contributes to the Court's mystique and sense of remoteness. In fact, the building is designed in a way that justices can enter and leave it without ever going through any public area. Until the Court had its own building, the justices had their own offices either at home or in other buildings. This might not have mattered in John Marshall's time when many justices, particularly in the early Marshall years, would board together, but later it certainly must have reduced the opportunity for informal interchange, with what possible consequences no one will ever be able to tell. Today, each justice has ample office space for the conduct of his or her work.

Justices are assisted in their work by their clerks. Today, each justice is allowed to have four clerks; they are generally hired directly out of law school. Serving as a clerk to a Supreme Court justice is both a high honor and as close as one can come to a guarantee of future success. Understandably, clerks comprise an extraordinarily able group of people. Today, many justices (but not all) rely on their clerks to produce first drafts of opinions that have been assigned to them, a practice that has engendered a certain amount of controversy over the years. All clerks do research and are involved in reviewing petitions for writs of certiorari (requests for the Court to review a case), which we will discuss more fully shortly. The justices' general penchant for privacy in the internal operations of the Court extends to their clerks as well. In fact, one scholar, Todd Peppers, researching a book on the role of the Supreme Court clerks, was even denied a copy of the *Law Clerk Code of Conduct*,[2] the Court's behavioral guide for incoming clerks, though he was subsequently able to find a copy in Thurgood Marshall's papers at the Library of Congress. Justices generally tend to hire clerks whose points of view are compatible with their own, a trend that has apparently increased in recent years.[3] While questions regarding the influence of the clerks will never completely cease, Professor Peppers has concluded that the modern clerkship provides fewer opportunities than in the past for a clerk to exercise "an inordinate amount of influence" on his or her justice.[4] Ironically, one of the few persons ever to attempt to make an issue of undue clerkship influence was the late Chief Justice Rehnquist himself, when, in 1957, as a young Phoenix lawyer, he wrote an article for *U.S. News & World Report* accusing clerks of being to the left of their own justices in showing extreme solicitude for both communists and criminal defendants.[5] Rehnquist had clerked several years earlier for Justice Jackson.

As in any other line of work, some justices work harder than others. Justice Souter, a bachelor, was known for putting in twelve-hour workdays, seven days a week. Justice Souter's work habits, in addition to reflecting his deep dedication to the law, were undoubtedly made easier by the absence of the commitments of family life and his reserved nature, which led him to shun the kinds of social functions that more gregarious justices undoubtedly enjoy. Most justices work hard, if not at the pace of Justice Souter. One major difference among justices, however, is how easily the opinion-writing and decision-making processes come. Justice Douglas had little trouble making up his mind on most cases and was known for his ability to turn out opinions quickly. In contrast, Justice Blackmun was known for agonizing over decisions and struggling with the opinion-writing process.

You may recall from our earlier discussion how shocked Justice Douglas was by the quiet of his new surroundings. There is, in fact, a monastic quality to life on the Court that complements the Court's sense of special mission. That mission, phrased most grandly, is to help realize the great promise of a free society. However much justices may disagree as to how to do their job, they all believe what they do is important, sometimes even critical, to the country's welfare. It is this sense of common purpose and the corollary understanding that, at the end of the day, individual egos and even bruised feelings need to be overcome, which accounts for the well-known shaking hands ritual (each justice shaking hands with every other justice) that precedes each meeting of the justices. The fact is that, for all their differences, there is a communal life on the Court that almost all the current justices speak of with affection and that often makes the departure of one justice and replacement with another a trying moment in the life of the Court.

With all its sacrifices and demands, being a Supreme Court justice is not a bad job, and most justices seem to have liked it well enough, retiring, for the most part, only when declining health or vitality, or family circumstances, dictate. Here again Justice Souter is an exception, retiring simply out of a desire to return to his beloved New Hampshire.

It should be noted that, in recent times, justices seem to time their retirements with an eye to assuring a successor with views similar to their own. In a comprehensive study of retiring justices, Artemus Ward concluded that direct or circumstantial evidence indicated that the timing of the retirements of Chief Justices Warren and Burger, and Justices Harlan, Stewart, White, Blackmun, Douglas, and Powell were all influenced to some degree by this consideration.[6] Justice Souter also clearly postponed his retirement until after the 2008 presidential election to allow a new president to appoint his successor. An exception to this recent trend was Justice Thurgood Marshall, who joked that he would retire only when his wife told him to do so. At 82 and in failing health, Marshall, true to his word, retired in June 1991 at the urging of his wife, only to have President Bush appoint Clarence Thomas, Marshall's ideological opposite, as his successor. Justices retire on full salary, which obviously makes the decision easier from a financial standpoint.

Ethical Standards for Supreme Court Justices

The standards expected of a Supreme Court justice have changed considerably over time. Joseph Story is regarded as one of the great Supreme Court justices. Appointed by President Madison in 1811, he was a legal scholar whose strong commitment to a broad reading of national powers complemented Marshall's own views. Yet while on the Court, Story also wrote speeches for Daniel Webster, served as president of a local bank, and even ran for president of the Massachusetts Constitutional Convention of 1820. In 1829, he also began his long tenure as a professor of law at Harvard, during which time he wrote many scholarly books. No justice today could or would do what Story did—first, because of the obvious conflict of interest many of these activities might have presented, and second, because the workload of today's Court, not to mention the need to be in Washington, D.C., for most of the year, would preclude any one human being from managing what Story did.

In one sense, this earlier account of justices' activities should not be too shocking. Most justices came from the circuits that they traveled. They were probably perceived of as local as well as national figures for whom an active civic life was not inconsistent with one's position on the Court. Moreover, conflicts just don't seem to have been as much a part of nineteenth century concern as they are today. Consider, for example, that it was an accepted part of the system that a justice would render a decision in his circuit-riding capacity that would later be reviewed by both himself and his colleagues in their appellate function in Washington.

The impartiality of a Supreme Court justice must be beyond question. Any contact that casts doubt on that impartiality is open to serious criticism. Even the most honest justices can occasionally allow themselves to be drawn into potentially compromising situations. In 1934, for example, Justice Brandeis had lunch with agricultural officials highly interested in his position on the constitutionality of the Agricultural Adjustment Act; they "took away from the meeting a sense that the justice was demonstrating a new flexibility in his position on the overall legality of the AAA."[7] This meeting should probably never have taken place given the clear understanding that justices should not allow themselves to be lobbied on matters coming before them. In today's world, even social contacts and friendships can present problems occasionally, as, for example, when it was suggested that Justice Scalia should recuse himself from a case in which Vice President Cheney was clearly interested after it was revealed that the two had been on a hunting party together. Justice Scalia refused, stating that he was fully capable of objectively deciding any case involving the vice president's office.

Very occasionally, justices, being human, will deliberately cross a line that they know shouldn't be crossed even if they can justify it to themselves. Something like that probably occurred with Justice Frankfurter. As recounted in *Scorpions*, by Noah Feldman, Frankfurter continued his contacts with his former law clerk, Phil Elman, by then a lawyer in the Solicitor General's Office, even after the government had joined the case in *Brown v. Board of Education*. Frankfurter wanted to make sure that the executive branch would be in support of the Court if it opted to end segregation, and Elman apparently proved useful in this effort, a kind of surrogate for the lobbying that Frankfurter couldn't do directly and, given Elman's position, should not even have been done indirectly.[8]

Frankfurter's lapse was hidden among the corridors of power. A different kind of question involves the propriety of the attendance of justices at certain functions. A speaking appearance at a partisan political rally or even a candidate fund-raiser would not be proper for a Supreme Court justice. On the other hand, justices are human and, like most of us, gravitate in their friendships and contacts toward people and audiences with similar beliefs. If one condemns Scalia's speeches before the Federalist Society, as some have done, one must also question Justice Breyer's presence at Renaissance Weekend, an annual gathering of serious-minded policy makers and scholars originally started by President Clinton. Some, including the *New York Times* in a June 11, 2011, editorial, have recommended that Supreme Court justices be made subject to the same code of ethics to which other federal justices are subject; but that would mean, among other things, putting lower federal court justices, who enforce the code, in a position of authority over Supreme Court justices. (Making justices subject to an ethics code enforced by a congressional body would obviously raise serious separation-of-powers issues.) While reasonable people can certainly disagree, relying on Supreme Court justices to police themselves seems appropriate given the enormous trust we already place in them.

The most important lapse in ethical standards in modern times cost a potential chief justice his seat on the Court. Abe Fortas was a prominent lawyer in the nation's capital and close friend of Lyndon Johnson, dating from the time Fortas successfully defended Johnson's razor-thin, 87-vote victory to the U.S. Senate in 1948, a victory that launched Johnson on his role in national politics. Johnson appointed Fortas to the Court in 1965. In 1968, Johnson nominated Fortas to be chief justice to replace the retiring Earl Warren. It was not a popular choice for many reasons, and a combination of Republicans, who hoped to preserve the nomination for the next president, expected to be Nixon, and Southern Democrats, antagonistic to many Warren Court decisions, derailed his nomination. During this process, it was also revealed that Fortas had accepted $15,000 from American University to teach a course while on the Court, a considerable amount given that the salary of an Associate justice at the time was $39,000. In 1969, it was further revealed that Fortas had accepted $20,000 pursuant to a consulting contract with the Wolfson Foundation for services to be rendered while on the Court. While Fortas subsequently returned the money, revelation of the arrangement, coupled with the fact that Wolfson himself had been convicted of stock market manipulation, sealed Fortas's fate, and he resigned from the Court. While Fortas had not broken any laws, he had behaved in a way that was simply no longer acceptable for a Supreme Court justice.

The Effect of Personality

Political scientists do not spend much time considering the role of personality in the work of the Court, perhaps because it is not an easy subject for regression analysis. However, in a recent book (*The Supreme Court: The Personalities and Rivalries That Defined America*), Jeffrey Rosen, legal affairs editor for the *New Republic* and a professor of law at George Washington University, compared several pairs of justices, and for each pair concluded that the more flexible of the two, the one more willing to moderate the application of his own principles for the sake of the country, was the more effective justice. In comparing, for example, Chief Justice Rehnquist with Justice Scalia, he notes that initially it was the witty and brilliant Scalia who was deemed likely to be the more effective justice. In the end, however, it was Rehnquist's political savvy and willingness to support prior precedents that he didn't necessarily agree with, that made him, in Rosen's view, the superior justice. I should add, parenthetically, that this particular comparison may be unfair to Justice Scalia, who is said to pride himself on never lobbying and in any event is not a chief justice, from whom leadership is expected. Moreover, Scalia has been effective in bringing many justices on the Court to share his distrust of legislative history as a basis for interpreting statutory language.

One clear difference among the justices is between those who actively seek to lobby other colleagues and those who do not. Personality surely plays an important role here. In his autobiography, Justice Douglas wrote: "There have been, while I have been on the Court, three active proselytizers: Stone, Black and Frankfurter. Most Judges content themselves with making up their own minds, but these three were evangelists, each in his own right, each sincere, eloquent, and unrelenting."[9] Interestingly, Douglas did not mention Justice Brennan, who was also known for attempting to exercise his considerable Irish charm on colleagues. He is reputed to have continually reminded his law clerks that with five votes around here, you can do anything. In contrast to Brennan, some justices, perhaps many, are personally reluctant to even appear to lobby colleagues. Christopher Eisgruber, who clerked for Justice Stevens, describes how weeks went by after Stevens had circulated his opinion in an abortion case without his receiving any comment from Justice O'Connor. He had shaped part of the opinion to win her support and one day shared with his clerks his anxiety over her silence. They suggested he walk down to her office and ask her. Eisgruber recalls: "Stevens rejected our suggestion. The opinion, he told us, ought to stand or fall on the force of its reasons. He would feel uncomfortable talking to O'Connor about the opinion because she might feel pressured by the conversation. Instead, he waited, and eventually she joined the opinion."[10] According to Jeffrey Toobin, of the justices on the recent Court, only Justice Breyer enjoys actively lobbying for his positions, Souter and Thomas being "downright reclusive," Stevens and Ginsburg "tend[ing] that way," Kennedy also "keep[ing] to himself," and, as mentioned, Scalia priding himself "on never lobbying."[11]

Personality and temperament are most important on the Court when it prevents natural allies from coming together. Some speculate that Justice Scalia might have had more influence on Justice O'Connor had he tempered his criticisms of her opinions, although this is pure speculation and in this writer's view unwarranted, given Justice O'Connor's strong personality and her own set of strong convictions. The personality clash that undoubtedly led to lost opportunities was between Felix Frankfurter on the one hand and other Roosevelt-appointed justices, particularly Justices Black and Douglas, on the other. Given his undisputed intellect, many expected Frankfurter to have a major influence on the Court's direction. Frankfurter himself seemed to envision this role. To Justice Reed he wrote, "The fact is that I am an academic and I have no excuse for being on this Court unless I remain so."[12] Not surprisingly, however, justices, even potentially sympathetic colleagues, did not like being treated as inferiors and lectured to fifty minutes at a time. His pedantic air and constant invocation in conference of the words of Holmes and Brandeis even irritated the usually unflappable Justice Brennan. For Justice Douglas, not noted for his talent for human relationships, Frankfurter was simply impossible. Once, after a particularly long harangue by Frankfurter, Douglas announced, "When I came into this conference I agreed in the conclusion that Felix has just announced. But he's talked me out of it."[13] Frankfurter's personality had its effect on the Court's morale. Melvin Urofsky, a Frankfurter biographer, has observed: "We can see the disastrous effects of Frankfurter's personalization of issues in the disintegration of the Court during the war years . . . Frankfurter, of course, does not share the full blame. . . . There is no doubt, however, that Frankfurter's behavior poisoned the well of collegiality."[14] As mentioned above, one of the most challenging times to be a justice in terms of working environment was in the 1940s and early 1950s when, in addition to Justice Frankfurter's personality to contend with, a bitter feud, never reconciled, arose between Justices Black and Jackson over Justice Jackson's belief that Justice Black had deliberately derailed his appointment as chief justice. "*Scorpions*" by Noah Feldman, provides a fascinating account of this period.

As rancorous as disagreements may sometimes be—and most historians would deny that rancor is the norm—there are moments when the feeling that all of them have for the Court as an institution transcends everything.

One such moment occurred in connection with the announcement of the Court's decision in *Brown v. Board of Education*. On May 15, 1954, the Court in conference had agreed to announce its decision on the following Monday, subject to the approval of Justice Jackson who was in the hospital recovering from a heart attack. In his memoirs, Chief Justice Warren writes: "I went to the hospital early Monday morning, May 17, and showed the justice a copy of the proposed opinion as it was to be released. He agreed to it, and to my alarm insisted on attending the Court that day in order to demonstrate our solidarity. I suggested that it was unnecessary, but he insisted, and was there at the appointed time."[15]

Today's Court works hard to preserve its collegiality and, by most accounts, has largely succeeded. Justice Ginsburg, for example, disclosed in an October 2008 talk at Princeton University how each justice's birthday is celebrated with a cake and how the justices often lunch together, observing only one rule—no shop talk. Occasionally, the justices even invite special guests to their lunches to discuss a particular topic.

Because it is a human institution, the quality of leadership on the Court can sometimes make an enormous difference. Unanimity in *Brown v. Board of Education*, for example, was not achieved easily. Since segregated schools existed (even in the District of Columbia) and were not challenged at the time the Equal Protection clause was adopted, historical analysis did not support the Court's position. Justices Reed, Frankfurter, Jackson, and Burton all needed to be won over for a unanimous opinion; each had reasons that might have led him to dissent. Warren understood each of their concerns and was able to craft an opinion acceptable to everyone but Stanley Reed, a Southerner. George Mickum, Justice Reed's clerk, has given this account of Chief Justice Warren's final conversation with the justice. It is worth quoting in full: "He [Warren] said, 'Stan you're all by yourself in this now. . . . You've really got to decide whether it's really the best thing for the country.' He was not particularly eloquent and certainly not bombastic. Throughout the Chief Justice was quite low-key and very sensitive to the problems that the decision would present to the South. He empathized with Justice Reed's concern. But he was quite firm on the Court's need for unanimity on a matter of this sensitivity."[16] Frederick Vinson was chief justice when the Court first agreed to hear *Brown v. Board of Education*. Vinson was not a strong leader, and some scholars believe that *Brown v. Board of Education* not only would not have been a unanimous decision but might actually have come out the other way, had Vinson not died and been replaced by Earl Warren. Justice Frankfurter, knowing the importance of the case, is reputed to have said that Vinson's passing was for him the first real evidence of a divine providence.

As with any other group, some justices' views are more highly valued than others because the justices themselves are more highly respected. This in turn can affect the dynamics of decision making and how justices try to influence each other. In his insightful recent biography of Justice Brandeis, Melvin Urofsky notes the great respect that Justice Brandeis had for Justice Van Devanter, even though they held very different views on many matters: "Brandeis compared Van Devanter to a 'Jesuit General' in the suppleness of his mind and believed that during much of the 1920s the real leader of the Court was not Chief Justice Taft but Justice Van Devanter, whose advice Taft sought constantly. When the Court divided, Brandeis would say that if he could convince Van Devanter, the opposition would collapse."[17]

8. The Litigation Process: From Complaint to Supreme Court Opinion

How Cases Begin

Anyone can bring a case that ends up being heard by the Supreme Court. Constitutional cases, of course, must be initiated by an aggrieved person, one who has suffered injury in fact, for which the Court can provide relief. This is the *standing* concept we have previously discussed. Beyond that requirement there is no limitation on the motives or circumstances surrounding constitutional cases.

Major legislation enacted by Congress will almost invariably be tested in the courts by those persons or groups who were opposed to the legislation. The constitutionality of even our most iconic pieces of legislation, such as the Social Security Act, the Public Accommodations Act of 1964, and the Voting Rights Act of 1965, has been tested in the courts.

It is not unusual for groups with a particular slant on how a constitutional provision should be interpreted, to seek out plaintiffs whose personal qualities or specific circumstances make an appealing case for challenging a particular practice or a settled doctrine of constitutional law. This was often done by the NAACP Legal Defense Fund in its half-century legal struggle to end segregation in the South, a struggle that culminated in *Brown v. Board of Education*, but was preceded by many cases that slowly built the foundation for that epic decision. This story has been brilliantly recounted in *Simple Justice* by Richard Kluger.[1]

The right to help bring test cases by organizations interested in shaping the development of law is itself safeguarded under the First Amendment. In the *National Association for the Advancement of Colored People v. Button*,[2] the Court held that the activities of the NAACP in advising parents of the legal steps necessary to challenge the State of Virginia's efforts at resisting school desegregation, including providing forms authorizing the NAACP to retain legal counsel for the parents, were constitutionally protected. Virginia had sought to discourage these activities by making it illegal for an organization to employ, retain, or compensate any lawyer in connection with a lawsuit in which the organization itself had no pecuniary right or liability. In his majority opinion, Justice Brennan emphasized the importance of litigation in advancing constitutional rights, noting that, in the context of the NAACP's objectives, "litigation is not a technique of resolving private differences; it is a means for [achieving] equality of treatment for members of the Negro community; [it] is thus a form of political expression. Groups which find themselves unable to achieve their objectives through the ballot frequently turn to the Courts. . . . litigation may well be the sole practicable avenue open to a minority to petition for redress of grievances."[3]

Sometimes test cases can create unwanted precedents. The leading example is undoubtedly *Plessy v. Ferguson*,[4] the famous 1896 test case to set aside a Louisiana statute requiring railroads to provide separate but equal rail car accommodations. The case was supported by an interesting combination of railroads, who objected to the increased costs imposed by the statute, and blacks and creoles who had organized into a citizens committee for the purpose of bringing suit. Unfortunately for both the plaintiffs and the course of civil rights history, the Court's decision ended up establishing the constitutional basis for "separate but equal" treatment of the races.

Very often constitutional cases arise from the ordinary conflicts and circumstances of everyday life. A student wears an arm-band to class to protest the Vietnam War, another gives an off-color speech to a school assembly, a third is upset at an attempt at censorship of the student newspaper by the school administration, a fourth holds up a sign at a parade. Each of these simple acts in an ordinary school day led ultimately to Supreme Court cases that have shaped the First Amendment rights of public high school students. None of the plaintiffs in these cases ever planned to have their name affixed to a litigation caption. Life just happens. It is also true, however, that many groups, such as the American Civil Liberties Union, take a strong interest in any free speech case.

The initiation and evolution of the landmark case of *Shelley v. Kramer* illustrates the interesting dynamic between individual story and group interest that is often the stuff of constitutional law. In 1945 J. D. and Ethel Shelley moved into their new home in a better part of St. Louis, Missouri, having fled a crime-ridden ghetto for a better life for themselves and their six children. The sale, however, violated a restrictive racial covenant, and a white couple living about ten blocks away sued to evict them. The Shelleys liked their new home and wanted to fight but did not have the financial resources to do so by themselves. Fortunately for them, the NAACP Legal Defense Fund had decided to take on the issue of restrictive racial covenants as part of its long-term goal to end legal segregation in the United States. The Fund thought the Shelley's situation provided an attractive opportunity to challenge the covenant and represented the family all the way to the Supreme Court, where the Court held the covenant to be unenforceable under the Equal Protection clause of the 14th Amendment.

The Jehovah's Witnesses have a long history of litigating important First Amendment cases. One case in particular illustrates how a simple act, in this instance the refusal by a seventh-grader in a Minersville, Pennsylvania, elementary school to salute the flag, a normal part of her class's morning routine, set off a chain of events that ultimately established a First Amendment right against compelled speech. Lillian Gobitis certainly never envisioned that she would become the catalyst for an important doctrinal change in constitutional law. This was not a decision forced on her by her parents. After a hearing before the local school board, she was expelled from school along with her fifth-grade brother. The Jehovah's Witnesses took the case to the Supreme Court and lost 8–1. This decision, in the words of the adult Ms. Gobitis, "just set off a wave of persecution. It was like open season on Jehovah's Witnesses. That's when the mobs escalated. The Kingdom Hall in Litchfield, Illinois was totally destroyed by a mob, and more than three thousand Witnesses were arrested every year for the next three years."[5] But the Witnesses did not concede defeat. In 1943, in *West Virginia State Board of Education v. Barnette*, another case brought by the Witnesses, the Court changed its mind and in a 6–3 decision held that forcing children to pledge the flag against their religious convictions violated the First Amendment.

Not everyone whose grievance moves constitutional law forward is necessarily a model citizen. Jay Near was an anti-Jewish, anti-Catholic, and anti-black newsman who published a weekly newspaper in Minneapolis filled with defamatory material. Yet, he also attacked the corrupt alliance between Minneapolis politicians and local gangsters and refused to back down when the establishment was able to temporarily shut down his newspaper relying on a state public nuisance law that allowed a judge without a jury to enjoin the publication of a "malicious, scandalous and defamatory newspaper." His cause was taken up by the newly formed American Civil Liberties Union and then the *Chicago Tribune*, which as a major newspaper had its own interest in the case. The Supreme Court heard the case and in

Near v. Minnesota[6] made clear what it had earlier hinted at—that the First Amendment applied to the states and that the prior restraint on publication authorized by the Minnesota law was unconstitutional.

Events themselves, of course, can trigger important constitutional decisions. The imprisonment of the Japanese during the Second World War, the civil suit against President Clinton, the discovery of President Nixon's tapes, Daniel Ellsberg's transmittal of the Pentagon Papers to the *New York Times*, a state libel judgment against the *New York Times*, the success of the Term Limits movement in the late 1980s and early 1990s, all of these are examples of events that have led to important constitutional law decisions.

So the answer to the question, how do constitutional cases arise, is: in every conceivable way—sometimes in response to important events, other times as a result of a simple act performed in the course of daily life by a person with no intention of ending up with the lead billing on a landmark litigation caption; and sometimes as part of a well thought out strategy by organizations devoted to the well-being of particular groups or to a particular view of a constitutional provision.

Deciding What Cases to Hear

Almost all cases heard by the Supreme Court today result from an exercise of the Court's discretionary jurisdiction, but this is a comparatively recent development. For the first century of its existence, the Court did not have much discretion as to what cases it would hear. This was not originally a problem, but after the Civil War, an increasingly complex industrial economy caused more and more cases to be brought to the Court. By 1890, it was clear that the workload was unsustainable. The Judiciary Act of 1891 solved part of the problem by creating today's Circuit Courts of Appeal and eliminating the remaining circuit traveling responsibilities of Supreme Court Justices. At the same time, Congress gave the Court more control of its calendar by providing that certain cases could be further appealed from the newly created circuit courts only if the Supreme Court *at its discretion* granted a writ of certiorari. The act achieved its immediate purpose— within a year the Court's workload had plunged to a sixth of its workload in 1890.[7] Nevertheless, a great deal of the Court's appellate jurisdiction remained obligatory, including cases involving constitutional questions. In the Judiciary Act of 1925, a bill actually written by the Supreme Court justices (and therefore aptly called "the Judges' Bill"), Congress further removed a large number of obligatory cases from the Court's docket. Finally, in 1988 Congress removed a last class of cases (roughly 10 percent of the Court's calendar) that could be appealed to the Court as a matter of right.

Is the Court's complete control of its own docket a good thing? In September 2009, a host of well-known scholars gathered for a half -day conference at the National Press Club to address this very question. The declining number of cases handled by the Court in recent years and the growing feeling that the Court might be ducking important legal issues have led to suggestions for a separate court, composed of experienced appellate judges, to decide what cases the Court should hear. It is not an idea likely to be adopted soon but the suggestion and the conference itself underscore the importance attached to the basic issue of how the Court decides what cases to take.

When the Supreme Court decides to hear a case, it means it will read briefs submitted by the parties and hear oral argument in order to answer a question or questions raised by the party seeking the Court's review. A request for such review is presented in the form of a writ of certiorari, more familiarly called a "cert. petition." The number of cert. petitions has grown astronomically in recent years. While the numbers vary, it is now not unusual for more than 9,000 petitions to be filed in a given year, of which less than 1 percent are accepted by the Court. The growing number of cert. petitions filed has led to the development of a pool system for reviewing them. The initial intake is effectively divided among the justices participating in the pool (currently all except Justice Alito). A memo for each petition is then prepared by a law clerk in the assigned justice's chambers and, after review by the justice, is circulated to the other justices with a recommendation whether or not to hear the case. It has been suggested that the pool system may, in part, be responsible for the decline in the number of cases heard by the Court, the theory being that young law clerks are risk-averse and do not want to risk potential embarrassment by suggesting that the Court hear cases that it does not ultimately accept.

The final disposition of a cert. petition is made by the justices as part of their regularly scheduled weekly conferences, which currently occur on Wednesdays and Fridays. If four justices vote to hear a case, then by what is known as "the Rule of Four" (actually an informal rule that did not even come to light until revealed by Justice Van Devanter in 1924), the writ of certiorari is granted and a record of the proceedings s forwarded to the Court. There is no doubt that internal decisions and procedures can affect the number of cases the Court decides to hear. In the early 1970s, Chief

Justice Burger helped institute a new kind of vote, the "Join Three" vote, in which a justice agreed to supply the fourth vote, if necessary, to hear a case but would otherwise vote to deny. The "Join Three" vote, plus a decision in 1971 to reduce oral argument in a given case from two hours to one hour, likely were the main contributors to a spike in the number of cases heard by the Court from 1970 to 1985. Since 1985, the number of cases accepted by the Court has been sharply reduced to the point that, for the 2007 term, the Court rendered opinions in only sixty-seven cases, the lowest number since the 1950s. This could be the result of several circumstances, including the stated desire of Chief Justice Roberts for the Court to maintain a low public profile and the fact that the Republican Party was largely in control of the appointment process for the federal judiciary for twenty-eight out of the forty years between 1968 and 2008, resulting in fewer conflicting decisions among the Circuit Courts requiring resolution.

Political scientists and legal scholars are anxious to find patterns in the Supreme Court's selection of cases. We need not concern ourselves with this research, which seems to be inconclusive at best, but there are some things we know for certain about the process.

First, no justice is anxious to accept a case that will likely result in a Court decision not to the justice's liking. A Court closely divided on numerous important issues may logically take fewer cases than normal, owing to the unpredictability of outcome. Second, sometimes justices themselves are on the lookout for a case raising a particular issue. Chief Justice Warren, for example, was very interested in expanding the right to counsel and asked his clerks to review cert. petitions with his interest in mind. The ultimate result was *Gideon v. Wainwright*[8] which established a defendant's right to counsel in all state felony cases. Third, the Court has a particular interest in cert. petitions filed by the Office of Solicitor General. The solicitor general plays an important role in the development of constitutional law. As the U.S. government's chief litigator, the solicitor general represents the government in all cases in which the United States is a party. Because of the respect accorded that office and because of the importance of the United States government itself as an instrument of the people's sovereignty, the Court is particularly responsive to the government's cert. petitions, granting them on average more than 50 percent of the time, some 50 times more frequently than the average cert. petition. Fourth, while one might expect justices to consult with each other and even bargain over what cases the Court should take, that expectation appears to be unfounded. A 1991 study by H. W. Perry

Jr. found the case selection process to be "relatively atomistic with decisions being made within chambers and the outcome . . . being primarily the sum of nine individual processes."[9] He did note that the threat by a justice to dissent publicly to a denial of cert. can lead to the granting of cert., particularly in cases where there are already two or three justices who want to hear the case.[10] Perry cited as possible explanations for the lack of bargaining and horse trading, time pressures and the feeling that individual cases are not that important since if a case presents a significant legal question, it will come up again. The lack of bargaining might also reflect a general consensus of the justices as to what kinds of cases are appropriate for hearing. Finally, studies of the Court's case selection process have generally concluded that individual justices are much more likely to vote to grant cert. petitions in cases where they wish to reverse the decision below.[11]

I should note here the important role that the Solicitor General's Office plays in the governmental structure. Historically, the Court has accorded great weight to the views of that office and often seeks its opinion by requesting the government to file amicus briefs in cases in which the government is not a party. This respect is due in part to the fact that the solicitor general has been perceived as nonpolitical, representing the long-term interests of the government, rather than the short-term partisan interests of a particular president. Indeed, the solicitor general even maintains an office in the Supreme Court Building itself.

The case selection process does have one flaw that once provided an extraordinarily embarrassing moment for the Court, for while it only takes four justices to decide to hear a case, it takes five to stay the proceedings below.[12] A stay requires that no further action be taken in relation to the case by either party. Undoubtedly one of the worst moments for the Court occurred because of this anomaly. In the 1980's, the Court was bitterly divided over the issue of capital punishment and more particularly on how tolerant the Court should be in allowing death row inmates chances to appeal. The more conservative justices on the Court had become increasingly aggravated by what they saw as a virtual campaign by the four more liberal justices (Brennan, Marshall, Blackmun, and Stevens) to obstruct executions. Things reached such a point that the four conservative justices refused to grant a stay in one death row case for which the Court had granted cert., even though the potential fifth vote for a stay, Justice Powell, was recovering from a cancer operation at the Mayo Clinic in Minnesota and was therefore unavailable to vote. With only four votes for a stay, the execution went forward even though the Court by the Rule of Four had voted to hear the case. Brennan, Marshall, Blackmun, and Stevens all issued a public dissent protesting the denial of the stay, prompting an incredulous *New York Times* editorial with the headline: KILL HIM 4–4.[13]

Denials of cert. rarely occasion much public outcry but there are exceptions. Take the case, which the Supreme Court didn't, of Khaled e-Masri, a German citizen of Lebanese descent. Mr. Masri was vacationing in Macedonia in 2003 when, at the behest of the United States, he was seized and transported to Afghanistan where he was tortured. It turned out that Mr. Masri was not a terrorist and his abduction was a mistake. The U.S. government secured dismissal of Khaled's civil suit against it by invoking the rule that allows exclusion of evidence that would reveal state secrets. Since the case had been well publicized, the denial of cert. evoked strong public and editorial reaction. Illustrating how strategic considerations can loom large, however, even the *New York Times* recognized that liberal justices might not have wanted to take the case out of a fear that the Court might actually have approved the seizure as a legal though unfortunate exercise of executive power.

Hearing the Case and Reaching a Decision

The formal process for deciding a case is easy to describe. It involves the submission to each justice of the Record of the Proceedings below, the writing and submission of briefs by each party setting forth their positions, oral argument before the justices, a discussion of the case by the justices in conference at which a tentative vote is recorded, and the assignment, drafting, issuance, and announcement of the final opinions in the case. The purpose of the process is to assure that each side has a full opportunity to be heard and that the justices thoroughly discuss and explore the issues in the case before reaching a judgment.

The decision-making process is all about the art of persuasion. It has two elements—first, the attorneys representing the parties (and other interested persons through amicus briefs) try to persuade the justices; then the justices try to persuade each other. Advocates have their moment in the brief writing and oral argument stage; justices when the case is discussed in conference and during the opinion-writing stage.

Amicus Curiae Briefs

When the Court grants cert., it specifies the issue or issues that it wants the parties to brief. In important cases, there are often many persons and groups, other than the litigants themselves, who may have a strong interest in the outcome of the case. These persons and groups will often file what are called *amicus curiae* (friend of the court) briefs, supporting the position of one of the two litigating parties.

Today, amicus briefs are filed in 85 percent of all cases; sometimes as many as eighteen hundred different organizations sign on to at least one Supreme Court brief during a term.[14] In *District of Columbia v. Heller*, the Court's recent case dealing with the right to bear arms, more than seventy-five amicus briefs were filed, including a brief filed on behalf of thirty-one States and another on behalf of 55 members of the United States Senate and 250 members of the United States House of Representatives. Other groups filing briefs included the Brady Center to Prevent Gun Violence; the D.C. League of Women Voters; Police Chiefs for the Cities of Los Angeles, Minneapolis, and Seattle; the Cato Institute; the Congress of Racial Equality; and Pink Pistols and Gays and Lesbians for Individual Liberty. The full list of amicus briefs filed in the case runs to four single-spaced pages.

In his comprehensive study of amicus briefs,[15] Paul Collins Jr. concluded that the sheer number of briefs filed supporting a particular position can influence case outcomes: " when the justices are faced with asymmetric amicus participation—in the sense that a large number of briefs are filed supporting a particular ideological position—the influence of the briefs is rather dramatic." One example of this phenomenon probably occurred when early in Chief Justice Rehnquist's tenure, the Court asked whether a major civil rights decision, *Runyon v. McCrary*,[16] holding that the Civil Rights Act of 1866 prohibited a private employer from engaging in racial discrimination in the making of a contract, should be reversed. This was a stunning development. Briefs opposing the Court's overruling of *Runyon* "inundated" the justices.[17] One was signed by seven major historians, including three Pulitzer Prize winners; another by 66 members of the United States Senate and 118 members of the House of Representatives. Perhaps most telling of all was the brief signed by 47 of the 50 states' attorneys general.[18] In the end, the Court voted unanimously not to reverse *Runyon*. It is hard not to believe that the amicus briefs had a major impact in this case. I should add that amicus briefs, even from the most powerful, do not guarantee success. In *Snyder v. Phelps*, the First Amendment case previously mentioned involving picketing at a soldier's funeral, the Court held in favor of the picketers notwithstanding an amicus brief from 42 U.S. senators, including the leadership of both parties, and another from 48 of the 50 states' attorneys general, urging that the jury verdict in favor of the aggrieved family be sustained.

Unlike the briefs of parties in a case, amicus briefs are filed on the same date and don't respond to each other. Substantively, they are probably most useful in bringing to the Court perspectives that help it evaluate the potential consequences of its decisions. To take just one example, in *Grutter v. Bollinger*,[19] a case we will discuss in more detail later, amicus briefs filed by General Motors, 3M, and retired military personnel described the importance of a diverse work force and officer corps for their work. Justice O'Connor cited these briefs as evidence of a compelling state interest in a diverse student body. In the case of *Terry v. Ohio*,[20] the amicus brief of Americans for Effective Law Enforcement is thought by some to have persuaded the Warren Court to allow police to stop and frisk persons acting suspiciously.[21]

Very occasionally amicus briefs may urge the Court to take a position or examine an issue that has not been taken or raised by either party to the litigation. This happened most dramatically in *Mapp v. Ohio* when the Ohio and American Civil Liberties Unions urged the Court to apply the federal rule excluding the admission of improperly obtained evidence in criminal trials to the states. You may recall from our earlier discussion that the Court subsequently adopted this position, making *Mapp* a landmark case.[22]

Amicus briefs are important not only because of their potential influence in a case but because they give an opportunity for the world at large to express its opinion. It is another way in which the least democratic branch can keep itself in contact with civil society, an important consideration for an institution that has few such avenues. It is, of course, also a good way for the Court to measure how important interest groups, often represented by formidable organizations, are thinking. The fact that the Court receives amicus briefs from so many parties not directly involved in a litigation speaks to the important reverberations of so many constitutional decisions for the larger society and underscores how those decisions can influence public policy by expanding or restricting the rights of journalists, minorities, corporations and many others.

Oral Argument

After the written briefs are in, the Court will hear oral argument on one of the days on the calendar set aside for that purpose. Currently, oral arguments are held on Mondays, Tuesdays, and Wednesdays of the first two weeks of each calendar month through April. They occur in the Court's main chambers and, as noted, are open to the public. Today, an hour is usually set aside for each case (each side having a half-hour to make its presentation) but there are occasional exceptions. In 2003, the Court held a four-hour hearing in *McConnell v. Federal Election Commission*, the case which addressed the constitutionality of the Bi-Partisan Campaign Reform Act of 2002, the first time the Court had allotted so much time to a case since the Nixon Watergate Tapes hearing.

The idea of limiting oral argument to an hour would have shocked our earliest generations of Supreme Court justices. In, for example, the pivotal case of *McCulloch v. Maryland* discussed earlier, oral argument lasted ten days with three different attorneys on each side allowed to make presentations. In an era when average citizens would happily attend Fourth of July orations four or five hours long, oral argument included embellishments that today would be unthinkable. In *McCulloch*, the attorney for the bank "paid his respects to both justices and opposing counsel. He had fulsome praise for the Court . . . he awarded compliments to his opponents for their 'polished elocution' and to Martin {Luther Martin] in particular, for his 'robust and hardy wit.'"[23]

Justice Story's reaction to the presentation by one of the bank's attorneys underscores just how effective a good oral argument can be: "I never in my life heard a greater speech; his elocution was excessively vehement, but his eloquence was overwhelming. His language, his style, his figures, his arguments, were most brilliant and sparkling. He spoke like a great statesman and patriot, and a sound constitutional lawyer. All the cobwebs of sophistry and metaphysics about State rights and State sovereignty he brushed away with a mighty besom."[24]

Undoubtedly, the high point of nineteenth century oral argument eloquence was the famous closing argument of Daniel Webster on behalf of Dartmouth College:

> This, sir, is my case. It is the case not merely of that humble institution [Dartmouth College]; it is the case of every college in our land. . . . It is more. It is, in some sense, the case of every man who has property of which he may be stripped. . . . Sir, you may destroy this little institution. It is weak. It is in your hands. I know it is one of the lesser lights in the literary horizon of the country. You may put it out. But if you do so, you must carry through your work. You must extinguish, one

after another, all those great lights of science which, for more than a century, have thrown their radiance over our land. It is, sir, as I have said, a small college and yet there are those that love it.[25]

This was not all. According to an eyewitness account, as retold by one historian, "Here Webster, the consummate actor, pretended to break down. His lips quivered, his voice choked, his eyes filled with tears. . . . Marshall bent his tall, gaunt figure forward as if straining to catch every word. His eyes seemed wet. Joseph Story still sat, pen in hand, as if to take notes, which he never took. The rest of the justices, too, seemed to be transfixed."[26] Needless to say, Webster won his case.

Today, at the time oral argument occurs, the justices have already had an opportunity to read the written briefs. They are likely to have discussed the case with their law clerks. Oral argument allows the justices an opportunity to question the lawyers about aspects of the case they find troubling. If a justice has made up his or her mind about a case, however, it also affords an opportunity to ask questions in a way that exposes weaknesses in the other side's position. In effect, oral argument becomes a vehicle for the justices to talk to each other.

Oral argument, then, is a complex affair with attorneys addressing justices and justices sometimes addressing each other in the guise of addressing attorneys. This can lead to humorous moments. Once, Justice Douglas stepped in to suggest a useful answer to a question posed by Justice Frankfurter. "I thought you were arguing the case," an irritated Justice Frankfurter said to the lawyer. "I am," he replied, "but I can use all the help I can get."[27]

The late Bernard Schwartz, a wonderful constitutional scholar, believed that oral argument also serves an important institutional purpose. "A lifetime's study of the high bench has . . . convinced me that the principal purpose of the argument before the Justices is a public relations one—to communicate to the country that the Court has given each side an open opportunity to be heard. Thus not only is Justice done, but it is publicly seen to be done."[28] The second Justice Harlan, however, did see more than a public relations purpose to oral argument, believing that "the lawyer who depreciates the oral argument as an effective instrument of appellate advocacy . . . is making a great mistake."[29] For Harlan, "the first impressions that a judge gets of a case are very tenacious . . . and those impressions are actually gained from the oral argument, if it is an effective job."[30] Harlan also believed that "there is no substitute . . . for the Socratic method of procedure in getting at the real heart of an issue."[31] A number of justices, including Justice Brennan and Chief Justice Rehnquist, have expressed similar views.[32]

The effect of oral argument on actual Supreme Court decision making has been a matter of considerable focus among political scientists. An interesting recent article by Timothy Johnson, Paul Wahlbeck, and James Spriggs II, appearing in the *American Political Science Review*, concludes that "oral arguments can influence Supreme Court justices' decisions by providing information relevant to deciding a case."[33] To anyone who has spent time reading transcripts of oral arguments, the authors' emphasis seems appropriate. Certainly, written briefs are not always as clear as they could be and, on that score alone, oral argument can be helpful in alleviating confusion. The authors also contend that the effectiveness of oral argument in any given case depends in part on the perceived credibility of the attorneys in the eyes of the Court and that this in turn can be influenced by a number of factors, including the frequency of counsel's appearing before the Court, the most experienced counsel having the most credibility.

The Conference

Currently, cases argued on Monday are usually discussed at the Court's Wednesday afternoon conference, those argued on Tuesday and Wednesday, at Friday's conference. No one other than the justices themselves attend the Wednesday and Friday conferences. The chief justice begins the discussion of a case with a brief description, emphasizing his view of the issues at stake. Most chief justices also state their own position at that time. This is one of the moments when the great chief justices can leave their imprint on a Court. Justice Fortas believed that "It was [Chief Justice] Warren's great gift that, in presenting the case and discussing the case, he proceeded immediately and very calmly and graciously to the ultimate values involved—the ultimate constitutional values, the ultimate human values."[34]

While there are no formal written rules governing conference procedures, the practice historically has been for justices to present their views on a case generally in order of seniority, with the most senior justice speaking first. It appears that relatively little debate occurs among the justices at the conference and recollections can occasionally differ as to what transpired, differences usually uncovered during the opinion-writing process. If the chief justice is in the majority, he will assign the writing of the majority opinion to himself or to someone else in the majority. If he is not in the majority, the most senior justice in the majority will assign the opinion.

Assigning opinions is an important source of power for a chief justice. Chief Justice Warren was noted for his fairness in assigning opinions, one of the many personal qualities that endeared him to his colleagues. Chief Justice Rehnquist was regarded as very fair as well. Chief Justice Burger, on the other hand, was sometimes accused of joining the majority simply to be able to assign the opinion. By virtue of their experiences before coming to the Court, some justices have a strong expertise in certain areas of the law, and case assignments will sometimes take advantage of this background. Thus, for example, Justice Stevens over the years has been regularly assigned antitrust cases, and Justice Breyer cases involving complex regulatory matters.

The assigning justice sometimes chooses a justice to write an opinion who most clearly represents the assigning justice's own views of a particular case. This is perfectly legitimate. Other times, strategic considerations enter into the choice. If the assigning justice is worried, for example, that a majority in the conference is tenuous, he or she may assign the opinion to a justice who is regarded as the least convinced member of the majority or the justice most likely to write an opinion that will hold the majority together. The views expressed in conference give both the assigning justice and the opinion writer a good sense of the reasoning of the various justices forming the majority.

There is nothing final about the positions taken in conference. Much happens during the opinion-writing process. It is not at all unusual for a justice who votes one way in conference to discover that the draft majority opinion reveals a weakness in the case not previously seen. To fully understand this process, we need to consider the different kinds of opinions that can be handed down in a case.

Kinds of Opinions

Court opinions come in many flavors—majority, plurality, concurrence, concurrence in the judgment, dissent, per curiam—each of which serves a specific function. Additionally, when the Court decides a case, it will either affirm or reverse each contested part of the decision below. Sometimes the Court's decision represents a final disposition of the case, but other times the Court sends the case back for additional factual findings or for a new trial.

Other than in the case of a per curiam (unsigned) opinion or the rare jointly authored opinion, in which more than one justice signs the opinion, a justice will either write his or her own opinion or join another opinion; sometimes a justice does both.

Let's assume a case in which a majority of the nine justices agree on both the result of the case (whether to affirm or reverse) and on the reasoning that led to the result. In that case, as mentioned, there will be an *Opinion of the Court.* Sometimes a justice who has joined the Opinion of the Court wants to add some thoughts of his or her own. In that event, the justice will write a *concurring opinion*, which other justices in the majority may also join. If a justice votes for the same result as the majority but disagrees with the reasoning of the majority and does not join the majority opinion, the justice will write *an opinion concurring in the judgment.* A good example of this kind of opinion occurred in *Lawrence v. Texas* in which Justice O'Connor refused to join in the opinion of the Court holding that Texas's statute criminalizing same-sex sodomy violated the liberty interest of homosexuals under the Due Process clause but agreed that the Texas statute violated the Equal Protection clause. Just how little concurrence there can be in a "concurrence in the judgment" is illustrated by Justice White's statement in an important free speech case: "I join the judgment, but not the folly of the opinion."[35]

It is not unusual in today's Court for there to be no Opinion of the Court because there are not five justices willing to join the same opinion. Sometimes part of an opinion will draw the support of a majority of justices and part will not. In that case, only part of the opinion will represent an Opinion of the Court. If there is no majority opinion on a point, the opinion representing the view of the most justices is called a *plurality opinion.* A justice who disagrees with both the result and the reasoning in the case will issue or join a *dissenting opinion.* There can be more than one dissent and more than one concurrence in any case.

It is worth noting that there were no dissents or concurrences in the very earliest Court decisions since each justice was expected to issue an opinion in each case. Strictly speaking then, there was no majority opinion of the Court. One can see that, if such a practice persisted, the system of precedent on which the Court ostensibly relies today, could not really have developed. Chief Justice John Marshall felt strongly that the Court should speak as one voice and it was his leadership that led to the system of Court opinions we are familiar with today. Marshall also did his best to discourage dissents.

The value of the concurrence is sometimes overlooked. A recent paper by Samuel Estreicher and Tristan Pelham-Webb[36] has pointed out how Justice Powell's concurrences sometimes were more influential than the majority opinion in shaping the development of the law by the lower federal Courts. As a good illustration, the paper cites *Branzburg v. Hayes*,[37] a 5–4 decision that refused to recognize a journalistic First Amendment privilege respecting a refusal to disclose sources. While Powell joined in the majority opinion, he also wrote a short concurrence clearly confining the majority opinion to the facts of the case. The essay notes, "Powell's separate opinion actually spurred recognition of a 'qualified reporter's privilege' in many subsequent lower court cases. Many of these courts adopted the line of thought that because Powell cast the 'deciding' vote to create the majority, his analysis stands as that of the Court."

While concurrences can prove a useful tool, particularly in the hands of a savvy centrist justice, dissents are valued for a different reason, for there is a rich tradition of passionate dissents that lived to triumph in another day. One thinks of Harlan's dissents in the Civil Rights Cases and the dissenting voices of Holmes and Brandeis to protect freedom of expression. Dissents, of course, are always at the expense of unity and sometimes are criticized for that reason. Others, however, argue that a false showing of unity is deceptive and that there is great value in the full expression of all points of view. This writer shares the latter view since constitutional law advances best as the result of reasoned argument and to stifle dissents is to stifle part of the argument.

The great dissents are almost always powerfully written with a memorable phrase often encapsulating for future justices the essence of the argument. Thus, Holmes's dissent in *Abrams v. United States* argued that "the best test of truth is the power of the thought to get itself accepted in the competition of the market." Today, the need to protect the "marketplace of ideas"—a metaphor for Holmes's argument first offered by Justice Brennan in a 1965 decision—is accepted as a fundamental purpose of the First Amendment.[38]

Dissents are sometimes written strategically as a way of luring members of the majority to change sides and make the dissent the majority opinion. In a close case, a justice who voted with the majority in conference might respond to a draft of the opinion with a note that he or she will await a draft of the dissent before commenting further, an excellent way to make the drafting justice receptive to further changes that the commenting justice might request. Not all justices appreciate the role the dissent plays in the Court's internal deliberations. Justice Robert Jackson, for example, once noted:

> There has been much undiscriminating eulogy of dissenting opinions. It is said they clarify the issues. Often they do the exact opposite. The technique of the dissenter often is to exaggerate the holding of the Court beyond the meaning of the majority and then to blast away at the excess . . . Then, too, dissenters frequently force the majority to take positions more extreme than was originally intended. The classic example is the Dred Scott case, in which Chief Justice Taney's extreme statements were absent in his original draft and were inserted only after Mr. Justice McLean, then a more than passive candidate for the presidency raised the issue in dissent.[39]

In contrast to Justice Jackson, Justice Scalia has written: "The most important internal effect of a system permitting dissents and concurrences is to improve the majority opinion."[40]

Nine Separate Law Firms? Not Always

In 1954, shortly before his death, Justice Jackson wrote: "The fact is that the Court functions less as one deliberative body than as nine, each justice working largely in isolation except as he chooses to seek consultation with others. These working methods tend to cultivate a highly individualistic rather than a group viewpoint."[41]

While Jackson's remark seems generally true, there are occasions when coalitions or informal groups do form. In the mid 1930s, Justices Cardozo, Brandeis, and Stone met at Brandeis's apartment on Friday evenings before a Saturday conference as a response to the regular habit of the conservative bloc of four—Butler, McReynolds, Sutherland, and Van Devanter—to drive together before arguments and the Saturday conference.[42] It is likely no coincidence that these meetings on both the liberal and conservative sides—so out of character for the Court generally and certainly for Justice Cardozo—occurred at the pivotal moment when the Court seemed to be rushing into a critical confrontation with the political branches.

More recently, in two highly visible cases—one dealing with capital punishment, the other with abortion—two different sets of justices met to form coalitions intended to prevent landmark cases from being overturned, in the process reversing a tentative conference vote. They are worth a moment's attention.

In 1972, the Court had held in *Furman v. Georgia*[43] that a death sentence imposed by juries operating with unbridled discretion was inherently arbitrary and violated the Eighth Amendment's prohibition of cruel and unusual punishment. Over 600 prisoners on death row had gained a temporary reprieve, but large segments of the public were enraged. State legislatures, in response, passed laws either imposing mandatory death sentences for certain categories of crimes or providing some standards for juries in deciding capital cases. A few years later, the Court addressed the constitutionality of five of those acts (two imposing mandatory death sentences and three providing discretionary guidelines) in cases collectively called *Gregg v. Georgia*.[44] At the time, three justices (Burger, White, and Rehnquist) were in favor of upholding all five statutes, while two (Brennan and Marshall) would have ruled against all of them. Blackmun was troubled by North Carolina's mandatory law but was willing immediately after the Conference to go along with upholding all five. Justice Powell had dissented in Furman, arguing that standards for capital punishment should be left for the state legislatures. He should therefore have been the fifth vote upholding all five statutes. He was also, however, a strong believer in precedent and did not want the Court to be seen as overruling a case so recently decided. Powell, Potter Stewart, and a newly sworn Justice Stevens met for lunch to discuss the situation and ultimately worked out a compromise position upholding the discretionary but invalidating the mandatory statutes, which preserved Furman but began to provide some guidance to the states as to how capital punishment could be constitutionally administered. Their opinion was jointly signed.

Another centrist coalition formed around the abortion issue in *Planned Parenthood of Southeastern Pennsylvania v. Casey*.[45] This time Justices Souter, O'Connor, and Kennedy, working in secret, jointly authored an opinion upholding a woman's right to choose while modifying the trimester analysis that had provided the framework for the Court's *Roe* decision. Chief Justice Rehnquist had written a draft majority opinion following the conference that would have severely undermined *Roe* and overruled it in all but name. We will have more to say about this case in Chapter 11.

In both these cases, the original conference vote tentatively created 5–4 majorities that would have effectively neutered, if not directly overruled, the prior landmark cases. In both cases, the writer of what was supposed to be the majority opinion (White in the case of capital punishment and Rehnquist in the case of abortion) was unable to keep the majority intact (if it in fact ever existed). For our purposes, the cases illustrate both the tenta-tiveness of conference votes and the way in which justices at extraordinary moments do meet and coalesce in ways that go beyond mere commenting on draft opinions from the security of their separate chambers.

Most times, however, justices attempt to persuade each other through their draft opinions and comments on the draft opinion of others. This can be a long process and often results in the most difficult cases being decided late in the term.

The opinion writing process is a collective enterprise, and justices gen-erally circulate their draft opinions to all other justices, although very occasionally, for strategic reasons, a justice writing a majority opinion will circulate it initially only to other colleagues in the majority. Generally, the author of the majority opinion is the first to circulate his or her draft. That starts the ball rolling. Then, those who voted with the majority in confer-ence will join the opinion, offer comments, suggest changes, or indicate a desire to see the draft dissent. The process at this point is much more fluid than one might expect. During the Burger Court, a justice voted with the majority in conference but later circulated or joined a dissent in 396 cases (17.3 percent).[46] Sometimes the vote change reflects reconsideration of a tentative vote. Sometimes a draft dissent can turn a vote. Justice Brennan has remarked, "It is a common experience that dissents change votes, even enough votes to become the majority."[47]

The most important consequence of this transparent and thorough pro-cess may simply be the benefit that accrues to the development of constitu-tional law as a whole. Justices may disagree sharply in their final opinions in a case, but it is rarely because they have misunderstood each other or not had sufficient opportunity to contest their views.

It should be clear by now that justices do not exchange votes on cases the way that legislators do. The reason is simple. Legislators represent constituen-cies. They build coalitions to achieve the objectives of their constituents. In coalition building, horse trading is part of the coin of the realm. Judges do not represent constituencies. The only thing we ask of our judges is that they apply the law to the best of their abilities. It would be highly inappropriate for Justice Scalia to agree to vote against his own beliefs in an establishment of religion case in exchange for Justice Breyer voting his way in an abortion case and there is no record of this kind of behavior on the Court.

The Court's decision-making process occurs completely out of public view and with no formal record of any oral discussions concerning the case.

The discussions and debates among the justices become public only to the extent that individual justices reveal them. This confidentiality is vigorously defended by the justices. Justice Powell likely expressed the views of most of the Court when he remarked that "this unstructured and informal process—the making of the decision itself, from the first conference until it is handed down in open court— . . . simply cannot take place in public The integrity of judicial decision making would be impaired seriously if we had to reach our decisions in the atmosphere of an ongoing town meeting. There can be no posturing among us, and no thought of tomorrow's headlines."[48] Speaking of the Conference in particular, Chief Justice Rehnquist echoed Powell's thoughts, praising an atmosphere in which "no one feels at all inhibited by the possibility that any of his remarks will be quoted outside of the Conference Room, or that any of his half formed or ill-conceived ideas, which all of us have at times, will be later held up to public ridicule."[49]

The Different Meanings of Victory

For the litigants in a case, a win is determined by the immediate outcome, namely whether the Court sustained or rejected his or her appeal. For everyone else, however, the winner or loser very much depends on one's point of view and, often, whether the reasoning of the case is broad or narrow, meaning whether it will apply to many situations in the future or is only applicable to a narrow set of facts.

Let us take, for example, the Court's controversial decision in *Citizens United v. Federal Election Commission.*[50] This is one of the most important cases decided by the Court in recent years. We will be looking at it in more depth in Chapter II. The case arose when a nonprofit corporation, Citizens United, released a documentary critical of Hilary Clinton which it anticipated it would make available to cable television stations within 30 days of some presidential primaries. Citizens United was rightly worried that such action would violate that portion of the federal campaign finance law that prohibits corporations from publicly distributing electioneering communications paid for from its general funds within 30 days of a primary election. (For our immediate purposes, we will refer to this portion of the law simply as the "statute.") Citizens United filed an action for declaratory judgment in Federal district court, in effect seeking to have the court bless its distribution of the film. The district court decided that distribution of the film would violate the statute. Interestingly, Citizens United did not initially claim that the statute was unconstitutional. The Supreme Court itself, however, asked the parties to brief this question. The Court had a number of options available to it to resolve the case. First, of course, it could have sustained the district court's decision, which had held that the film could not be distributed within the 30-day time frame provided by the statute. It became fairly clear, however, during oral argument, that the district court's decision would not be sustained and the only question then was how broad or narrow the decision might be. A very narrow ruling would have been that, on the facts of the case, there was not a "public distribution" of the film within the meaning of the statute and therefore no violation of the statute. This would have been a decision based on statutory interpretation and would have been regarded as a defeat by those who wanted to have the statute declared unconstitutional—victory for Citizens United but not headline material. Alternatively, the Court might easily have taken a middle position and held that the statute was unconstitutional as applied to nonprofit corporations, leaving open the question whether the statute was still applicable to general for-profit corporations, such as pharmaceutical companies or defense manufacturers or any other corporation other than nonprofits—a victory for Citizens United worthy of attention but not a banner headline. The Court, however, chose neither of these options and ruled in the broadest possible way that the statute was simply unconstitutional, meaning that all corporations (and unions) are now free, as a matter of constitutional right, to spend as much money as they want from their general funds to influence the outcome of federal or state elections—victory for Citizens United every bit worthy of the rare banner headline it earned from the *New York Times*.

Decisions can create conflicting emotions for many reasons. Sometimes a litigant can establish his or her legal position but be found ineligible for the relief sought. This can be a victory or not, depending on the individual's particular motivation for bringing the case. Recently, for example, the Court had to decide whether the strip search of a female high school student was unreasonable and violated the Fourth Amendment. While searches outside the school environment must be based on probable cause, the Court has relaxed that standard in the school environment so that only a "reasonable suspicion" is required to conduct a search. After carefully assessing all the facts, in *Safford United School District #1 v. April Redding*[51] the Court concluded that the search did not meet the standard of reasonable suspicion. Victory for plaintiff? Not completely. Plaintiff had sued several school officials for damages resulting from the search, but public officials are constitutionally protected from liability under the Court's theory of qualified immunity, even when they act wrongly, if the Court decides that the law at the time the officials acted was not clearly established. In this case, the Court decided (Justices Ginsburg and Stevens dissenting) that its prior cases had left enough doubt as to the reasonableness of the search that qualified immunity was appropriate. Thus, even though plaintiff had clarified the law for future students and school officials, Ms. Redding lost her case against the school officials themselves (although her case against the district itself was still allowed to go forward).

You may be wondering what happens to the whole of a law if a single provision is found unconstitutional. This raises the issue of "severability." At the risk of oversimplification, the basic idea is that the rest of the law can survive if the unconstitutional provision is not integral to the law's general purpose and the law remains workable as a practical matter. Severability will be a major issue for the Supreme Court when it hears the case involving the provision in the 2010 federal health care law requiring individuals to pay a monetary amount to the government if they fail to obtain health insurance. The Court, which has set aside five and a half hours of oral argument for the case, has specifically asked the parties to argue the issue of severability, in other words, whether the rest of the health care act can survive if the individual mandate is found unconstitutional.

Whatever the fate of the litigants in a particular case, we are all potentially affected by the Court's holdings.

9. The Toolbox for Judicial Decision Making

Some Opening Thoughts

Let's begin with an analogy. At the end of each baseball season, the Cy Young award is given to the best pitcher in each league, based on the votes of a selected group of sports reporters. But what are the right criteria for judging the best pitcher? Should one decide solely on who has given up the fewest runs per game when that statistic can be skewed by the size of the pitcher's home park? The best won-loss record might be a good criterion, but is it when one pitcher's team scores many more runs in his support than another's? And maybe statistics should not be the whole story. How important is it that one pitcher may have won several crucial games late in the season?

Just as with the Cy Young Award, in applying the Constitution, some justices claim to look for the comfort of fixed criteria and clear rules while others seek a broader array of factors on which to base their judgment. There are, of course, vast differences between choosing a best pitcher and deciding a constitutional case, but both endeavors have these things in common: first, there has to be a winner; second, the deciders may have very different attitudes as to how to arrive at the best decision; and third, there is a clearly defined body of relevant information which different deciders will rely on for different purposes. There is, of course, one important difference. The reporters who vote on the Cy Young award do not have to disclose their vote or explain it; Justices do.

Scholars have long debated whether the Constitution can be said to have an objective meaning, but one set of scholars has wisely noted, "We act as if the Constitution has inherent meaning because only if it has such meaning does it make sense to say that the Court got a particular decision right or wrong."[1]

Justices and scholars over the years have contended for various approaches to constitutional law. Innumerable labels have been used to describe these approaches. Justices have been variously described as originalists, textualists, majoritarians, realists, pragmatists, minimalists, activists, and moral constitutionalists, to name only some of the most prominent labels. These categorizations should not obscure the essential untidiness of constitutional interpretation. The fact is that each justice struggles in his or her own way to define what the Constitution means, and while they do have perspectives on how to find that meaning, there is probably no justice in the history of the Court that has been completely consistent in applying his or her own criteria. This is not surprising if what Chief Justice Hughes told a newly appointed Justice Douglas is true: "Justice Douglas," Hughes said, "you must remember one thing. At the constitutional level where we work, 90 percent of any decision is emotional. The rational part of us supplies the reasons for supporting our predilections."[2]

To cite one example of what Chief Justice Hughes might have meant, take the position of Justice Black, who liked to think of himself as a textualist. If the Constitution said something, he took it pretty literally. He was famous for saying that when the First Amendment says, "Congress shall pass no law" limiting freedom of expression, it meant no law. Correspondingly, if the Constitution didn't say something, he was not about to read something into it. Thus, as we discussed, he resisted the whole notion of substantive due process. Recall, however that Black also believed, based on his view of its legislative history, that the Fourteenth Amendment completely incorporated the Bill of Rights. The amendment, however, said not a word about incorporation. Black could never satisfactorily answer this simple question: if the amendment was meant to incorporate the Bill of Rights, why didn't it simply say so?[3] It is hard to resist the conclusion that Black had an emotional investment in the idea of constitutional certainty, that he was not comfortable with ambiguity, and that his positions on substantive due process and total incorporation are best understood as efforts to maintain the kind of Constitution he wanted it to be.

The above is not to say that generalizing about approaches is a meaningless exercise. On the contrary, it is the only currency we have to evaluate the continuing exchange over how the Constitution should be applied to real cases, but we should note that these descriptions are approximations of what scholars (and sometimes even the justices themselves) think justices should do, not necessarily what justices actually do. Why individual justices favor one approach over another depends a great deal on how they view the Constitution. This, of course, depends in part on a justice's broader system of values and beliefs. To pretend that justices' personal philosophy, which in turn obviously impact their political beliefs, do not inform their approach to the Constitution and its broad phrases would be nonsensical. Does this mean that all this discussion about how to interpret the Constitution—however interesting intellectually—is so much window dressing? I don't believe so. While this is a difficult subject, let us approach it in the brief space we can devote to it by considering the career of Louis Brandeis, appointed by Woodrow Wilson in 1916 as the Court's first Jewish justice.

Justice Brandeis and the Problem of Objectivity

In the early years of the twentieth century, law began to be viewed less as a formal set of rules based purely on logic and abstract thinking and more as an evolving set of rules heavily influenced by events and ongoing economic, scientific, and social changes. Louis Brandeis welcomed this attitude. Both as an advocate and later as a justice, he wanted justices to understand the harsh realities of urban and industrial life that were producing much of the progressive state legislation that the Court was striking down in the name of abstract concepts like "liberty of contract."

In *Muller v. Oregon* (1908),[4] a case considering the constitutionality of a state law providing for a maximum ten-hour work day for women, Brandeis, as the attorney for the state, did something unprecedented—he spent only a couple of pages of a 100-page brief on legal precedents and devoted the rest to a detailed description of various studies and findings showing why the legislation was a reasonable response to the plight of working women. Just a few years earlier, as you may recall, in *Lochner v. New York*, the Court had invalidated legislation providing for a maximum ten-hour work day for bakers. Nevertheless, Brandeis won in *Muller*, and his brief led to a pronounced shift in the manner in which attorneys argued, sometimes successfully, sometimes not, for the constitutionality of progressive legislation. The kinds of fact-laden briefs introduced by Brandeis in *Muller* became known as "Brandeis Briefs."

Brandeis continued to press his views when he was appointed to the Court, and they ultimately prevailed when the Court simply ceased invalidating economic legislation. Brandeis drew a sharp distinction, however, between economic legislation and legislation that interfered with civil liberties. For the latter type of legislation, he was unwilling to give Congress much deference. In the 1920s, he dissented eloquently from decisions of the Court upholding criminal convictions based upon the Espionage Act and other statutes that he believed violated the First Amendment.[5] So upset was Brandeis by these decisions that he finally wrote to Felix Frankfurter (then a professor of law at Harvard) suggesting that certain professors of their mutual acquaintance explore, through law review articles, ways of overcoming them.[6]

There is no question that Brandeis was an economic progressive with a strong personal commitment to freedom of expression. There is also no question that the Constitution as he interpreted it was wholly in accord with those views. Does this mean that Brandeis was imposing his own personal views on the Constitution?

In 1948, a Yale law professor, George Braden, after carefully considering the supposedly objective constitutional approaches of both Justice Black and Justice Frankfurter, concluded:

> There is no objectivity in constitutional law because there are no absolutes. Every constitutional question involves a weighing of competing values. Some of these values are held by virtually everyone, others by fewer people. Supreme Court justices likewise hold values. The more widely held are the values in society, the more likely the Supreme Court will hold them; the more controversial the values, the more likely the Supreme Court is to divide over them.[7]

Braden's statement suggests that the question whether one is imposing one's views on a hapless Constitution is essentially meaningless. The real question is not whether Brandeis's personal philosophy informed his opinions, but whether he translated that philosophy into a constitutional view that he consistently and conscientiously sought to apply without regard to the kinds of things he shouldn't consider, like which political parties the litigants belonged to, whether he personally liked one of the attorneys more than the other, or even what result he personally wanted.

That judicial decisions inevitably reflect personal values does not mean that consideration of interpretive approaches is a waste of time, for justices must still publicly defend their opinions with reasoning that attempts to be cogent and persuasive. And in arriving at those opinions, they are constrained by the existing body of law applicable to a case and their presumed desire to be consistent with their own prior opinions. Above all, even assuming that there is no objectivity in constitutional law, whatever that might mean, the fact is that the cumulative effect of a continuing clash of values is the development of a Constitution of accreted meaning, with extraordinary consequences for society as a whole. This makes the clash both worth understanding and worth fighting over.

As to the justices themselves, Justice Brennan perhaps best captured their perspective on interpreting the Constitution when he stated, "My relation to this great text is unmistakably public. That is not to say that my reading of the text is not a personal reading, only that the personal reading perforce occurs in a public context and is subject to critical scrutiny from all quarters."[8]

What justices decide and how they defend their decisions in their opinions is more important than their inner motivation because it is the public clash of viewpoints that moves the law forward. We will consider some of these viewpoints shortly, but first let us look a little more closely at how justices' perspectives might have been affected by their life experiences.

The Impact of Life Experiences

The role that background and experience play in the development of a judicial philosophy is not always easy to assess but is impossible to deny. Chief Justice Warren surprised many people by his liberalism and sympathy for the underdog when he became chief justice. Yet Warren came from a working-class family. His father was initially a railroad repairman who later became a building contractor. As a young prosecutor, Warren saw not only the power of law enforcement but also its potential for misuse. His experiences as attorney general and governor of California also influenced him. He came to regret his role in the internment of the Japanese during World War II, an event that undoubtedly made him more aware of the ease with which the majority can oppress minorities with plausible but ultimately fallacious excuses for racial discrimination. If Warren's experiences helped shape him as a justice, so did his personality. His gregariousness and informality made him an effective chief justice; his impatience with theory (he was just an average law student at Berkeley) and desire to engage the real world also presaged a justice who would preside over an activist Court not afraid to make bold decisions.

It may be no more than a coincidence, but it is interesting that four of the most liberal justices on the late Warren Court (Warren, Douglas, Black, and Fortas) all came from modest, sometimes very challenging economic circumstances. Douglas's father died when he was only five; his mother had to take in washing to make ends meet. Black was raised in rural Alabama; his father managed a small country store. Fortas's family was Orthodox Jewish; he was raised in Memphis, Tennessee, where his father eked out a living for the family doing a variety of jobs. Even Brennan, who grew up in Newark, New Jersey, in relative security as the son of a successful local politician, knew that his father had started out as ordinary day laborer and that his family was dependent on the votes of working people for its own success. Byron White, appointed by President Kennedy, was raised in a small rural town in Colorado; his father helped manage a local lumber supply business and White paid for Yale Law School out of his earnings as a star professional football player. Meanwhile the three more conservative Justices (Harlan, Stewart, and Clark) all came from more prosperous, politically active families.

It is not unreasonable to believe that these backgrounds may have influenced the Justices in their various approaches to the law. Certainly Justice Brennan made no secret of the role his upbringing played. "What got me interested in people's rights and liberties was the kind of neighborhood I was brought up in. I saw all kinds of suffering—people had to struggle."[9] Justice Douglas believed that his experience growing up in the Cascade Mountains and the love of nature it fostered in him profoundly shaped his views on the Court. A more recent example of the shaping role of experience is Justice Scalia, an only child raised by first-generation American, devoutly Roman Catholic parents. His father was a professor of romance languages at Brooklyn College, an expert on Dante, and a believer in the value of literal translations.[10] It is hard to separate Justice Scalia's textualism and his fondness for clear rules and principles from his own intellectual upbringing and his four years at Xavier High School, which, according to Joan Biskupic, "established Antonin's academic prowess, entrenched his regard for Catholicism, and reinforced his rule-oriented nature."[11]

Searing life experiences also undoubtedly influence a justice. Justice Holmes generally refused to invalidate legislation based on objections to substance, believing that the Court had almost no role to play in overseeing the results of the political process. As previously mentioned, Justice Holmes was wounded three times during the Civil War. Though he came from a highly idealistic, strongly antislavery, New England household, Holmes developed a disdain for moralizing and abstract ideals. When Holmes wrote that if the people want to go to hell it was his job to help them get there, he was stating not only a judicial philosophy but a view of life that had little use for grandiose visions, at least of the kind that the Court was supposedly duty-bound to enforce through the Constitution.

The Building Blocks of Constitutional Meaning

In Chapter 8, we discussed the various kinds of Supreme Court opinions, but of what do Supreme Court opinions consist? Almost all opinions begin with a recitation of the major facts underlying the case, usually as determined in the lower court proceedings. The opinion will also recite the procedural posture of the case—how the case got to the Supreme Court and the specific issue that the Court is considering in the case. With these preliminaries out of the way, the decision and the Court's reasoning will be set out.

Legal opinions consist of reasons marshaled to justify an outcome. Justices often reach different outcomes because they begin with different premises and ideas of what constitutes a sound decision. All Justices, however, need to cite the specific materials—let's call them building blocks—that allow them to reason their way to their decision. Conceptually, we need to divide these building blocks into two types. The first type simply consists of all the opinions previously rendered by the Court that might be relevant to the matter at hand. These opinions are consulted when the Court is seeking to determine what, if any, precedents may control the current case. So important is the role of precedent that we will consider it separately in the next subsection. The second type of building block is consulted when the Court is trying to determine directly the meaning of the constitutional text without reference to how the Court might have applied that text in the past. For the most part, these materials will be drawn from the following: (1) the text of the Constitution itself, including amendments; (2) statements claimed to illuminate the intent behind or meaning of the text; (3) historical context, meaning any relevant aspect of the social, political, economic, and legal environment at the time of drafting and ratification of the text; (4) tradition, meaning the acceptance or nonacceptance of certain practices or beliefs over a period of time; and (5) current context, meaning the Court's understanding of contemporary beliefs and practices, particularly as those beliefs and practices may be affected by the Court's decisions. Let us look at these building blocks a little more closely but before we do, I should note here the work of Charles Black, a distinguished scholar who argued that sometimes cases are best decided not by a specific reliance on a particular provision of the constitutional text but rather by intuiting the proper outcome from the broader "structures and relationships created by the constitution in all its parts or in some principal part."[12] Space does not permit us to elaborate on Black's work, but it should be recognized as an approach to deciding cases that implicates neither precedent nor a direct search for the meaning of individual provisions of the text. Certainly, however, most cases do involve an examination of text. Let us look at the building blocks justices rely upon in that search.

The Text

Since the Constitution is a legal document, the starting point for any case is to identify the particular constitutional provision or provisions at issue. While, as we have discussed, the Constitution's broader concepts—due process, equal protection of laws, full faith and credit, freedom of speech and religion—pose the most enduring challenges to the Court, the Court is often required to consider the meaning and applicability of very specific terms and instructions in the Constitution as well.

The passage of time means that some words and phrases in the Constitution must be amplified beyond their original meaning. To cite an easy example, one of the enumerated powers of Congress is to provide for an army and navy. Clearly, the intent of this authority was to provide the necessary forces to defend the country, but without some escape from a tyrannical literalism, we might need a constitutional amendment to have an air force, an absurd result.

You might be thinking, "Well wait a minute. If words or phrases can be changed or added to willy-nilly, then what's the point of a text at all?" How do you limit this freedom from becoming the world of Alice in Wonderland, where words mean only what people want them to mean? It's a fair question. There is certainly no one clear answer that everyone would agree upon. William Blackstone, the eighteenth-century legal theorist whose *Commentaries* exerted great influence on American legal thinking, did provide a partial answer by allowing an escape from plain meaning when the words "bear either none, or a very absurd signification, if literally understood."[13] However, according to one scholar, "the absurdity issuing from literal application had to be a matter of logic, not merely a disfavored policy result."[14]

A better escape hatch perhaps is offered by what is referred to as the structuralist approach to textual interpretation, which allows for a discovery of the meaning of the text through an evaluation of the overall purpose of the Constitution at its founding and the way various elements of the Constitution work together. The structuralist position does appear to offer a more plausible basis for slipping away from clearly undesirable results. In speaking of the Commerce clause, for example, just one of the provisions Akhil Reed Amar believes benefits from a structural approach, he writes:

"Each of the document's clauses must be read not in isolation, but through the prism of the Constitution's overarching structures and purposes. That is how Americans in fact ratified the so-called Commerce clause, and that is how sensitive and sensible interpreters today should read it."[15]

Sometimes even a relatively conservative Court will embrace the idea of a living constitution to justify an expansion of the text. Consider, for example, how the Court in the *Kelo* case discussed earlier, justified the way in which the term "public use" in the Eminent Domain clause had been expanded to include "public purpose":

> This "Court long ago rejected any literal requirement that condemned property be put into use for the general public." [Citation omitted] Indeed, while many state courts in the mid-19th century endorsed "use by the public" as the proper definition of public use, that narrow view steadily eroded over time. Not only was the "use by the public test" difficult to administer . . . but it proved to be impractical given the diverse and always evolving needs of society. Accordingly, when this Court began applying the Fifth Amendment to the States at the close of the 19th century, it embraced the broader and more natural interpretation of public use as public purpose.[16]

Of course, there are limits to this liberality. No one seriously suggests that the age limits for qualifications for federal office can be amended by judicial fiat to reflect our much longer life spans or that the right to a trial by jury in cases where the sum in controversy exceeds $20 can be judicially changed to reflect inflation. On the other hand, even though Congress's enumerated power is only to "coin money," few now question the government's authority to issue paper currency, although, as previously discussed, this was a matter of great dispute in the 1860s. When and how textual liberalities are taken depends, of course, on many things, most importantly, common sense.

Statements Contemporaneous with Enactment

To interpret the Constitution, justices often turn to statements made by the Framers and others at the time of the Constitutional Convention and enactments of amendments. As one scholar has noted, "Virtually everyone agrees that the specific intentions of the Framers count for something" and "occasionally specific intentions are decisive."[17]

James Madison took it upon himself to act as unofficial secretary of the Constitutional Convention. His *Notes* provide, in the words of Charles

Evan Hughes, "the most direct approach to the intention of the makers of the Constitution" that we have.[18] Because Madison refused to publish the notes while any member of the convention was still alive, they were not published until after his death on July 4, 1831. Consequently, the Supreme Court did not have the benefit of this extraordinary record of the Constitutional Convention for more than four decades. Other notes and records of the convention (most notably *The Records of the Federal Convention of 1787*, ed. Max Farrand, 4 volumes) are invaluable to scholars, but it is Madison's *Notes* that bring the delegates and the debates most visibly to life.

As important as Madison's *Notes* have been for the development of constitutional law, they do not fully reflect everything that went on at the convention because (a) much of the important work, particularly as the convention progressed, was done by committees whose debates he was not able to witness; (b) the secrecy surrounding the convention's deliberations means that there was no reporting on its proceedings and, among other things, we can only guess at the discussions held and deals struck at taverns, boarding houses, and elegant dinners during that long Philadelphia summer; and (c) Madison's *Notes* themselves seem to thin out as the convention wore on, perhaps a reflection of his own fatigue.

Statements made during ratification can also be illuminating. We have already described the importance of the *Federalist Papers* as an aid to understanding the contemporary view of the Constitution. The nearest thing to a direct reply to the *Federalist Papers* was a series of sixteen essays signed "Brutus" appearing in the *New York Journal* at the same time as the Federalist essays. Many other Anti-Federalist pamphlets and essays also appeared, including a widely circulated minority dissent signed by 21 of the 23 delegates who had voted against the Constitution at the Pennsylvania ratifying convention. Patrick Henry made an impassioned speech against the Constitution at the Virginia ratifying convention that conveys the depth of feeling and fears engendered by the proposed government. There are a number of excellent collections of documents recording the debate over ratification.[19]

As we have already discussed, ratification of the Constitution involved an intense state-by-state struggle. The debates engendered by this struggle, and the pamphlets and essays that they produced, are important because they give us a real sense of the concerns the document aroused and place the document as a whole in historical context. For those justices who place great importance on the original meaning of the words of the Constitution at the time of enactment, these debates shed important light on how those words were understood both by the Constitution's proponents and by its opponents. The debates are important, however, to others as well. Even those most comfortable with the notion of the Constitution as a living document not to be ruled by the dead hand of the past, look to the Constitution as an expression of basic values and principles that are illuminated by these debates.

For some justices, perhaps most, the statements made at the Constitutional Convention have particular importance because of their direct relationship to the document. On the other hand, Justice Scalia has made a point of saying that contemporaneous expressions of others have just as much importance to him as the statements of the Framers. Justice Scalia writes, "I will consult the writings of some men who happened to be delegates to the Constitutional Convention—Hamilton's and Madison's writings in the *Federalist*, for example. I do so, however, not because they were Framers and therefore their intent is authoritative and must be the law; but rather their writings, like those of other intelligent and informed people of the time, display how the text of the Constitution was originally understood. Thus I give equal weight to Jay's pieces in the *Federalist* and to Jefferson's writings, even though neither of them was a Framer."[20]

Historical Context

Historical context—meaning the laws, customs, beliefs, and traditions existing when the Constitution or the amendment at issue was enacted— can also be an important source of understanding. Let me give just one example of a case where context assumed considerable importance. Earlier we discussed the case in which the Court declared unconstitutional state-imposed congressional term limits on the basis that such limits constituted an impermissible additional qualification for office. The key dispute in that case was whether the Constitution allowed the states to impose such additional qualifications. Justice Thomas pointed out in his dissent that some states, at the beginning of the Republic, required Representatives to live in their congressional districts. This, of course, was an additional qualification and was cited by Thomas to support his position that the list of qualifications in the Constitution was not exhaustive and the states were free to add to them. For Justice Stevens, writing for the majority, however, Justice Thomas was letting a single tree block the forest. For him, what was really significant was not the minor matter of residence qualifications, but the other qualifications that some states imposed on their state officeholders, but not on their federal counterparts. For Justice Stevens, this general reticence of the states to impose state office qualifications on their federal representatives was important evidence that the states recognized that the Constitution's qualifications were generally meant to be exclusive. While Thomas and Stevens came to different conclusions, they both agreed on the relevance of context—in this case meaning the legal setting around the time of enactment.

Context can also play an important role when the continued legitimacy of a prior Supreme Court precedent is under review. If the Court in a prior case utilized reasoning based on a set of circumstances that no longer exist, the case's value as a precedent may have significantly eroded. For example, when the Court began to adopt an intermediate level of scrutiny for sex discrimination under the Equal Protection clause, there were older precedents in place approving legislation that denied women the right to pursue careers, such as bartending and even law. The context in which those decisions were made—a then near universal belief that a woman's proper place was in the home and that she by her very nature was ill-suited for the professions—made it easier to disregard those precedents as relics of a different era.

Historical context was also important in assisting the Court to determine whether a law enacted after Watergate was a bill of attainder that Congress, under Article I, section 9, is prohibited from enacting. The law directed President Nixon's presidential papers (consisting of 42 million documents and 880 tape recordings) to be collected and examined by the administrator of General Services and prohibited their destruction except as provided by law. The law specifically applied to President Nixon's papers and only his papers, and on the surface appeared to be a classic bill of attainder, namely, a law directed against a particular individual or group of individuals as punishment without benefit of trial. Punishment without trial is, of course, a classic deprivation of due process. In holding by a vote of 7–2 that the act was constitutional, the Court in part undertook a review of the origins and development of bills of attainder and concluded, "no feature of the challenged Act falls within the historical meaning of punishment."[21] Here we see the Court struggling to apply an old term to a new situation and looking at history to help find the right answer.

Sometimes, context can present an obstacle to a decision that the Court wants to reach. In *Brown v. Board of Education*, the Court found segregation in public schools unconstitutional under the Equal Protection clause, notwithstanding that Congress had approved segregation of public schools in the District of Columbia at the time the Equal Protection clause was adopted and most public schools, even outside the South, were segregated when the Amendment was adopted. These facts made clear that, viewed in historical context, the Fourteenth Amendment itself was not deemed inconsistent at the time of enactment with a system of racial segregation in the public schools. In the end, the Court determined that separate could simply never be equal and that this newer understanding trumped historical context.

Tradition

The Constitution provides the framework for our governmental system. It is not, however, the entire system. Customs and practices develop that become part of the accepted order of things. The Constitution, for example, states that the president shall "from time to time give to Congress Information of the State of the Union," a requirement that has led over the years to the president's annual State of the Union message delivered in January to a joint session of Congress. The address is now part of our political tradition. Courts are reluctant to overturn traditions, not only because forcing change is never easy but also because a practice's long acceptance can itself establish legitimacy. Consider, for example, these words of Chief Justice Rehnquist in *United States v. Morrison*,[22] the case that invalidated a federal law creating a civil remedy for gender-motivated violence: "The regulation and punishment of intrastate violence that is not directed at the instrumentalities, channels or goods involved in interstate commerce has always been the province of the States."[23] Implicit in this statement is the idea that a long-standing practice or tradition can be so embedded in our constitutional structure as to preempt an assertion of federal authority that runs counter to that tradition.

It can be argued that sometimes justices, both liberal and conservative, can be too sensitive to tradition. The Court, for example, seems to have accepted that the two major parties will often gerrymander congressional and state legislative districts to protect their respective incumbents, notwithstanding that this has led to fewer and fewer genuinely competitive races for these offices.[24] This acquiescence is surprising since the Framers believed strongly in accountability and were very aware of the danger that officeholders might easily resort to manipulations to perpetuate themselves in power.[25]

Tradition does not always win out. The fact that the political patronage system was, for most of our history, an accepted part of the political landscape, did not protect it when the Supreme Court in a series of cases effectively ended the system on First Amendment grounds.[26]

We should add that tradition itself cannot rewrite the Constitution. George Washington, for example, set a precedent when he refused to run for a third term as president, a precedent honored until Franklin Roosevelt ran for a third term a century and a half later. Roosevelt won a third term handily and even a fourth during World War II. No one could reasonably claim that Roosevelt's action violated the Constitution even though it violated a strong political tradition. President Roosevelt's four terms led directly to the Twenty-Second Amendment, which prohibits a president from serving more than two terms.

Current Context

While text, contemporaneous statements, historical context, and tradition are all important sources of meaning, they look backward. Sometimes, however, the Court turns to more contemporary evidence to help resolve constitutional problems, particularly when it is trying to assess the future impact of its decisions. Current context is particularly important for those justices who believe that constitutional law must reflect and take account of contemporary realities. We will be discussing this approach shortly, but we should note that these justices will look to changes in contemporary culture to evaluate the continued relevance of past precedents. As mentioned, the Court's heightened scrutiny of sex discrimination owed a great deal to changing views on a woman's proper role in society and a realization of her growing economic importance as a breadwinner. In *Brown v. Board of Education*, the Court cited current sociological and psychological studies showing the crippling effect of mandated segregation on black children's sense of self-esteem, to support its conclusion that separate facilities could in fact no longer even be considered equal.

Sometimes, unfortunately, the Court applies its notion of reality through rose-colored glasses. In 1979, for example, the Court upheld a Georgia statute that allowed minors to be committed to mental institutions without benefit of either a pre- or post-commitment hearing. The majority opinion, written by Chief Justice Burger, cited the "natural bonds of affection" between parent and child as sufficient assurance that the best interests of the child would always be protected as long as a neutral professional signed off on the child's admission. In a strong dissent, Justice Brennan took the Court to task for ignoring contemporary studies that showed that "parental decisions to institutionalize their children often are the results of dislocation in the family unrelated to the children's mental condition."[27] Justice Brennan cited the fact that a National Institute of Health Study had found that only 36 percent of persons under the age of twenty admitted to a mental hospital actually required such hospitalization.

The Role of Precedent

Supreme Court decisions now take up hundreds of thick volumes of *U.S. Reports*. Yet in one sense, time does not exist for the Court, for when today's Court refers to a decision made a hundred years ago, it still says "We did so and so" as if the justices on the current Court actually made that century-old decision. The reason is that the Court is always the Court, one institution that speaks with one collective (if sometimes changing) voice over time.

The basic principle of *stare decisis* (which literally means, "let the decision stand") is that the Court should be consistent in its application of the law and, therefore, that similar cases should be decided similarly, unless there is a basis for overruling, ignoring, or distinguishing the prior cases. It is this goal and this system that binds the generations of justices together.

Justifying the Use of Precedent

Many social scientists question whether Supreme Court justices really feel constrained by prior decisions. They seek to explain voting patterns of justices based on various models (the attitudinal model and rational choice models being the most popular) that assert that the factors which explain voting behavior are "external to the law, such as the justices' personal or policy preferences, and not factors internal to the law, including the Constitution or precedent."[28]

In an influential book, *Majority Rule or Minority Will*,[29] Harold J. Spaeth and Jeffrey Segal argue that justices follow their own instincts when it comes to deciding cases and that stare decisis is a particularly weak explanation for voting behavior on the Court when it comes to constitutional (as opposed to statutory) cases. The authors do not deny that there are instances when justices do feel constrained by prior decisions but question whether such behavior "exists at systematic and meaningful levels."[30] Their findings are based on a comprehensive survey of Supreme Court precedents from the very beginnings of the Court that focused particularly on the extent to which dissenting Justices subsequently followed precedents with which they initially disagreed. Their conclusion was that "precedent rarely influences United States Supreme Court Justices."[31] This view is by no means universally accepted. Michael Gerhardt, for example, argues that "precedent cannot play the role that many social scientists (and some legal scholars) insist that it must play"[32] and therefore their conclusions, based on their flawed view of the predictability that precedent should provide in constitutional decision making, are fundamentally unsound.

I would also take note here of a thoughtful recent work by Eileen Braman whose research, including interesting decision-making experiments with law students, has led her to conclude that, "influence is not an all-or-nothing proposition"; her account of judicial decision making, which she calls "motivated reasoning," "posits attitudinal influence, but suggests 'outer limits' on the ability of decision makers to reach conclusions consistent with their preferences."[33]

Whatever the scholarly literature may show, justices act as if precedent matters, and it would be hard to imagine a viable system of decision making that did not recognize precedent. It has been estimated that roughly four-fifths or more of the authorities cited by Supreme Court justices in constitutional cases are of past decisions of the Court itself.[34] This is not difficult to explain. A Court that did not at least purport to value precedent would undermine the values of predictability and stability that a rule of law brings to society. It would also be imposing on itself an unsustainable workload, ignoring the accumulated wisdom and guidance of generations. As Justices Kennedy, Souter, and O'Connor stated in their unusual joint opinion in *Planned Parenthood v. Casey,* "no judicial system could do society's work if it eyed each issue afresh in every case that raised it."[35]

Precedent also allows the Court to create an orderly framework for adjudication of cases. In the area of constitutional law, particularly, the Court has constructed frameworks for deciding many kinds of cases. We have already discussed, for example, how the Court applies different levels of scrutiny to cases arising under the Equal Protection clause. Lawyers litigating those cases argue within an established methodology for decision making. These frameworks direct arguments into well-worn channels carved out by precedent. Without them, every lawsuit would be a free-for-all.

Michael Gerhardt has pointed out that precedent also plays "an important function" in "framing the Court's agenda on whether to grant certiorari" since it is "practically impossible for the Court to decide any constitutional issue without initially determining the scope, legitimacy, and coherence of prior case law."[36]

In the absence of a system of precedent, the Courts would likely be overwhelmed by litigation. As David Strauss has stated, "an awful lot of issues, constitutional and common law and otherwise, simply do not get litigated. People just know what the law is, and they live with it. Or, if they litigate, the case is settled very quickly. In those cases—the vast majority—precedent is often the principle constraining force. Precedent puts many arguments and positions off limits—so clearly off limits that we do not realize how much work the precedents are doing."[37]

In an essay on how Supreme Court justices do their work, Justice Frankfurter noted that the Court rarely encounters a case where there is only one "so-called" constitutional principle at stake.[38] He then quotes Justice Holmes: "The boundary at which conflicting interests balance cannot be determined by any general formula in advance, but points in the line, or helping to establish it, are fixed by decisions that this or that concrete case falls on the nearer or farther side."[39]

Prior cases are the single best guide that justices have to help them determine exactly which side of a line conflicting principles fall upon, because only prior cases involve the concrete application of those contending principles. By way of example, in *Lee v. Weismann*,[40] the Court had to decide whether a prayer performed by a Rabbi at a public school graduation ceremony was constitutional. Two sets of precedent and tradition were meeting head on—one approved recognition of prayer on public occasions and the other disapproved prayer in a school setting. The Court, in a highly contested 5–4 decision, found that the graduation event was such a critical event in the life of a child and family that simply avoiding the event was not an acceptable option. "The State," wrote Justice Kennedy, "cannot require one of its citizens to forfeit his or her rights and benefits as the price of resisting conformance to state-sponsored religious practice."[41] In effect, the majority saw the case as having more in common with the compulsory setting of a classroom than the kinds of public occasions—opening of legislative sessions, inaugurations— in which prayer was traditional and did not violate the Constitution. Prior precedent fueled the discussion of both the majority and dissenting opinions.

Even when the Court is arguably breaking new ground, centrist justices in particular keep a close eye on precedent. In *United States v. Lopez*,[42] Justices Kennedy and O'Connor, although they joined the opinion of Chief Justice Rehnquist striking down the federal Gun Free School Zones Act of 1990, wrote a lengthy concurrence in which they emphasized the need for consistency in the Court's Commerce clause decisions:

. . . the Court as an institution and the legal system as a whole have an immense stake in the stability of our Commerce Clause jurisprudence as it has evolved to this point. [*Stare decisis*] operates with great force in counseling us not to call in question the essential principles now in place respecting the congressional power to regulate transactions of a commercial nature. . . . *Congress can regulate in the commercial sphere on the assumption that we have a single market and a unified purpose to build a stable national economy.* (my emphasis)[43]

Why the Supreme Court Overrules Precedents

The Supreme Court is always free to overrule prior precedents and has done so frequently over the years. There are no hard and fast rules explaining when the Court should or will reverse itself.

Sometimes the Court reverses itself because events have shown that it has gotten something seriously wrong. As discussed earlier, the Court reversed itself in a matter of only a few years after it originally decided by an 8–1 vote that a school district could constitutionally require children to salute the flag regardless of a student's religious beliefs. The strong editorial reaction against the original decision, the violence that Jehovah's Witnesses experienced after its issuance, and the recognition of the importance of freedom of conscience at a time when we were fighting against Hitler and fascism, all likely played a part in the Court's 6–3 reversal.

Sometimes the Court itself needs time to adjust to a new reality. In 1965, for example, the Warren Court refused to overturn the conviction of a black man by an all-white jury, even though the use of peremptory challenges by prosecutors had kept blacks from ever serving on juries in that county.[44] (Peremptory challenges allow attorneys at the jury selection stage of a trial to excuse potential jurors without giving any reason for the challenge.) The Court cited the long tradition of peremptory challenges to justify its decision. Twenty-one years later, the Court reversed itself, holding that racial exclusion was no longer a permissible trial strategy; tradition no longer trumped racial discrimination.[45]

Sometimes subsequent cases reveal that the Court's prior ruling is simply incapable of principled application. Such was the case with *National League of Cities v. Usery*,[46] where the Court initially held that Congress had no authority to regulate states as states when they were acting in their traditional governmental capacity. *National League of Cities*, however, soon proved unworkable because of the difficulties in distinguishing traditional and nontraditional areas of government activity. After less than a decade, the Court decided that there was simply no way that the test could be consistently applied and abandoned the distinction in favor of a broad rule allowing for federal governmental regulation.[47] Another example is provided in the area of right-to-counsel in criminal cases. For years the Court tried to distinguish between felony cases in which a defendant was entitled to counsel because he or she would be seriously prejudiced without one and cases in which counsel was not required. The case-by-case approach created numerous instances of overturned convictions and finally, in *Gideon v. Wainwright*,[48] the Court held that a defendant had a right to counsel in all felony cases.

Often a change in personnel on the Court will cause a reversal of recent decisions. This kind of decision, if done often enough, could erode respect for the Court. Dissenting in a case, Potter Stewart once noted, "A basic change in the law on a ground no firmer than a change in our membership invites the popular misconception that this institution is little different from the two political branches of government."[49] And when a newly appointed Justice Burger suggested in 1972 that some recent double jeopardy be overruled, Justice White, who had dissented in those cases, cautioned against it, explaining that a judgment so recently reached "is entitled to at least some period for clinical observation before it is interred."[50] But changes in justices can have an immediate impact, as shown most dramatically in the case of *Citizens United v. Federal Election Commission*, in which the Court overruled its decision of just a few years earlier, following the replacement of Justice O'Connor by Justice Alito.

Changing societal attitudes also play a role in overruling prior precedents. This was certainly the case when *Lawrence v. Texas*[51] overruled *Bowers v. Hardwick*. As previously noted, *Lawrence* represented a real shift in values for a majority of the Court, which had finally come to believe that the state cannot "demean" the "existence of homosexuals or control their destiny by making their private sexual conduct a crime."[52] That attitude mirrored changing attitudes in society, reflected in the sharp decline in the number of states that continued to treat sodomy as a crime and the growing public perception of gays as a minority group often facing irrational discrimination.

Qualifying Precedents without Overruling Them

Sometimes the Court will establish a broad precedent that subsequent decisions will narrow or qualify without overruling it.

The Court's rulings on the free speech rights of high school students provide a case in point. In 1969, the Court, in *Tinker v. Des Moines Independent School District*,[53] upheld the right of students to wear black arm bands to class to protest the Vietnam War. Writing for the majority, Chief Justice Fortas boldly declared that students did not "shed their constitutional rights to freedom of speech or expression at the schoolhouse gate."[54] The case came to stand for the proposition that high school students were free to express themselves as long as their expressions did not cause substantial disruption to the life of the school. In 1986, however, the Court qualified its position.[55] A student had given a sophomoric, somewhat suggestive speech on behalf of a candidate for school office at a school assembly. In upholding the principal's disciplining of the student, Chief Justice Burger noted, "Surely it is a highly appropriate function of public education to prohibit the use of vulgar terms in public discourse. . . . Nothing in the Constitution prohibits the States from insisting that certain modes of expression are inappropriate."[56] Just two years later, the Court, in a case involving the content of a student newspaper, held that "educators do not offend the First Amendment by exercising editorial control over the style and content of student speech in school-sponsored expressive activities so long as they are reasonably related to legitimate pedagogical concerns."[57] Most recently, the Court held that a principal "may consistent with the First Amendment, restrict student speech at a school event, when that speech is reasonably viewed as promoting illegal drug use."[58]

One might legitimately ask how much is left of *Tinker* when schools can censor out of pedagogical concerns and discipline what they regard as inappropriate or dangerous language. Yet clearly erosion is not the same thing as overruling and since none of the narrowing cases involved political speech, *Tinker* still stands at a minimum for the proposition that political expression, responsibly expressed, is protected in the public high school as long as it does not cause substantial disruption. Perhaps that was all that it was meant to stand for in the first place. The desire to qualify rather than overrule past precedents reflects a natural desire not to admit previous error or criticize prior Courts. It is also a way for the Court to move incrementally, an approach embraced by numerous justices.

How Strong Should the System of Precedent Be?

Justice Douglas, one of the most liberal justices ever to have served on the Court, and Justice Clarence Thomas, certainly one of the most conservative, have one important thing in common: a belief that justices should *not* feel greatly restrained by precedent in interpreting the Constitution. What Douglas said to the American Bar Association in 1948 could easily have been said by Justice Thomas today: ". . . it is the Constitution which we have sworn to defend, not some predecessor's interpretation of it. Stare decisis has small place in constitutional law."[59]

Let's suppose that a clear conservative majority gains ascendancy on the Court. Assuming one doesn't accept unreservedly the Douglas/Thomas view, what criteria should guide this new majority in deciding how far to go in reversing Warren-era precedents with which it disagrees? One restraint would be the degree to which landmark decisions have gained public acceptance. Michael McConnell, for example, has acknowledged that numerous current precedents, including some as basic as "protection against sex discrimination under the Equal Protection clause . . . expansion of the Commerce Clause to permit federal regulation of intrastate commercial activity, or prohibition of gross malapportionment of state legislative districts" violate his basic principles.[60] Yet, he suggests that the overwhelming public acceptance of these principles "constitutes a mode of popular ratification, which gives these decisions legitimacy and authority."[61] Interestingly, McConnell here sounds like Bruce Ackerman, who has written extensively on how events occurring outside the formal legal process can themselves constitute "constitutional moments." McConnell's assertion of popular ratification would certainly qualify as such a moment, even if occurring over a much longer time frame than the moments that Ackerman describes. A related but distinct restraint would ask how deeply embedded a precedent has become in the fabric of the nation's political, social, and cultural life. It would demand a close examination of the potential consequences of trying to put the genie back in the bottle. Even today, for example, the *Miranda* warnings are not wildly popular. Nevertheless, to the surprise of many, Chief Justice Rehnquist, who had previously taken the position that the *Miranda* warnings were not constitutionally required—wrote a strong opinion for the Court denying the power of Congress to abrogate or revise the *Miranda* rules, reaffirming *Miranda* as a precedent of the Court in *Dickerson v. United States*.[62] Rehnquist noted that "Miranda has become embedded in routine police procedure to the point where the warnings have become part of our national culture."[63]

Adherence to precedent allows the Court to speak with a consistent voice over time. Justices who worry about that consistency are especially concerned about overruling prior cases. In *Baker v. Carr*, Justice Potter Stewart tentatively voted with a five-person majority in conference to allow a suit challenging a failure to reapportion to go forward on Equal Protection grounds. Stewart, however, had made it very clear to Justice Brennan that he would stay with the majority only if Brennan could show that the proposed decision would not violate any earlier precedents. Justice Brennan did an exhaustive research job and convinced Stewart that no prior precedent would be violated. With some humor, Justice Douglas recounts in his autobiography how Justice Clark at the last moment changed his mind and made a six-justice majority, rendering all of Brennan's work somewhat unnecessary.[64]

In summary, our new hypothetical conservative majority would need to consider at least three things in deciding whether to overturn past decisions with which it disagreed: (1) their degree of public acceptance, including acceptance by other branches of government; (2) the practical consequences of a reversal; and (3) the effect of a reversal on the Court's prestige and reputation for consistency.

The Unwritten Constitution

The importance of an independent judiciary, now deeply rooted in our constitutional and political tradition, is an excellent example of an idea that is sometimes referred to as the unwritten Constitution. The term "Good Behavior" could have been interpreted in any number of ways. As noted, it was in fact decided in 1805 by the most political branch, the Congress, through the failure of the Chase impeachment, that the tenure of Supreme Court justices should not be pawns in the nation's political struggles. That decision now forms part of our unwritten Constitution, the "swirling sea of assumptions and experiences" that include "the lessons drawn from thinking about the Constitution and its presuppositions and from the history of the struggle to make it real."[65]

This idea of an unwritten Constitution is accepted by both conservative and liberal Supreme Court justices. Chief Justice Rehnquist expressed the idea this way: "When the Constitution is ambiguous or silent on a particular issue, this Court has often relied on notions of a constitutional plan—the implicit ordering of relationships within the federal system necessary to make the Constitution a workable governing charter and to give each provision within that document the full effect intended by the Framers. The tacit postulates yielded by that ordering are as much engrained in the fabric of the document as its express provisions, because without them the Constitution is denied force and often meaning."[66] For Rehnquist, the constitutional plan is part of the fabric of the document, though based on "tacit postulates." For others, the unwritten Constitution is broader, dealing not only with structure and organization, but with the whole way in which actions taken by the Congress and the president have implicitly infused meaning into the document. For this latter group, Jefferson's decision to go forward with the purchase of Louisiana is as much a part of our constitutional heritage as any decision of the Supreme Court, and equally valuable as a contribution to our understanding of the Constitution.

10. Crafting a Constitution

Nine Perspectives

What follows is an imagined discussion among potential Supreme Court nominees, each representing a particular perspective on interpreting the Constitution, who have been asked by the president to present their views.

Candidate One—The Originalist Perspective

Mr. President, constitutional cases require the Court to apply the Constitution as it was understood when it was drafted and ratified. The purpose of the Constitution and the Bill of Rights was to fix the essential structure of government and to guarantee certain rights for all time. The Constitution was all about fixing definite rules. If we want to add or subtract from these rules, we can amend the Constitution. The Constitution is a legal document. As such, its words do have definite, ascertainable meanings and we need to first look at those words, ascertain how they were understood when written and apply that understanding to the problem at hand. Sometimes the text is not clearly understood. We then have to look at the traditions and context giving rise to the text and apply that tradition to the problem. What we can't do is force our own subjective views of what the Constitution should have said, or might have said, to create a new Constitution, since then the Constitution will have failed in its essential purpose. I believe that Orginalism is the only approach to the Constitution that draws its legitimacy from the people themselves who actually ratified the Constitution. This is an important consideration in a system that is rooted in the idea of the consent of the governed.

Candidate Two—The Moral Reading Perspective

I disagree profoundly with my colleague. Most of the critical phrases in the Bill of Rights and the Fourteenth Amendment guaranteeing individual rights embody general principles that the drafters knew and expected would have to be applied to situations that they themselves could not contemplate. To pretend that such words can be applied as if they were in an ordinary business contract is to ignore their most important aspects: their level of generalization and the essential moral commitments to fairness, equality, and autonomy that these words and the Constitution as a whole embody. Thus, when we apply the Constitution to individual cases, our approach must always be informed by the need to be true to the general principles that are its foundation. Candidate One's reference to the amendment process—a difficult task in any event—does not mean that the Constitution belongs in a strait jacket. My approach infuses a moral dimension into constitutional interpretation but does not mean that we ignore history or language or that we can read whatever we want into the document. We can't just make it up as we go along or choose our own set of policy goals (for example, there is no commitment to economic equality in the Constitution) but within appropriate parameters we can and should make the Constitution the best document it can be. The soaring phrases of the Constitution must be allowed a trajectory of their own or else they are something less than what the founders intended them to be. That trajectory may, even must, recognize changes that occur over time that call for new applications of older principles. As the Supreme Court said in *Brown v. Board of Education*, explaining how segregation could be unconstitutional in 1954 under the Fourteenth Amendment even if it had not been in 1868 when the amendment was adopted, "We must consider public education in the light of its full development and its present place in American life."[1]

Candidate Three—The Majoritarian Perspective

I am concerned that Candidate Two places too much faith in the ability of justices to do the right thing. More fundamentally, the key for any justice of the Supreme Court is to recognize that Congress and the legislatures of the States speak for the people. Unelected Supreme Court Justices are far removed from the political process and must give great deference to the voice of the people as expressed through their elected representatives. It is not for us to substitute our opinions for theirs. As the good Justice Holmes said, "If the people want to go to Hell, I will help them. It's my job."[2] Unless acts of Congress or a state legislature for that matter are clearly unconstitutional, they should not be overturned.

Candidate Four—The Democracy Reinforcement Perspective

If we are to let the people go to Hell, we need to be damn sure that it is the people that have spoken. Consequently, one thing the Court must do is assure that democratic processes are working as they should. If, for example, free speech is denied to minority viewpoints, then the lawmaking power itself is called into question, because the opportunity to change or contest legislation has been denied. Except for overseeing the democratic processes, the Court has little business declaring legislative acts unconstitutional.

Candidate Five—The Autonomy and Dignity Perspective

What bothers me about the views of both Candidates Three and Four is that they see the Constitution only as an insurer of fair processes. Democracy, however, is about freedom and is rooted in the autonomy and dignity of the individual. When government infringes on that dignity and autonomy, it attacks the basic premises on which the Constitution was founded. We must always be vigilant to protect that dignity when balancing the interests of the state and the individual. Only such an approach can make the Constitution the living, organic document that it was meant to be. The Court owes the powerless and the historically discriminated against a particular duty of vigilance when it comes to assessing the strength of the interest the state or federal government advances to justify its actions. That is part of what animated the Court, properly in my judgment, to void a Texas statute that allowed counties to exclude children of illegal immigrants from attending public school. To deny these children an education, a deficiency that would haunt them throughout their adult lives, simply because they were undocumented, a circumstance itself beyond their control since they had been brought to the United States by their parents, was properly subjected to strict scrutiny for which no compelling government interest was found.

Candidate Six—The Neutral Principle Perspective

I very much admire the spirit of the sentiments expressed by Candidate Five, but they suggest that the Court should be oriented in its decisions to favoring certain classes of people and certain results. When the Supreme Court interprets the Constitution it must do so in a principled way. Principled decisions can't be made on the basis of the identity of the litigants. Principled decisions can only be made on the basis of neutral principles that are applicable to all cases. Otherwise the Court has forfeited the objectivity that is the basis of its right to review in the first instance. If the Court does not develop objective, neutral principles, then Congress and the president have just as much right to be the final arbiters of constitutional meaning as the Supreme Court. The role of the justice is not to make value judgments but to act as an impartial umpire.

Candidate Seven—The Minimalist Perspective

It would be a wonderful world if all our constitutional decisions could be closely reasoned, based on well-articulated, neutral principles universally applicable to all cases. The problem is that such principles may not exist at all. Moreover, highly theorized decisions may decide too much, leaving little elbow room for future cases to refine earlier constitutional positions. They also leave little opportunity for the executive and legislative branches to contribute to the constitutional dialogue. Rather than looking for a way to apply broad, neutral principles, the Court should try to decide constitutional cases on as narrow and fact-based a basis as possible, leaving as much open to future development as possible. In interpreting the Constitution, narrow fact-based rulings are a very good thing, broad rules generally are not.

Candidate Eight—The Demystification Perspective

I think there is a certain lack of candor going on here. Let's be honest. Supreme Court justices deal with cases that involve clashes of values. Values are ultimately personal, and most times a justice will want a result that will accord with those values. The justice's first instincts in deciding a case, therefore, will be visceral and will lead him or her directly to the desired result. Precedent may be used to persuade. It will not be used to decide. This is not necessarily a bad thing. What is bad is trying to cover one's tracks by pretending that there is an objectivity to law that simply does not exist. We would all be much better off if judges, including Supreme Court justices, were much more honest about the bases for their decisions.

Candidate Nine—The Pragmatism Perspective

I think Candidate Eight distorts the decision-making process for a judge, at least for a Supreme Court justice. It is not just about a justice aligning a case with his or her own ideology. Justices are constrained by the very public nature of the process, the need for the Court's opinions to be accepted by the political branches of the government, and by the force of public opinion. Moreover, the Court as a whole must be seen as consistent, which means that justices who care about the Court as an institution—and that would be all of them—cannot simply ignore its prior decisions. But I do agree with Candidate Eight that the Court's reliance on precedent sometimes leads it to decide and/or defend cases as a matter of logic when, in constitutional law particularly, we need to examine the practical consequences of our decisions. There is, or at least should be, a pragmatism about constitutional decision making that does not ignore principle or precedent, but at the same time insists on thinking through problems not just as exercises in logic or applications of precedent but as real-life problems with real-life impacts.

Analyzing the Debate

All of the perspectives presented above represent important points of view in the conversation over how to apply the Constitution. They certainly do not represent the entire universe of ideas on the subject, and they are presented in very basic form. Nevertheless, they do encompass some ideas about constitutional interpretation that are worth a slightly closer look.

Justice Scalia is currently the Court's most articulate exponent of the originalist point of view. Often, *Originalism* is used interchangeably with *Strict Constructionism*, but such usage is incorrect. Strict Constructionism is a form of textualism that seeks to embrace the narrowest possible meaning of a word or phrase. Originalism does not demand such construction. While Originalism limits the Court's ability to create "new" constitutional rights, it does not mean that rights found in the Constitution, when interpreted in accordance with their original meaning, should necessarily be interpreted narrowly. Justice Scalia, for example, would point to the Court's decision upholding the right to burn the flag as a correct but hardly narrow view of the First Amendment. The originalist impulse places a high value on predictability and questions the ability of fallible human beings to interpret a Constitution free of their own prejudices. The solution for originalists is to bind justices to a fixed text and a fixed moment in time.

Originalists come in many shapes and sizes, and originalists and quasi-originalists debate with each other as much as they debate with nonoriginalists. One particularly interesting discussion occurred in a 2006 *Yale Law Journal* colloquium,[3] with an introduction by Justice Breyer, focusing on the works of two scholars, Jed Rubenfeld and Akhil Amar. Rubenfeld, among other things, distinguishes in his work between what he calls "Foundation Application Understandings," which he believes the Court has always and should always adhere to (the prohibition of prior restraints on speech would be an example) and "No Application" understandings (for example that the Equal Protection clause as originally understood did not prohibit racial segregation in schools), which he believes represent mere intentions, not fundamental commitments to Foundational Understandings, and which the Court is free to modify or disregard. By way of example, recall that the Equal Protection clause is now viewed as requiring intermediate scrutiny of laws that discriminate against women, a major departure from nineteenth-century decisions of the Court practically endorsing such discrimination as a societal good. Rubenfeld endorses this new application of the Equal Protection clause, though many originalists, including Justice Scalia, do not, and they would question whether it is even appropriate to call Rubenfeld an originalist though he clearly regards certain historical understandings as binding on subsequent generations. Rubenfeld also emphasizes original understandings, as opposed to original meaning of the text, which would also separate him by many degrees from Justice Scalia on the originalist spectrum.

While not all the perspectives of the nine candidates are mutually exclusive, certainly the originalist and moral reading perspectives represent very different approaches. Scholar Ronald Dworkin is associated most closely with the moral reading perspective. Dworkin does not assert the authority of justices to create constitutional rights without reference to the constitutional text but does assert that the rights specified in the text have a dimension in moral principle that is inconsistent with a constitution of entirely pre-determined meaning. At the most fundamental level, Scalia and Dworkin differ about what a constitution—at least the American Constitution—is supposed to be. For Scalia, it is an anchor against the winds of change; for Dworkin, a compass for an unknown future.

Dworkin's philosophy makes a critical distinction between concepts and specific conceptualizations of that concept. *Concepts* are the overarching principles embodied in key constitutional phrases, and *conceptualizations* their particularized expressions. In effect, conceptualizations articulate the meaning of the concepts. Dworkin uses the example of fairness. *Fairness* itself is a concept; what might or might not constitute fairness in any given situation is a conceptualization of that concept. Dworkin argues that the *right* to free speech, the *equality* commitment embodied in the Equal Protection clause, and the *due* in due process represent concepts that justify, even demand, what he calls the "Moral reading of the Constitution." Dworkin writes, "According to the moral reading, these clauses must be understood in the way their language most naturally suggests; they refer to abstract moral readings and incorporate these by reference, as limits on government's power."[4]

Thoughtful nonoriginalists recognize in Originalism the strength of a constitutional approach rooted in respect for the Constitution as law and concede the need for a theory that provides a principled means of deciding constitutional cases. They reject, however, the view implicit in Originalism that it is the only acceptable basis for applying the Constitution. For one thing, they do not concede that the Framers themselves intended that future generations should be bound by the contemporary meaning of the provisions they were enacting. More fundamentally, nonoriginalists believe that there is no justification for tethering today's understanding of the Constitution to the past since the Constitution's "status as law" depends, in the words of Richard Fallon, "on practices of acceptance."[5] In other words, given the choice between a reading of the Constitution that would accord with an originalist understanding but would be totally unacceptable in today's world—think attitudes toward slavery here for starters—and a reasoned, principled alternative, Originalism hardly seems an inevitable choice. Critics of Originalism also point out that some of the most important areas of constitutional law have developed in ways that the founding fathers might not only have not expected but would have disapproved. As David Strauss has noted, for example, "there is . . . good evidence that the people responsible for adding the First Amendment to the Constitution would have been comfortable with forms of suppression that would be anathema today."[6]

The Majoritarian perspective has been associated with numerous Supreme Court justices, including Justice Holmes and Justice Frankfurter. Deference to legislative acts does not necessarily favor liberal or conservative political outcomes. Today's liberals would have favored deference when the Court was outlawing progressive legislation, while many conservatives today see deference as a way of restricting activist justices. But even here matters get muddled. Chief Justice Rehnquist gave very little deference, for example, to federal legislation that he believed intruded on matters confided by the Constitution to the states. Deference today seems more a rhetorical flourish than a factor in actual decision making. Consider that the Rehnquist Court struck down, in whole or in part, 42 state or local statutes and 32 federal statutes between 1994 and 2002.[7] Deference to legislative majorities does tend to be invoked more by originalists than by nonoriginalists since it provides a convenient avenue of attack against the judicial activism that Originalism is designed to constrain. Of course, as one scholar has observed, "originalist theory itself prescribes that judges should invalidate at least some legislation that is supported by political majorities—namely, legislation that is incompatible with the original understanding."[8]

The Democracy Reinforcement perspective complements the majoritarian perspective since it too is generally willing to trust to the substantive results of the democratic process. The perspective was articulated originally in a famous footnote in an otherwise rather minor case decided in

1938, *United States v. Carolene Products Co.*[9] John Hart Ely elaborated this footnote into a coherent, much-discussed constitutional theory. In Ely's hands, judicial review becomes severely circumscribed because it "can appropriately concern itself only with questions of participation, and not concern itself with the substantive merits of the political choice under attack."[10] In Ely's view, legislation, no matter how crazy, cannot be declared unconstitutional. He admitted, for example, that legislation making it a crime to remove a person's gall bladder except to save his or her life could not be declared unconstitutional under his theory of judicial review. For those troubled by this conclusion, he simply argues that the solution, when representatives act crazy, is to vote them out of office or lobby to repeal the legislation. He also argues that a constitutional theory does not need to concern itself with a kind of legislation that could never possibly pass in the first place. Ely's view was echoed by Justice Frankfurter in one case when Frankfurter noted: "The process of Constitutional adjudication does not thrive on conjuring up horrible possibilities that never happen in the real world and devising doctrines sufficiently comprehensive in detail to cover the remotest contingency."[11]

Candidate Five's position echoes to a large extent the views of Justice William Brennan, a Democrat appointed by President Eisenhower in 1956 who served until 1990. Brennan believed that the Constitution could and should be used wherever possible to protect the dignity and autonomy of the individual. His views are not compatible, to put it mildly, with those of either the originalists or the majoritarians. Brennan, for example, dissented when the Court upheld an Air Force regulation prohibiting a Jewish officer from wearing his yarmulke while on duty[12] and when it sanctioned disciplinary action taken against an assistant district attorney who had sent around a questionnaire to his fellow employees soliciting their views on work-related issues and possible grievances.[13] Brennan stood with these vulnerable individuals against assertions of state authority, even when those assertions of authority had a reasonable basis. The Air Force certainly had a reasonable interest in promoting esprit de corps and the district attorney a similar interest in preserving morale and unity in his office.

Candidate Six echoes the views associated with Herbert Wechsler, a Columbia Law School professor. His 1959 law review article[14] (based on a lecture he had delivered at Harvard) argued for neutral principles of constitutional adjudication and questioned the constitutional basis for such important cases as *Shelley v. Kramer* and *Brown v. Board of Education*. Wechsler applauded the results of both these cases but could not find a satisfactory neutral principle that would justify the result. Wechsler's views forms an interesting contrast with those of Justice Black. Justice Black, unlike Justice Brennan with whom he often ended up agreeing, did not welcome the idea of a constitution alive with ever-changing purpose reflecting the needs of a new generation. For him, that was too malleable a document. Yet he saw a constitutional system with a spirit that was hardly neutral when it came to deciding real cases. "Under our constitutional system," he wrote in 1940, "courts stand against any winds that blow as havens of refuge for those who might otherwise suffer because they are helpless, weak, outnumbered, or because they are non-conforming victims of prejudice and public excitement."[15] It is not surprising that Black, unlike Wechsler, did not have a difficult time reconciling *Shelley* and *Brown* with his larger constitutional philosophy. Perhaps because Wechsler demanded so much of his neutral principles—namely, that they be capable of application in all instances—his views do not seem as influential today as they were forty-five years ago. Wechsler's approach also seems to ignore how vigorously the meaning of the broad phrases in the Constitution are contested. Christopher Eisgruber, for example, has noted that the meaning of *equal protection* "takes judges straight to the nerve center of American ideological controversy."[16] Since the "meaning of equality is fundamentally contested," Eisgruber concluded, "judges cannot appeal to some uncontroversial standard of equality that exists outside and apart from competing theories about equality."[17] If Eisgruber is correct, and I believe he is, Wechsler's search for all-encompassing neutral principles seems doomed from the start.

The minimalism embraced by Candidate Seven is an orientation closely associated with Justice Sandra Day O'Connor. It encourages highly nuanced rulings that avoid sweeping statements of constitutional principle. One of today's leading constitutional scholars who embraces minimalism, Cass Sunstein, has noted that minimalists try to do two things: they "try to decide cases rather than to set down broad rules,"[18] and they "generally try to avoid issues of basic principle" because they want "people who disagree on the deepest issues to converge."[19] In wishing to leave as much as possible to the democratic process, minimalism echoes, even if it does not embrace, the views of John Hart Ely. Sunstein's defense of minimalism is itself very case specific—that is, he does not contend minimalism is always the right approach for every constitution and every country. Rather, he believes minimalism particularly appropriate for the U.S. Constitution, because it best fits with salient characteristics of our own system and history, where "the original public meaning of the Constitution is not so excellent," "the democratic process good but not great," and judges likely to "do poorly if they strike out on their own."[20]

Critics of minimalism object that it provides little basis for predicting outcomes of future cases and consequently fails to provide the necessary guidance for people (and lower court judges for that matter) who want to follow the law. Minimalism may also result in the delay of validating important constitutional rights as the Court slowly wends its way to a decision that it could arguably have reached much earlier applying basic principles. The tension between minimalist and broadly theorizing justices is very real, best illustrated by the sharply worded criticisms that many of Justice O'Connor's opinions elicited from Justice Scalia. This is not necessarily a liberal/conservative issue. Chief Justice Warren would likely have been as uncomfortable with minimalism as Justice Scalia; at least such is implied by Warren's statement that "in the Supreme Court, the basic ingredient of decision is principle, and it should not be compromised and parceled out a little in one case, a little more in another, until eventually one receives the full benefit."[21]

Candidate Eight states views associated with, if perhaps in slightly more robust terms than he would himself, Richard Posner, a distinguished judge of the U.S. Court of Appeals for the Seventh Circuit and the author of numerous books and articles. Judge Posner views the judicial claims of transparency and objectivity with disdain. "Legal doctrine," he writes, "is something a court of last resort can always (well, almost always) get around and it will do so if the judges' feelings are sufficiently engaged."[22] Though regarded as a conservative judge himself, Posner is equally distressed by claims of impartiality by justices all along the ideological spectrum, and it is their pretense that ideology doesn't matter that bothers him the most. He writes, "Does Justice Scalia think that his appointment to the Supreme Court by President Reagan was due solely to the opinion that the appointing authorities held of his impartiality, judgment, and lawyerly acumen, and not at all to his ideology?"[23]

Candidate Nine expresses the views of Justice Breyer as set forth in his book, *Active Liberty*. Like Judge Posner, Justice Breyer is not enamored of decision making that purports to rest simply on the logical application of abstract principles. But whereas for Posner legal doctrine is something that justices can always get around, for Breyer it is very real. To Breyer, constitutional provisions are alive with purpose and identifying that purpose and then seeing how that purpose applies to the concrete issue at hand is the essence of constitutional decision making. We will see Justice Breyer's approach at work in our consideration of the Ten Commandments cases in Chapter 11.

Justice Breyer's views harmonize well with those of a leading scholar, David Strauss, who argues that constitutional law is best understood when viewed as a species of common law, not statutory interpretation. For Strauss, the common law method, with its simultaneous respect for tradition but openness at appropriate moments to change, best explains not only how the Supreme Court has acted but how it should act. He writes: "American constitutional law is preoccupied, perhaps to excess, with the question how to restrain judges, while still allowing a degree of innovation; the common law has literally centuries of experience in the use of precedent to accomplish precisely these ends."[24] One senses in Breyer's approach the same values that Strauss admires in the common law tradition—"humility, the limits of human reason and distrust of abstract argument."[25]

Originalism and the Moral Reading

While all of these perspectives are important, it is the argument between originalists and those advocating the moral reading perspective that engages the deepest passions and denudes the largest part of the forest; it is worth a little more space. The battle gets played out along many academic fronts, including whether, as mentioned, constitutional theory demands an originalist approach; whether twenty-first-century justices can determine the original understanding of words used two hundred years ago, or should even have to try; whether there can ever be a sufficient consensus about history to make it the basis of constitutional adjudication; and whether language itself is capable of conveying fixed meanings.

Dworkin's perspective (as well as Brennan's) is often associated with the idea of a "living" constitution. Like Orginalism and Strict Construction, the notion of a living constitution is sometimes caricatured, in this case as a license to do anything a justice wants. Neither Brennan nor Dworkin, however, would argue that the Court can simply step in and remedy problems that legislatures have failed to address, unless that failure itself has risen to the level of a constitutional violation. Interestingly, the Court in a 5'4 decision very recently found just such a violation in the overcrowded prison conditions in California and took the unusual step of ordering a release of prisoners to remedy the violation.[26] While Justice Scalia railed against the decision as a violation of separation of powers and unwarranted intrusion by the judiciary into the operations of government, the majority, whether one agreed with it or not, was simply enforcing its view of what the Eighth Amendment's prohibition of cruel and unusual punishment demanded.

While a detailed examination of the debates surrounding Originalism and Moral Reading is beyond the scope of our project, let me illustrate by one example what seems to be a major weakness of the originalist approach. Today, in trials involving mobsters and members of other exceedingly dangerous groups, the "anonymous jury" is emerging as a powerful tool to protect jurors.[27] Criminal defendants have resisted these juries, arguing that they violate their Sixth Amendment right to a public trial. The historical evidence is mixed on this point, but suppose for a moment that the evidence was indisputable that in 1787 anonymous juries were viewed as improper and that the right to a public trial included knowing the identity of your jurors. Should that fact be the last word on the question? I would say no. There seems to be no plausible reason why today's judicial system could not note the vast difference in circumstances respecting the jury system of 2007 and the jury system of 1787, not to mention the simple fact that the problem of mobster defendants intimidating defenseless jurors was simply not an issue in eighteenth-century America. Here Dworkin's distinction between *concepts* and *conceptualizations* appears quite useful. Few would dispute that the basic normative principle animating the Fifth and Sixth Amendments is the right to a fair trial. The ingredients of a fair trial are indisputably the right to present evidence in open court to a disinterested fact-finder free to render an impartial verdict. Even assuming that anonymous juries were not acceptable at the end of the eighteenth century, is it not more reasonable to provide today for a limited exception to that rule to preserve our normative idea of a fair trial in which intimidation (from either the defendant or the state or the community) should play no part? The originalist impulse to freeze the Constitution into a single moment of time would suggest a negative response and, in so doing, reveals a fundamental weakness. I should add here that Justice Scalia often refers to himself as a faint-hearted originalist, meaning that he is not always willing to follow Originalism's suggested results in extreme cases; this hypothetical might provide one of those instances.

The Moral Reading of the Constitution, as articulated by Dworkin and others, is criticized by originalists for, among other things, its disregard of textual discipline, its assumption that federal judges have the capacity to make disciplined moral judgments that are more than just a reflection of their subjective feelings, and its tendency to short-circuit the political process with decisions that supplant the fundamental principle of majority rule. For originalists, the poster child for a bad constitutional decision is *Roe v. Wade*, which, they argue, epitomized each of these shortcomings.

Originalists are not the only people with reservations about an approach that seems to elevate moral principle above all else. Laurence Tribe, for example, has argued that "the moment you adopt a perspective as open as Dworkin's, the line between what you think the Constitution *says* and what you wish it *would* say becomes so tenuous that it is extraordinarily difficult, try as you might, to maintain that line at all" (emphasis in the original).[28] Taking a slightly different tack, Richard H. Fallon criticizes Dworkin for maintaining an unrealistic view of what constitutional law is all about. He writes, "Dworkin's theory remains at an important remove from what actually occurs in constitutional practice. His continuing depiction of constitutional adjudication as a pervasive contest of principles does not adequately reflect the role of the empirical, the contingent, the predictive, and the tactical."[29] Interestingly, Fallon's own views reflect the deep tensions that underlie the question of what it means to interpret the Constitution. On the one hand, he seems to endorse a kind of muted form of Moral Reading:

> If constitutional language, historical understandings and judicial precedents will reasonably bear more than one interpretation, then there is at least a strong presumptive case that the Justices should adopt the interpretation that will make the Constitution, in Dworkin's words, "the best it can be" (without twisting it into something else). Where alternative interpretations are otherwise reasonably plausible, does anyone really think that a Justice should be indifferent to issues of ultimate right or fairness?[30]

At the same time, however, Fallon recognizes an important role for deference to political majorities when there is reasonable disagreement about "what the Constitution means or how it should be implemented," particularly when a reasonably founded resistance to a Court decision may be expected or when costly litigation, not justified by the benefit from the standpoint of "overall substantive justice," is likely to result.[31] Fallon concedes a profound ambivalence about *Roe v. Wade* even after decades of reflection on the case,[32] a fact not too surprising given that his own instincts appear to simultaneously pull in opposite directions.

I have referred to the general untidiness of constitutional interpretation as actually practiced by Supreme Court justices, so it may not be surprising that the line between Originalism and the Moral Reading of the Constitution, so sharp in academic debate, begins to blur in practice. The fact is that, in the heat of battle, nonoriginalist justices will display their Originalist side and Originalists their nonoriginalist side. Supreme Court justices themselves are neither wholly from Venus or Mars, no matter what even they say. When, for example, the Warren Court suddenly discovered that the Constitution required "one person, one vote," a fact that had somehow escaped the Court's notice for the previous 170 years, it turned to its reading of the debates on population equality at the Constitutional Convention to justify its conclusion. On the other hand, when the moment demands it, as it did for Justice Scalia in the affirmative action cases that we will discuss in Chapter 11, he had no problem finding that the Equal Protection clause protects whites as well as blacks, a principle he deduced without any support from the history of the clause.

Before leaving this subject, we should note that neither Justice Scalia nor Professor Dworkin claim perfection for their approaches. Scalia has acknowledged that Originalism is "not without its warts. Its greatest defect, in my view is the difficulty of applying it correctly."[33] The title of his article, interestingly enough, was "Originalism: The Lesser Evil." On the other end of the spectrum, Dworkin has acknowledged (though perhaps not so candidly admitting it as a weakness) that, under his moral reading of the Constitution, "intractable, controversial, and profound questions of political morality that philosophers, statesmen and citizens have debated for many centuries" will be decided by justices "whose insight into these great issues is not spectacularly special."[34]

Let us now consider some of the issues that have produced the deepest disagreements on the Court and among the public at large.

11. The Court in Action: Contemporary Constitutional Controversies

The Establishment Clause and the Ten Commandments
A Brief Introduction to the Establishment Clause

The Establishment Clause of the First Amendment provides that Congress "shall make no law respecting an establishment of religion." The Court did not significantly address this provision until 1947 when, in *Everson v. Board of Education*,[1] it confronted the issue whether parochial school parents could constitutionally receive reimbursement for transportation costs from public funds. The program obviously benefited the parochial school system if only by relieving financial pressure on tuition-paying parents. Did the program violate the Establishment clause? The first question, of course, was whether the Establishment clause applied to the states; the Court said yes, adding the clause to the list of rights held incorporated into the Fourteenth Amendment. The Court, however, also held that the program did not violate the Establishment clause, because otherwise parents who were simply exercising their constitutional right to send their children to private schools would be unfairly penalized and also because the program, in the Court's view, did not amount to an endorsement of religion.

A much different Establishment clause issue arose, however, in the early 1960s, over the issue of prayer in public schools, and the Court, in *Engel v. Vitale*,[2] held that prayer did violate the Establishment clause. The decision aroused a great storm of protest. It is still widely disapproved of by social conservatives, particularly black African American Protestants.[3] Interestingly, while more than 80 percent of the public still embraces some form of prayer in public schools, a majority, by a wide margin, prefer "silent prayer" to either "general prayer" or "Christian prayer."[4] The Court, however, in 1985, in *Wallace v. Jaffree*,[5] overturned an Alabama law that required each school day begin with a moment of silence or meditation, on the ground that the Alabama legislature had been motivated solely by a desire to advance religion. Since *Wallace*, several Circuit Courts (the Eleventh, the Fourth, the Fifth, and the Seventh) have upheld state moment-of-silence statutes, finding a sufficient secular purpose (e.g., to calm students and ready them for the school day) in the statutes; one (the Third) has found such a statute unconstitutional. This is a subject the Supreme Court may well choose to revisit in the future.

The Establishment clause is only one side of a two-sided First Amendment coin dealing with religion. The other side restricts Congress from enacting laws prohibiting the "free exercise" of religion. Together, these provisions are responsible for the widely held metaphorical conception that the Constitution creates a wall separating church and state. The basic idea is that government will neither aid nor hinder religion, but this statement is obviously not an accurate description of how things actually work: nobody would suggest, for example, that the Fire Department should let a church building burn to the ground to avoid aiding religion nor would a religious institution be exempted from the full sanction of the criminal law if it engaged in torture to stamp out heresy among its members. These are obviously extreme examples but once the metaphorical wall is breached, as it must be simply in the nature of things, the closer questions become extremely difficult because the wall metaphor, as Christopher Eisgruber and Lawrence Singer have pointed out in a challenging but rewarding work,[6] offers no real guidance as to how to decide actual cases. This is a fascinating and difficult subject, one unfortunately we can just get a glimpse of.

The Supreme Court, in an attempt to bring some order to Establishment clause cases, did attempt a basic analytical framework in *Lemon v. Kurtzman*,[7] an early Burger Court decision (Burger served as chief justice from 1969 to 1986), holding that Pennsylvania and Rhode Island statutes providing public funds to parochial and other nonpublic schools (as well as public schools) directly in support of teacher's salaries and textbooks violated the Establishment clause. To avoid violating the Establishment Clause, the Court held, the law or action at issue must (1) have a secular purpose; (2) not have the primary effect of promoting or harming religious activity; and (3) not entangle government too closely with religion. The *Lemon* framework is still good law but barely, since four current justices (Roberts, Alito, Thomas, and Scalia) would probably overrule it. Justice O'Connor, whom Justice Alito replaced, articulated an alternative test in her review of Establishment cases, a test that simply asks whether the action or law in question would be perceived by a reasonable observer with full knowledge of all the facts as an endorsement of religion.

In recent years, the Court has definitely tilted toward a view of the Establishment clause that gives a fairly wide berth to religious activities. The Court, among other matters, has had to address (1) whether a publicly funded voucher program helping parents pay for private school tuition was constitutional in a city where virtually all the parents were using the payments to pay for parochial school tuition (the Court in *Zelman v. Simmons-Harris*[8] approved the program) and (2) whether a public university was required to subsidize the activities of religious student organizations on the same terms that it subsidized secular student organizations (the Court in *Rosenberger v. Rector and Visitors of the University of Virginia*[9] said yes.) These cases, however, do not mean that the Court has endorsed direct aid to religion. On the contrary, in *Zelman* the Court stressed that parents, not the state, were deciding how the money was to be spent, and *Rosenberger* was ultimately treated by the Court as a free speech case in which the university did not have the right to discriminate against a religious viewpoint. Both of these were 5–4 decisions.

Justice Scalia has long espoused the view that the First Amendment allows the government to favor religion over irreligion, although not one religion over another. Current Supreme Court doctrine is to the contrary. It provides that the "First Amendment mandates governmental neutrality between religion and religion, and between religion and non-religion."[10] As you might expect, this concept of complete neutrality was behind the Court's landmark decisions eliminating prayer in public schools.

In 2005, the Court took up two cases addressing whether displays of the Ten Commandments violated the Establishment clause. The cases excited wide interest, but the results were confusing to the public, since in one case the Court allowed the display and in another prohibited it. To understand the divergence in the two cases is to get a good taste of the complexities of constitutional law and the particular dilemma posed by the Establishment clause.

McCreary County, Kentucky, v. the American Civil Liberties Union[11]

In 1999 two Kentucky county legislatures ordered the Ten Commandments to be displayed (Display 1) in a very high-traffic area of their respective county courthouses. Large, gold-framed copies of the text were accordingly located in prominent places in the courthouses. The county legislatures had made no effort to conceal their goal of promoting religion. The American Civil Liberties Union sued in Federal District Court to stop the display.

The two county legislatures responded by adopting new resolutions referencing the Ten Commandments as the "precedent legal code" upon which Kentucky law is based and authorizing additional displays of documents in smaller frames to surround the Ten Commandments (Display 2). These additional documents also had religious references, making them odd choices if the intent was to make the Ten Commandments appear part of a more secular exhibit. The District Court ruled against Display 2. Following this ruling, the courthouses installed a third exhibit (Display 3) emphasizing the historic importance of the Ten Commandments and surrounding the Commandments with a different set of documents, including the Magna Charta, the Declaration of Independence, the Bill of Rights, and the lyrics of the Star Spangled Banner. The entire collection was entitled "The Foundations of American Law and Government Display."

It was Display 3 whose constitutionality was before the Supreme Court in *McCreary County*. The key question for the Court was whether the earlier history of Displays 1 and 2 could be used as evidence of an impermissible religious purpose in a case involving Display 3. In a 5–4 decision, the Court found that these earlier events were relevant and established a religious purpose for Display 3 that caused it to flunk the first prong of the *Lemon* test requiring a secular purpose. Without its prior history, the Court might have approved Display 3, particularly in view of the Court's decision in *Van Orden v. Perry*, decided on the same day as *McCreary County*.

Van Orden v. Perry[12]

In *Van Orden v. Perry*, the Court *approved* the display of a monument inscribed with the Ten Commandments on the Texas State Capitol grounds. The monument, donated by an organization dedicated to fighting juvenile delinquency, was only one of 21 historical markers and 17 monuments surrounding the Capitol. It was the only marker or monument with an explicitly religious theme and enjoyed no particular prominence on the grounds. Moreover, the Ten Commandments display had been on the grounds for forty years, without exciting any controversy, before the suit was brought challenging its constitutionality.

How They Voted

Eight of the nine justices voted consistently in both cases to either approve or prohibit the displays. Justices Souter, O'Connor, Ginsburg, and Stevens voted to prohibit both installations. Chief Justice Rehnquist and Justices

Scalia, Thomas, and Kennedy approved both displays. Justice Breyer was the swing vote, voting to prohibit the installation in *McCreary* but approving the installation in *Van Orden*.

Recall our earlier discussion that an opinion only has clear precedential effect if it is signed on to by a majority of the Court. In *McCreary*, Justice Breyer joined Justice Souter's opinion, making it a majority opinion and thereby giving it precedential effect. He did not, however, join Chief Justice Rehnquist's opinion in *Van Orden*, instead writing his own opinion "concurring in the judgment." Thus, there was no "Opinion of the Court" in *Van Orden*. By joining Justice Souter's opinion in *McCreary*, Justice Breyer helped reaffirm the principle that the First Amendment must be neutral between religion and nonreligion. Justice Souter's opinion in *McCreary* and Justice Scalia's dissent in that case sharply frame their differences on this question.

Scalia's Attack and Souter's Response

In *McCreary* Justice Scalia mounted a frontal assault on the idea that government needs to be neutral when it comes to religion. His opinion starts on an unusual note describing a personal incident at an international conference of lawyers and judges in Rome, Italy, on September 11, 2001. One of the justices from an unnamed European country had heard President Bush conclude his address to the nation that night with the words "God bless America." The next afternoon, the justice commented to Justice Scalia that, much to the justice's distress, it would be impossible for the leader of his country to ask God to bless it. Indeed, it would be absolutely forbidden. Scalia then contrasts this exclusion of religion from the public forum in many European nations with what he regards as the much more religiously welcoming American model. After citing early examples of religion in the public square—including Washington's addition of "so help me God" to the presidential oath, the First Congress's decision to open every session with a prayer, and John Marshall's decision to open sessions of the Supreme Court with "God save the United States and this Honorable Court"—Scalia asks, "What is more probative of the meaning of the Establishment Clause than the actions of the very Congress that proposed it, and of the first President charged with observing it?"[13]

In his dissent Justice Scalia had to address the fact that the Ten Commandments are part of the Judeo-Christian religious tradition so, putting aside the issue of religion versus nonreligion, didn't the display of the Ten Commandments violate the Establishment clause in relation to Moslems,

Buddhists, and Hindus, among others? Here Justice Scalia finds himself on very difficult terrain, arguing that Moslems are not harmed by the display of the Ten Commandments because they acknowledge only one God just as the Jews and the Christians do. He writes, "There is a distance between acknowledgement of a single creator and the establishment of a religion,"[14] and concludes, "Publicly honoring the Ten Commandments is thus indistinguishable, insofar as discriminating against other religions is concerned, from publicly honoring God"[15] (my emphasis). As for the poor polytheists and atheists, Justice Scalia simply writes them out of the Establishment clause's ambit of protection: "It is entirely clear from our Nation's historical practices that the Establishment Clause permits this disregard of polytheists and believers in unconcerned deities, just as it permits the disregard of devout atheists."[16]

Justice Souter admits that if the type of historical evidence cited by Justice Scalia "were all we had to go on," then the argument for complete government neutrality between religion and nonreligion might be weak.[17] But Souter cites a number of pieces of historical evidence in support of a principle of complete neutrality, including that the Establishment clause actually broadened the original draft version of the amendment, which had only prohibited the creation of a national religion, and that Thomas Jefferson refused to issue Thanksgiving proclamations on the ground that they violated the Constitution. Souter also quotes from letters of James Madison supporting abstinence on the part of the government respecting religious matters. Justice Souter takes on Justice Scalia's claim that the Establishment clause allows for governmental support for monotheism, finding in it an assertion "that the government should be free to approve the core beliefs of a favored religion over the tenets of others, a view that should trouble anyone who prizes religious liberty."[18]

Given the conflicting evidence, Souter concludes that "there was no common understanding about the limits of the establishment prohibition." He does not find this particularly troubling: "What the evidence does show is a group of statesmen, like others before and after them, who proposed a guarantee with contours not wholly worked out, leaving the Establishment Clause with edges still to be determined. And none the worse for that. *Indeterminate edges are the kind to have in a constitution, meant to endure*" (my emphasis).[19]

Here we come to a central difference between a Scalia and a Souter, a difference that may be as much about temperament as judicial philosophy.

For Souter, "indeterminate edges are the kind to have in a Constitution." Nothing could be more anathema to Justice Scalia, for whom the Constitution is about anything but indeterminate edges. With the "Historical evidence" supporting "no solid argument for changing course," Justice Souter concludes that there is no reason to abandon the sixty-year-old precedents supporting the principle of complete neutrality, particularly given the fact "that the divisiveness of religion in current public life is inescapable."[20] Note the pragmatic element in Souter's reference to the "divisiveness of religion in current public life." Not only is complete neutrality the better principled view but, for Souter, the potential consequences of abandoning that view could be particularly harmful. One can almost hear Scalia muttering under his breath that, of course, religion's role may be divisive, but settling divisive issues is exactly what democracy is all about. And, if Souter overheard him, one might also hear Souter replying, Yes, but taking religion out of politics is precisely what the Founders intended by the Establishment clause in the first place.

Justice Breyer Explains His Split Decision

What about the opinion of Justice Breyer? How did he reconcile his approving one display of the Ten Commandments but not the other? We come again to our critical distinction between stating what the law is and applying it to a given factual situation. We know from the fact that Breyer joined Souter's opinion in *McCreary* that he is comfortable with the basic concept of complete neutrality of government between religion and nonreligion. But in *Van Orden*, he felt that the Court would be expressing hostility, not neutrality, toward religion if it required the removal of a monument that had existed without controversy for forty years. He acknowledged that this was a "borderline case" for which "I see no test related substitute for the exercise of legal judgment."[21] For Breyer, the key determinate in *Van Orden* was "the context of the display." While he agreed that a religious message was communicated, he found a secular message as well; he found that the Eagles who donated the statue had "ethics-based motives"; and he found that "the physical setting of the monument . . . suggested little or nothing of the sacred." Justice Breyer also emphasized that the monument in question had been on display for forty years before its constitutionality was questioned. While acknowledging the danger of a slippery slope, he concluded that, "where the Establishment Clause is at issue, we must distinguish between real threat and mere shadow. Here we have only the shadow."[22]

Justice Breyer's interpretive approach is clearly based upon a kind of pragmatism that some might find unprincipled or even illogical but which he maintains is the essence of interpreting a democratic constitution. In his book, *Active Liberty*, Breyer discussed the *Van Orden* case (and *McCreary*) in just these terms: "given the religious beliefs of most Americans, an absolutist approach that would purge all religious references from the public sphere could well promote the kind of social conflict that the Establishment Clause seeks to avoid . . . my opinions sought to identify a critical value underlying the Religion Clauses. They considered how that value applied in modern-day America; they looked for consequences relevant to that value. And they sought to evaluate likely consequences in terms of that value."[23] In this case, Justice Breyer's pragmatism differentiated him from every other justice on the Court.

The Equal Protection Clause and Affirmative Action

Much constitutional law is about boundaries: who is protected within those boundaries and how those boundaries are defined. In the Ten Commandments cases just discussed, Justice Scalia placed atheists outside the protection of the Establishment clause. In the affirmative action cases we will now discuss, the Court had to decide whether the Equal Protection clause protects blacks and whites on the same terms or whether there is an enclave that allows some discrimination on the basis of race in favor of minorities. Just as the two Ten Commandments cases were decided on the same day with results pointing in opposite directions, so also did the Court decide two major affirmative action cases—*Grutter v. Bollinger* and *Gratz v. Bollinger*—on the same day, also with divergent results. (You may want to refer back to our discussion of the Equal Protection clause in Chapter 3 before continuing.)

The Bakke Case

The contours of both the *Grutter* and *Gratz* cases were determined by a 1978 Supreme Court case, *Regents of University of California v. Bakke*.[24] In *Bakke*, the Supreme Court reviewed a racial set-aside program that reserved 16 out of 100 seats in a medical school class for members of certain minority groups. The four most liberal justices then on the Court voted to approve the program on the ground that the government can use race to remedy disadvantages cast on minorities by past racial discrimination. The five other justices voted to strike down the program, but one of them,

Justice Powell, while voting to invalidate the program, also voted (with the four liberal justices) to reverse the state court's injunction against any use of race whatsoever in admissions programs. In other words, Justice Powell took the position that while the University of California's set-aside program was unconstitutional, some race-conscious admissions policies might be permissible.

In *Bakke*, the government had offered a number of interests to satisfy the requirement of a "compelling" state interest under the strict scrutiny standard. Powell rejected them all, except one: the attainment of a diverse student body. While Justice Powell wrote only for himself, his diversity rationale arguably represented the opinion of the Court, since the four justices allowing the use of race to remedy past racial discrimination were also of the view that diversity was a compelling state interest. Lest there be any doubt, Justice O'Connor in her majority opinion in *Grutter* announced "today, we endorse Justice Powell's view that student body diversity is a compelling state interest that can justify the use of race in university admissions."[25]

The Admissions Programs in *Grutter v. Bollinger* and *Gratz v. Bollinger*

Both the University of Michigan Law School and College used race-conscious admission programs for the purpose of creating racial diversity; the Court accepted the law school's program in *Grutter* but rejected the college's program in *Gratz*. The law school admissions policy in *Grutter* required admissions officials to evaluate each applicant based on all the information in his or her file, including a personal statement, letters of recommendation, and an essay describing how the applicant would contribute to the life of the law school. The policy also required grade point average and Law School Admission Test scores to be considered, because the expectation for each accepted applicant was that he or she would graduate without serious academic problems. The policy laid out no specific mechanism for achieving racial diversity but reaffirmed the law school's commitment to including minorities who without that commitment "might not be represented in our student body in meaningful numbers." The law school tracked on a daily basis the ethnic composition of the class in order to assure that it would attain a "critical mass" of minority students, but claimed not to have a specific percentage target for minority enrollment. An admissions officer testified that in some instances an applicant's race played no role and in other cases could be "determinative." The Undergraduate program in *Gratz* did not require individualized consideration of each applicant.

In fact, the admissions policy was based on a point system, with a maximum possible score of 150 points; any applicant scoring over 100 points was admitted. Under a "miscellaneous" category, each minority applicant was awarded 20 points automatically, the maximum available in that category. Nonminority students could also receive 20 points for a variety of factors, including athletic ability, socioeconomic disadvantage, or attendance at a predominantly minority high school.

How They Voted

In *Grutter*, Justices O'Connor, Souter, Breyer, Ginsburg, and Stevens voted to sustain the law school's program, with Chief Justice Rehnquist and Justices Thomas, Scalia and Kennedy in dissent. The importance of *Grutter* is that it approved racial diversity as a sufficiently compelling state interest to permit properly constructed race-conscious admission programs. In *Gratz*, Justices O'Connor and Breyer joined the four justices who had dissented in *Grutter* to reject the college's policy. *Grutter* was the critical case because it held that race-conscious programs could be valid. *Gratz* simply applied the *Grutter* precedent and found the College's policy wanting.

Why One Program Made It and the Other Didn't

In *Grutter*, Justice O'Connor relied in part on "numerous studies" showing that "student body diversity promotes learning outcomes" and "better prepares students for an increasingly diverse workforce and society."[26] Justice O'Connor also cited numerous amicus briefs, filed by corporations and even retired military officials, emphasizing the need for a diversified work force in which the races work harmoniously together.[27] Having found that the law school had a compelling interest in promoting diversity, the next question was whether the school's policy was narrowly tailored to meet the school's objectives. "To be narrowly tailored," Justice O'Connor wrote, "a race-conscious admissions program"[28] must not unduly burden individuals who are not members of the favored racial and ethnic groups. She concluded that the program was narrowly tailored because race was only used as a plus factor and all applications received individualized consideration. She also concluded that the law school had "sufficiently considered workable race-neutral alternatives."[29]

In contrast, in *Gratz*, Justice O'Connor found that "the procedures employed by the University of Michigan's (University) Office of Undergraduate Admissions did not provide for a meaningful individualized review of applicants."[30] She emphasized that the "mechanized selection index score, by and large, automatically determines the admission decision for each applicant" and "thus precludes . . . the type of individualized consideration the Court's opinion in Grutter requires."[31] Justice O'Connor's emphasis on individualized attention resonates with Justice Brennan's concern for the dignity and autonomy of the individual, not a justice she is normally associated with. Justice O'Connor was troubled by an admissions program that lacked focus on the individual, a conclusion perhaps not shocking for a justice who, at the age of six, could "shoot a .22 caliber rifle . . . mend a fence and ride horseback with the cowboys on roundups from dawn to dusk."[32]

Justices Scalia and Thomas Question the Diversity Rationale

In his dissent in *Grutter*, Justice Scalia wrote, "The Constitution proscribes government discrimination on the basis of race, and state-provided education is no exception."[33] This has been a long held position of Justice Scalia and therefore his dissent was not surprising. Justices Thomas and Scalia both pointed out that the law school could have achieved racial diversity if it was willing to lower its academic standards. Thus, for them, the case was not merely about diversity but about the school's desire to be both diverse and selective. Not only was it trying to maintain its elite status, it was trying to do so as a national law school. Justice Thomas noted that Michigan Law School "trains few Michigan residents and overwhelmingly serves students, who, as lawyers, leave the State of Michigan. By contrast, Michigan's other public law school, Wayne State University Law School, sends 88% of its graduates on to serve the people of Michigan."[34] He concludes, "The law school's decision to be an elite institution does little to advance the welfare of the people of Michigan or any cognizable interest of the State of Michigan."[35]

Justice O'Connor does not take Justice Thomas on directly. She seems to take it as a given that the law school is not required to abandon its academic selectivity, which she described as "the cornerstone of its educational mission."[36] Justice Thomas offers no reason why the State of Michigan should be precluded from deciding that a highly selective, publicly supported law school is in its interest or why the law school should be forced to transform itself if racial diversity is in fact a permissible objective. Implicit in Thomas's argument is the idea that a state can have no compelling interest in creating a national law school emphasizing racial diversity.

Justice Ginsburg's Dissent in *Gratz*

In *Gratz*, Justice Ginsburg found herself in the minority in wanting to approve the more statistically based undergraduate admissions policy. In her dissent, joined by Justice Souter, she asserts that "In implementing the equality instruction" behind equal protection, "government decision makers may properly distinguish between policies of exclusion and inclusion."[37] "Actions," she adds, "designed to burden groups long denied full citizenship stature are not sensibly ranked with measures taken to hasten the day when entrenched discrimination and its aftereffects have been extirpated."[38] Justice Ginsburg's opinion is, of course, diametrically opposite that of Justice Scalia. For Scalia, the words "Equal Protection" and the value those words represent clearly forbid any racial preference; for Justice Ginsburg, the history behind and immediate purpose of the Equal Protection clause permit a wide constitutional berth for such preferences.

The Pragmatic Court

Not surprisingly, affirmative action has been one of the most controversial public issues of our time since it calls for discriminating on the basis of color when such discrimination is precisely the legacy we are striving to leave behind. It is also an issue that reaches deeply into everyday life, affecting governmental employment and contracting decisions as well as educational opportunities. Just as in the Ten Commandments cases, we see the Court reaffirming a position—in this case, the acceptability of appropriately tailored racial preferences—while at the same time applying the position in a way that clearly marks its boundaries.

Grutter and *Gratz*, more graphically than most cases, raise the question, what should constitutional law be about? Is it simply a matter of getting the law right, and what does that mean? For Justice Scalia, the outcome of these cases was predetermined by his fixed view that the Equal Protection clause embodied a principle of complete racial neutrality that would be violated by any diversity program giving minorities a special advantage. The value of those programs, for society as whole, was simply not relevant. Only a justice so confident in his judgment of correct constitutional principle could afford to be so dogmatic. Yet it is difficult to explain how Justice Scalia could embrace complete neutrality so fervently in the Equal Protection context, while rejecting it with equal fervor in the Establishment clause context, particularly since Equal Protection historically sought to aid blacks (an argument against the complete neutrality which Scalia embraces for Equal Protection) while the

Establishment Clause clearly aimed at noninvolvement of government in the area of religious beliefs (an argument for the strict neutrality that Scalia rejects for the Establishment clause). On the other hand, Justice Ginsburg's dissent in *Gratz* seems unwilling to concede at all the degree to which affirmative action programs do offend a clear moral principle embodied in the language of Equal Protection—that everyone is entitled to be treated equally under the law. Affirmative action programs do violate that tenet. Perhaps neither Justice Scalia nor Justice Ginsburg can get it right completely because there are some cases for which principle cannot be the complete answer. Law, after all, does not exist in a vacuum and, perhaps, there is something to be said for decisions that rest not so much on a choice between competing principles as on their reconciliation for the benefit of society as a whole.

Postscript: *Parents Involved in Community Schools v. Seattle School District 1*[39]

It is impossible to leave our discussion of *Grutter* and *Gratz* without considering the Court's recent decision upholding constitutional challenges to certain local school board policies. In *Parents Involved in Community Schools v. Seattle School District 1*, the Court ruled that school assignment policies that gave preference to blacks over whites in some instances were not a permissible means to help maintain racial balance in public schools.

The swing vote in the 5–4 decision was Justice Kennedy. He declined, however, to join the parts of Chief Justice Roberts's opinion that "imply an all-too unyielding insistence that race cannot be a factor in instances when, in my view, it may be taken into account."[40] Kennedy added, "A compelling interest exists in avoiding racial isolation, an interest a school district in its discretion and expertise, may choose to pursue."[41] Thus, while the particular plans involved in the Seattle and a companion case were overturned, at least for the moment, a school board's compelling interest in promoting integration continues to be recognized.

Feelings ran high in this case, in part because the entire legacy of *Brown v. Board of Education* suddenly seemed at risk. Justice Stevens, in his dissent, made the rare assertion that "no member of the Court that I joined would have agreed with today's decision."[42] It was left to Justice Breyer to gauge the true impact of the decision: "Yesterday the plans under review were lawful. Today, they are not. Yesterday, the citizens of this Nation could look for guidance to this Court's unanimous pronouncements concerning desegregation. Today, they cannot. Yesterday, school boards had available to them a full range of means to combat segregated schools. Today, they do not."[43]

Campaign Finance Reform and Free Speech

In his 2010 State of the Union address, President Obama did something that hadn't been done in Washington in a long time, if ever. With several justices of the Supreme Court present, including Chief Justice Roberts, he sharply criticized the Court for its decision in *Citizens United v. Federal Election Commission* rendered less than a week earlier. This case, you may recall from our earlier discussion (see Different Meanings of Victory in Chapter 8) invalidated a restriction on corporations and unions that had been on the federal statute books since 1947. The Democrats applauded; the stunned justices, even those who had dissented from the 5–4 decision, didn't. President Obama was not the only one questioning the Court's decision. A few days after *Citizens United* was announced, Justice O'Connor, now retired, expressed particular concern about the impact of *Citizens United* on state judicial elections. "If both sides [corporations and unions] unleash their campaign spending monies without restrictions, then I think mutually assured destruction is the likely outcome."[44]

Citizens United is only another chapter in a long saga of attempts to regulate the influence of money in political campaigns. More than a century ago, Mark Hanna, President McKinley's astute campaign manager and political operative, famously remarked, "There are two things that are important in politics. The first is money, and I can't remember what the second one is."[45] Things have not changed. Money does not assure victory, but for any major office at either the state or federal levels, it is certainly necessary to assure a chance at victory. Shortly after Hanna's statement, Congress enacted the first attempt at campaign finance regulation by prohibiting corporations from making contributions to federal candidates in federal elections. In 1925, Congress also enacted the Corrupt Practices Act in response to the Teapot Dome scandal, wherein President Harding's Secretary of the Interior was convicted of accepting a bribe in return for awarding a lease without competitive bidding in Teapot Dome, Wyoming, a naval oil reserve. These different acts were ineffectual, partly because there was no active enforcement of their provisions and partly because campaign finance was simply not a big issue. After all, corporate money and big donor contributions, presumably more available to Republicans than Democrats, were not exactly turning the tide of battle during the twenty years (1932–52) that the Democrats controlled the White House and (for all but two years of that period) Congress.

Things began to change in the 1950s with the decline of the organizational strength of political parties[46] and the emergence of television as a dominant feature of American culture and communications. Both of these developments led to the emergence of candidate-centered politics, which in turn enhanced the role of money.

In 1971, Congress enacted *the Federal Election Campaign Act of 1971*, which severely limited the amount of money that could be spent on advertising by candidates for the House and Senate (as well as the presidency) and provided that only 60 percent of the overall advertising limit could be spent on broadcast advertising. In 1974, Congress enacted a comprehensive set of amendments to the 1971 act that put in place the modern statutory framework. The 1974 amendments put more stringent limitations on campaign spending than had the 1971 act. The amendments severely limited the total amount that could be spent on House and Senate campaigns and also limited to $1,000 the amount that an individual could spend independently to influence a federal election.[47] This precluded an individual from even placing a reasonable size newspaper ad in support of his or her candidate. The amendments capped individual contributions to an individual candidate at $1,000 per election, with an overall aggregate contribution limit for each individual of $25,000 for all federal candidates annually; tightened disclosure requirements for campaign contributions; established a system of public funding for presidential campaigns; and created the Federal Election Commission to enforce the provisions of the act.

Buckley v. Valeo and the Creation of the Contribution/Expenditure Dichotomy

The 1971 act as amended by the 1974 amendments (hereafter referred to as FECA) was promptly challenged, uniting folks not normally located on the same side of a litigation caption, such as the Mississippi Republican Party on the one hand and Eugene McCarthy on the other. What united such disparate plaintiffs was a common interest in raising money with as few restrictions as possible. Senator McCarthy (D.-Minn.) was an outspoken liberal and opponent of the war in Vietnam whose near victory in the New Hampshire Democratic primary in 1968 had led to President Johnson's decision not to seek reelection. The Mississippi Republican Party was just beginning to emerge as a force. As outsiders, both McCarthy and the Mississippi Republicans needed contributions, hopefully from a few big contributors, to fuel their very separate ambitions.

In *Buckley*,[48] the Court found that—because money had become so vital in facilitating speech in political campaigns—attempts to regulate its role in elections raised fundamental First Amendment concerns. The Court then fashioned a dichotomy between contribution limits and expenditure limits that it has continued to adhere to ever since and which has shaped the subsequent history of campaign finance reform.

The Court upheld the contribution limitations in FECA because it viewed them as only a "marginal restriction" on speech, since a contributor was still free to express his or her own views and because the Court believed there was a strong governmental interest in limiting corruption and the perception of corruption that large contributions encouraged. At the same time, the Court invalidated FECA's expenditure caps.

The Court rejected the expenditure limitations for two reasons. In the more widely quoted rationale, the Court held, "A restriction on the amount of money a person or group can spend on political communication during a campaign necessarily reduces the quantity of expression by restricting the number of issues discussed, the depth of their exploration, and the size of the audience reached. This is because virtually every means of communicating ideas in today's mass society requires the expenditure of money."[49] This is an interesting statement because it makes an empirical finding about expenditure limits—that they "necessarily reduce the quantity of expression by restricting the number of issues discussed"—without offering any corroborating evidence. Critics of the Court's position refuse to buy into that assumption. In a later case, for example, Justice Stevens ridiculed the premise implicit in *Buckley* that any limitation on expenditures necessarily resulted in loss of valuable political speech: "Just as a driver need not use a Hummer to reach her destination, so a candidate need not flood the airwaves with ceaseless sound bites of trivial information in order to provide voters with reasons to support her."[50] The Court's second rationale for holding expenditure limits unconstitutional goes much more to the heart of the constitutional dilemma that they pose. The Court wrote: "In the free society ordained by our Constitution it is not the government, but people—individually as citizens and candidates and collectively as associations and political committees—who must retain control over the quantity and range of debate on public issues in a political campaign."[51] Here the Court is saying that whatever its empirical impact, the government simply does not have a legitimate interest in regulating the amount of campaign expenditures. Of course, missing from this rationale is any notion that, in enacting campaign finance reform, the government is the people, a stance directly at odds with the majoritarian perspective discussed in Chapter 10.

In addition to the contribution/expenditure dichotomy, one other aspect of *Buckley* also deeply affected subsequent financing of federal elections: the distinction between issue ads and ads intended to aid a particular candidate. Financing of issue ads, *Buckley* held, was simply not subject to federal regulation. This created a huge loophole because, as subsequently interpreted by the Federal Election Commission, virtually any ad that did not expressly advocate the election or defeat of a candidate was an issue ad, not a campaign ad, and could be financed with unregulated money, an outcome that enabled corporations to continue to use their financial power to influence election outcomes. It was this loophole that Congress tried to close and that the Court struck down in *Citizens United*.

Campaign Finance after *Buckley*

The contribution limits upheld in *Buckley* produced a number of results.

First, eliminating large donations required candidates to spend more time raising money since they now had to cast a wider net to fill their campaign coffers. It also encouraged the development of political action committees that would take on the burden of raising money from many potential contributors.

Second, the contribution limits enhanced the importance of soft money contributions—those contributions not subject to the contribution limits of federal law. These included contributions to state political parties, which finance registration and get-out-the-vote drives for state candidates. Enhancing these activities will inevitably assist congressional candidates as well as state office candidates (and a presidential candidate) since elections for state and federal offices are held concurrently. The Federal Election Commission encouraged the raising of huge amounts of soft money by accommodating the requests of the national political party committees to use soft money to pay for party building activities and administrative costs of national and state parties.

Third, individuals, limited in what they could give to a candidate, began to form independent groups where they were free to spend as much money as they wanted in support of a candidate so long as they did *not* do so in coordination with the candidate. Such an independent group financed the famous and politically effective ads linking Governor Michael Dukakis, the Democratic candidate for president and Vice President George H. W. Bush's opponent, with Willie Horton, who, while on parole under a program initiated by Governor Dukakis, committed a brutal murder. The ad played to people's worst fears and prejudices.

As a result of these developments, during the 1990s federal candidates, particularly incumbents, became extremely active soliciting contributions not only for their own campaign coffers but also for soft money donations to the national political party committees as well as to the congressional campaign committees. Since the candidates were very aware of who contributed what to these party committees, the aim of the contribution limits—to discourage corruption and the appearance of corruption—had been partially if not wholly nullified. In addition, corporations and unions were taking advantage of the favorable interpretation of what constituted issue ads, as opposed to express advocacy ads, to use their general treasury funds to help influence elections.

The Bipartisan Campaign Reform Act of 2002

The net result of *Buckley* was, in the words of one scholar a "crippled FECA" that "affected chiefly the recruitment of money, ending the freedom of the fat cats and encouraging the development of PACs."[52] In response to these activities, after a decade of debate, Congress enacted the Bipartisan Campaign Finance Reform Act of 2002 (hereafter referred to as BCRA). Virtually every provision of the act was challenged on constitutional grounds in eleven different lawsuits totaling eighty plaintiffs. The Chamber of Commerce, the American Federation of Labor, the American Civil Liberties Union, and the National Rifle Association, among many other groups, were united in their opposition to provisions of the act.

The BCRA tried to close two major loopholes that were allowing candidates and the political parties to evade the contribution limits of FECA. Title I tried to close what we will call the "political party conduit loophole" by banning soft money donations to the national political party committees. Title II tried to close the corporation/union express advocacy loophole by prohibiting corporations and unions from financing "electioneering communications," essentially any broadcast advertisement naming a candidate for federal office paid for from general treasury funds and "distributed" within 30 days of a primary or 60 days of a general election.

McConnell v. Federal Election Commission Upholds the BCRA

In *McConnell v. Federal Election Commission*,[53] the Supreme Court upheld the essentials of both Title I and Title II of the BCRA. The Court recognized that Title I's ban on a national party's receipt of soft money prevented the national parties from supporting candidates for state office that, of course, were not subject to FECA, which only covers federal elections. Nevertheless, the Court was willing to tolerate this result as a necessary element of the congressional goal of limiting the influence of soft money in politics. The Court upheld Title II because it agreed that the bright line created by Title II's clear definition of prohibited "electioneering communications" was a reasonable response to the ways in which corporations and unions had essentially been able to do an end run around the law. The Court also pointed out that (1) corporations and unions interested in discussing issues within the proscribed time periods could do so as long as they didn't mention any candidates, and (2) they could still create their own PACs and use that money to pay for ads supporting the candidate of their choice.

Citizens United v. Federal Election Commission

Citizens United v. FEC was not supposed to be a landmark case. The petitioner, Citizens United, did not even claim that Section 203 (the section prohibiting the use by corporations and unions of their general treasury funds for the forbidden expenditures) was facially unconstitutional. Nevertheless, the Court asked for argument on this question and, as previously discussed, declared Section 203 unconstitutional on its face. The Court's reasoning was based on a simple proposition: corporations and unions, argued the majority, have broad First Amendment rights that cannot be circumscribed based on their identity as corporations and unions. According to the majority, corporations and unions had just as much right as anyone else to seek to influence an election outcome and therefore just as much right as individual citizens to make independent expenditures to achieve that result.

Justice Stevens, in a long and passionate dissent, took a different view, arguing that "In the context of election to public office, the distinction between corporate and human speakers is important."[54] Among other things, he argued that the tremendous economic power of corporations would allow them, as a result of the majority's decision, to potentially overwhelm the voices of individual voters and even candidates. Drowning out other voices is, he argued, a legitimate First Amendment concern. Justice Stevens also spoke of "the distinctive corrupting potential of corporate electoral advocacy financed by general treasury dollars."[55] Stevens took a much broader view of the kind of corruption that could legitimately concern lawmakers attempting to rein in corporate financial power: "Corruption can take many forms. Bribery may be the paradigm case. But the difference between selling a vote and selling access is a matter of degree, not kind."[56] He added: "In a democratic society, the longstanding consensus on the need to limit corporate campaign spending should outweigh the wooden application of judge-made rules. . . . At bottom, the Court's opinion . . . is a rejection of the common sense of the American people, who have recognized a need to prevent corporations from undermining self-government since the founding. . . . While American democracy is imperfect, few outside the majority of this Court would have thought its flaws included a dearth of corporate money in politics."[57]

Who Is Right?

The range of views among justices respecting the constitutionality of campaign finance reform is as wide as it possibly can be. Some justices think that all monetary limitations are unconstitutional, and others that any limitations are constitutional unless they are set so low as to prevent effective communication altogether. For Justice Stevens (and Justice White before him), money is not speech, and therefore regulating money in politics does not raise significant First Amendment concerns. On the other hand, for justices like Scalia and Thomas, the First Amendment simply does not allow for any regulation of money because contributing and spending money is so intertwined with speech and so necessary to facilitate its expression that it enjoys absolute First Amendment protection.

Money in politics poses especially difficult constitutional problems because, in the words of one noted scholar, "it forces the legal system to choose between transcendent commitments—liberty and equality—and yet the Constitution provides no guidance as to how that choice should be made."[58] Justice Scalia argues that there is no constitutional commitment to equality of influence in federal elections, but that there is a core First Amendment commitment to political speech, which both contribution and expenditure limits infringe upon. That is not a weak argument, but is it a full answer to the problem? Elections are the foundation of political legitimacy. Why shouldn't reasonable regulations intended to assure the democratic integrity of that process be allowed, particularly when the Constitution has specifically provided that Congress has the power to regulate the manner in which elections are conducted?

Abortion and the Constitution
Roe v. Wade

In 1971 Norma McCorvey was destitute, pregnant, and living in Texas, where abortions were illegal except to save the life of the mother. She wanted an abortion, to avoid both economic hardship and the social stigma of bearing an illegitimate child. She had not been using birth control pills for medical reasons on the advice of her doctor. Her class action (an action brought on one's own behalf and on behalf of people similarly situated) to have the Texas abortion statute declared unconstitutional was successful when the Supreme Court by a 7–2 vote upheld her claim. *Roe v. Wade* established a woman's constitutionally protected right to an abortion. It immediately invalidated laws in virtually every state in the union that, with various exceptions, made abortion criminal.

The Irony of Unintended Consequences

Roe is a troubling (though not necessarily incorrect) decision from a constitutional perspective because it took a contentious public issue out of the political process, the arena in which our disagreements are to be fought out. By 1973, as part of the emerging trend toward women's rights, a number of states had already reformed their abortion statutes and more were considering changes. These battles were being fought at a state level because exercise of the police power has traditionally been a matter for the states. Between 1967 and 1972, seventy-five national groups, including the American Baptist Convention, the YMCA, the American Medical Association, and the American Jewish Congress had advocated the repeal of all abortion laws.[59] The irony, of course, is that *Roe* did not remove abortion as a political issue. Quite the opposite, it altered the entire political landscape, galvanizing previously apolitical groups to work for its reversal and dividing the two major political parties into separate camps.

Roe v. Wade also nationalized the abortion issue. Every state in the union now had to recognize a woman's right to choose on the terms established by the Court. Other than amending the Constitution, the only way for opponents of choice to reverse *Roe* was to elect presidents who would select Supreme Court justices hostile to *Roe* who, at some point in the future, would be able to overturn it. This is exactly what they set out to do and had Justices Souter, Kennedy, or O'Connor voted to overturn the decision, as the Republican presidents who appointed them likely expected, *Roe v. Wade* would have been reversed.

Justice Blackmun's Opinion

Writing for the Court in *Roe*, Justice Blackmun anchored the right to choose in "the Fourteenth Amendment's concept of ordered liberty," which "is broad enough to encompass a woman's decision whether or not to terminate her pregnancy."[60] He emphasized the practical consequences of forcing a woman to continue an undesired pregnancy: "Specific and direct harm medically diagnosable even in early pregnancy may be involved. Maternity, or additional offspring, may force upon the woman a distressful life and future. Psychological harm may be imminent. Mental and physical health may be taxed by child care. There is also distress, for all concerned, associated with the unwanted child, and there is the problem of bringing a child into a family already unable, psychologically and otherwise, to care for it."[61] Justice Blackmun agreed that if the fetus was a person within the meaning of the Fourteenth Amendment, then the case for a woman's right to choose "collapses."[62] He concluded, however, that the word person as used in the 14th Amendment "does not include the unborn."[63] Justice Blackmun did not claim that a woman's right to choose was absolute and unlimited, for the pregnant woman is not "isolated in her privacy," and the state does have a "legitimate interest in protecting the potentiality of human life."[64] This was the basis for *Roe*'s famous and much-criticized trimester division of pregnancy, with a woman having an absolute right to an abortion in the first trimester, the state having some interest to legislate for the health of the mother from the end of the first trimester to the point of fetus viability outside the womb, and the state having a right after viability to legislate to protect "the potentiality of life."[65]

Some justices and scholars, uncomfortable with Justice Blackmun's reliance on the Due Process clause, prefer to ground the right to choose in the Equal Protection clause. Among others, Justice Ginsburg has expressed this view, feeling that a woman can simply not live a full life on the same terms as a man without the right to control her reproductive destiny. It also seems fair to say that when women are made to bear unwanted children, they are being forced to pay a price for an action in which a male shares an equal responsibility but certainly not an equal burden.

The Debate

The emotion *Roe v. Wade* engenders is not about democratic theory or textual interpretation but about the fundamental belief held by many that life begins at conception. Michael Paulsen of the University of Minnesota has argued that the whole question regarding the right of choice "is whether the unborn human fetus or embryo is a member of the human family to whom the state *may*, or perhaps *must*, provide basic protection of the laws, including his or her right to life, as against private violence" (emphasis in the original).[66] He then adds: "The answer to this question is straightforward. A conceived human embryo is biologically, human life. It is a separate, unique living human being. Embryology, fetology, all of medical science attest to this basic fact."[67] Given his premise, Paulsen concludes that *Roe v. Wade* "is wrong morally—the most awful human atrocity inflicted by the Court in our Nation's history."[68]

For many people who feel like Paulsen, no balancing of interests is warranted with the possible exception of a pregnancy to save the life of the mother, when termination of the pregnancy would be analogous to the right of self-defense. He acknowledges this when he suggests the state "*may*, or perhaps *must*," constitutionally forbid abortion. A conclusion that a fetus is constitutionally protected from the moment of conception would, of course also take the abortion controversy out of the democratic process, for under such a reading, no abortion could be constitutionally permitted. We should note here that this is not the view of Justice Scalia. He believes that states have a perfect right to permit abortion on demand; he simply insists that they also have the right to criminalize it. The choice is to be resolved "like most important questions in our democracy: by citizens trying to persuade one another and then voting."[69]

Roe Reaffirmed with Important Changes

In 1992 in *Planned Parenthood of Southeastern Pa. v. Casey*,[70] the Supreme Court reaffirmed a woman's constitutional right to choose but abandoned the trimester analysis in *Roe*, allowing instead for regulations at any time in the pregnancy as long as they did not place an undue burden on the right to choose. The case involved a challenge to a number of abortion regulations enacted by the State of Pennsylvania, including a required waiting period and parental and spousal notification requirements. Many conservatives had hoped that the Court in *Casey* would overturn *Roe v. Wade* outright. Past voting patterns of some of the justices and the presence of new Justices Thomas and Souter seemed to augur such a result. But, as previously described (see Chapter 8), Justices Kennedy, Souter, and O'Connor produced an opinion that reaffirmed a woman's constitutional right to choose but also recognized a role for the state to regulate abortion so long as it did not unduly burden the right to choose.

In *Roe v. Wade*, Justice Blackmun had attempted a middle ground between the competing interests of a woman's right to choose and a fetus's right to life by invoking a trimester analysis that seemed more like a legislative compromise than a product of constitutional logic. The *undue burden* standard that replaced it in *Casey* represented an alternative middle ground based on the more accepted premise that constitutional rights are not absolute and can be made subject to reasonable regulation, particularly when there may be important competing interests. With *Casey*, the right to choose is respected but the state is given the opportunity to express its concern about abortion by regulating the woman's decision-making process in a way that underscores the gravity of the decision, encourages reflection, and, in the case of a minor, actually limits the right of choice itself.

While *Casey* upheld *Roe*, it also upheld most of the state's regulations, including that a minor obtain parental consent for an abortion, provided there is an adequate judicial bypass procedure to protect the minor if she has reasonable grounds for fearing her parent's reaction to her pregnancy. The Court did reject a spousal notification requirement as an undue burden on the right to choose. In analyzing each requirement, the Court undertook to examine how the requirement itself would be experienced by the pregnant woman in order to determine whether it was a substantial obstacle to exercising her right to choose.

The basic approach outlined in *Casey* has the implicit endorsement of even such a rights-sensitive scholar as Ronald Dworkin. For Dworkin, the right protected in *Roe v. Wade* is the right not to be coerced by the state into having a child. That right for Dworkin is fundamental and cannot be compromised. Not every regulation of the right to an abortion is necessarily prohibited, however, because Dworkin also sees a legitimate governmental interest in affirming the sanctity of human life. Such an interest leads Dworkin to conclude that (1) the state may prohibit abortion, subject to certain exceptions, after the fetus has become viable; and (2) the state may also attempt "to persuade its citizens to take decisions about abortion seriously, to understand that such decisions do involve fundamental moral issues."[71] It is this latter point that leads Dworkin to conclude that noncoercive abortion regulations are permissible. To this writer at least, Dworkin's analysis carves out a constitutionally sound middle ground, although it certainly holds no appeal for anti-choice advocates like Michael Paulsen nor perhaps for pro-choice persons who regard any regulation of abortion as inherently coercive.

Is the Right to Choose Properly Grounded in the Constitution?

In his dissent in *Casey*, Justice Scalia called the undue burden standard "as doubtful in application as it is unprincipled in origin."[72] "By finding and relying on the right facts," Scalia writes, a district court judge "can invalidate [almost] any abortion restriction that strikes him as undue."[73] Scalia pulls no punches, analogizing *Roe* to the infamous *Dred Scott* decision that denied a black man could ever be a citizen. Both cases took a difficult issue away from the people. "The Imperial Judiciary lives"[74] he concludes.

Scalia's attack on the undue burden standard as unprincipled and basically a free pass for judges does seem to ignore the fact that there are numerous instances when the Court must determine whether a particular activity involves an undue burden on a conceded right or power. Recall, for example, that when examining the constitutionality of a state commercial regulation, the Court inevitably asks whether it imposes an undue burden on interstate commerce. Justice Scalia was certainly not the only person concerned about *Roe*. Archibald Cox, the solicitor general President Nixon caused to be fired in the famous "Saturday Night Massacre" during the Watergate crisis, worried that *Roe v. Wade* "can be supported only upon an exceedingly broad view of the creative lawmaking aspect of the Court's role in constitutional interpretation."[75] For Cox, the Court in *Roe* acted "like a body of Platonic Guardians, charged with bringing the Constitution up to date by deciding, according to the circumstances of our times, without regard to the past or the long-run sentiment of the people, whether a free and humane society should respect a woman's freedom of choice as fundamental."[76] Cox did not reject the idea that "there are times when constitutional decisions may be made to embody what the perceptive judge, still submerging his personal preferences, finds to be the teaching of our national ideals despite our inconsistent practices."[77] For Cox, *Brown v. Board of Education* represented such a decision. Cox, however, did not believe that accepted national ideals embodied a right to an abortion since he found the abortion laws rooted in a collective regard for the special sanctity for human life, which had not changed.

We are, of course, far from a national consensus about abortion, but a good portion of the public seems to accept the constitutional status quo, best summarized as a qualified acceptance of a constitutional right to choice, subject to the right of states to enact regulations forcing a woman to carefully consider that choice. Recently, the Court in *Gonzalez v. Carhart*, a 5–4 decision, sustained a federal statute that outlawed what it is generally known as "partial birth abortion," with no exception made for the health of the mother.[78] Whether this augurs a more radical change in the Court's position in the future may depend very much on the future membership of the Court.

One Person–One Vote

Would you object if your vote counted less in an election than someone else's? Maybe not if there seemed to be an acceptable reason. Shareholders in a corporation do not vote equally based on their status as shareholders. Someone with 10,000 shares has a vote 10,000 times more powerful than a person with one share. One Share One Vote seems preferable to One Share-holder One Vote because someone who has 10,000 times more invested in the success of the company should arguably have a proportionately larger role in its key decisions. You may recall that there were important property qualifications for voting in the early years of the Republic based in part on a similar notion that property owners had a greater stake in society. That view, however, was soon rejected in favor of a deepening commitment to citizen—at least, white male citizen—equality.

If we as citizens are all equally invested in the success of our government, it follows that our votes should all be counted equally, but what does counted equally mean? It can mean that within the same contest, everyone's vote should weigh the same. In 1962, most elections (though not all)[79] would have met that standard. If, however, "counted equally" means that, in a representative democracy, representatives should represent equal numbers of people, then our electoral system in 1962 was grossly inequitable because there were vast disparities in the numbers of people that Congress persons and state legislators represented. In 1962, to cite just one of many possible examples, the population of Michigan's 16th Congressional District was 802,994; its 12th Congressional District had a population of 177,431. A Special Report of the Congressional Quarterly Service showed twenty-one states in which the largest Congressional District in the State was at least twice the size of the smallest District.[80] Similar statistics could easily be quoted for state legislative districts. These disparities resulted for the most part from the unwillingness of rural dominated legislators to reapportion legislative districts to reflect population shifts away from the farms to cities and suburbs. From the standpoint of urban and suburban politicians, the resulting disparities were a huge problem. Expanding metropolitan areas were creating demands for services and infrastructure that rural-dominated legislatures resisted funding. Since state legislatures draw congressional district boundaries, this rural bias carried over into the House of Representatives as well.

The State of Tennessee mirrored these developments. After World War II, Memphis, Nashville, Knoxville and Chattanooga all experienced significant population growth as hundreds of thousands of people moved from farms to jobs in the expanding industrial and commercial South. The political power, however, "stayed behind on the cotton flats, the hills and the ridge land farms."[81] Charles W. Baker was one of many local politicians who became fed up with going hat in hand to a legislature that for sixty years had been ignoring the Tennessee state constitution's requirement to reapportion its legislative districts every ten years. The last apportionment had occurred in 1901. Baker's motivation for filing the lawsuit that Chief Justice Warren later referred to as the most important case in his tenure on the Court was simple. "We felt like if the legislature would reapportion itself according to the constitution, we would get a better break on state revenues coming back to our county"[82]—a simple motivation for a case that would ultimately lead to a national constitutional rule changing the way virtually all our elected officials are chosen.

Baker v. Carr

The key facts in *Baker v. Carr*, decided in 1962, are straightforward. As noted, the State of Tennessee had not readjusted its legislative districts, which were based on county lines, since 1901. The result was that at the time of the suit, Moore County, for example, with a population of 2,340 had the same number of state representatives (2) as eleven-times-larger Rutherford County (population 25,316). Just sixteen years earlier, in *Colegrove v. Green*,[83] the Court had rejected a claim that a failure to reapportion congressional districts violated the Equal Protection clause. In his plurality opinion in *Colegrove*, Justice Frankfurter had declared the requested relief beyond the Court's "competence to grant" and famously warned against the judiciary entering a "political thicket." Frankfurter's opinion was consistent with the historic position of the Court going all the way back to 1849 when, in *Luther v. Borden*,[84] the Court refused to hear a case that would have turned on which of two Rhode Island state governments was legitimate. In 1912, in *Pacific States Telephone and Telegraph Company v. Oregon*,[85] the Court similarly refused to consider whether passage of legislation by initiative (i.e., by direct vote of the people) was unconstitutional. In both cases, the claim was made that Article IV, section 4 of the

Constitution guaranteeing each state a Republican form of government (generally known as the Guaranty clause) had been violated, and in each case the Court held that such a question was not for the judiciary to decide since it involved a political question.

Given these precedents, it is not surprising that the plaintiffs in *Baker v. Carr*, including Charles Baker, did not invoke the Guaranty clause but instead claimed that the Tennessee legislature's failure to reapportion its districts for sixty years to reflect population shifts violated the Equal Protection clause of the Fourteenth Amendment.

In *Baker*, Justice Brennan reviewed in some detail all of the occasions when the Court had invoked the political question doctrine and found none of them applicable to the Tennessee case.[86] It is important to understand, in light of subsequent cases, that *Baker v. Carr* did not determine that Tennessee's unequal population districts violated the Equal Protection clause but only that such a case could be heard by the judiciary. It did not decide the merits of the case although Justices Warren, Douglas, Brennan, and Black were prepared to do so.[87] It didn't happen because Potter Stewart, then the newest justice on the Court, insisted that the Court not hear the merits. He wanted the case remanded to the lower courts to allow for the development of more factual evidence. He may have also wanted the lower Court to grapple with the issue of an appropriate standard for determining what degree of malapportionment was needed before the Equal Protection clause was violated. In this respect, Brennan had been less than candid when he asserted the existence of well-developed, judicially manageable standards for discovering when a state's districting plan violated the requirements of Equal Protection. Justice Frankfurter correctly pointed out in dissent that the Equal Protection clause supplied no "guide for the judicial examination of apportionment methods."[88] The Supreme Court would have to invent one. It would do so in a way that was both logical from the standpoint of the Court's needs and radical in its effect on the existing political structure.

The New Standard

Two years after it decided *Baker v. Carr*, the Supreme Court, in *Wesberry v. Sanders*,[89] declared: "We hold that, construed in its historical context, the command of Art. I, s2, that Representatives be chosen 'by the people of the several States' means that as nearly as is practicable one man's vote in a congressional election is to be worth as much as another's."[90] In other words, representatives in Congress must represent equal numbers of people.

In *Wesberry*, the Court was faced with congressional district lines that had not been redrawn in several decades. The case had been brought by voters in Georgia's Fifth Congressional District, which had almost 825,000 people. By contrast, the Ninth District had less than 275,000 people. It seems a fair assumption that a congressman representing 275,000 constituents can probably give them closer attention and better service than one representing 825,000 people. Justice Black's majority opinion had a very originalist flavor, relying as it did on its reading of history and especially the Constitutional Convention's debate between the big states and small states over the appropriate basis for representation. Black wrote:

> The debates at the Convention make at least one fact abundantly clear: that when the delegates agreed that the House should represent the people they intended that in allocating Congressmen the number assigned to each State should be determined solely by the number of the State's inhabitants. . . . It would defeat the principle solemnly embodied in the Great Compromise—equal representation in the House for equal numbers of people—for us to hold that, within the States, legislatures may draw the lines of congressional districts in such a way as to give some voters a greater voice in choosing a Congressman than others.[91]

Justice Harlan, in his dissent, zeroed in on the consequences of the Court's decision: "today's decision impugns the validity of the election of 398 Representatives from 37 States, leaving a constitutional House of 37 members now sitting."[92]

Textually, Black had asserted that since the House of Representatives is chosen "by the People of the several States," equal population districts are required. Extracting such a profound principle from such an innocuous phrase seemed ludicrous to Justice Harlan:

> Although many [delegates], perhaps most of them, believed generally—but assuredly not in the precise, formalistic way of the majority of the Court—that within the States representation should be based on populations, they did not surreptitiously slip their belief into the Constitution in the phrase "by the People," to be discovered 175 years later like a Shakespearian anagram.[93]

Since *Wesberry* dealt only with congressional elections, the question after *Wesberry* was whether one person, one vote also applied to the states and, if so, whether to both bodies of a state legislature or only one. The answers came four months later.

Reynolds v. Sims and *Lucas v. Colorado General Assembly*

Within nine months of the decision in *Baker v. Carr*, litigation had begun in 34 states challenging the constitutionality of state legislative apportionment schemes. With two-thirds of the state legislative districting regimes under attack, some guidance for litigants and the lower courts was necessary.

In *Reynolds v. Sims*,[94] the Court confronted an Alabama apportionment scheme clearly not based upon population equality and held, "as a basic constitutional standard, the Equal Protection Clause requires that the seats in both houses of a bicameral state legislature must be apportioned on a population basis."[95] Like the Tennessee legislature in *Baker v. Carr*, the Alabama legislative lines had not been changed since the turn of the century. In *Reynolds*, Chief Justice Warren, writing for the majority, drew a direct line from electoral fairness to equal population districts. He noted that weighing one person's vote more than another in the same election would violate Equal Protection. He then asserted, without offering any evidence or argument in support, that "the effect of state legislative districting schemes which give the same number of representatives to unequal numbers of constituents" is "identical" to weighing their votes differently.[96] With this equivalency established, he concluded:

> Since the achieving of fair and effective representation for all citizens is concededly the basic aim of legislative apportionment, we conclude that the Equal Protection Clause guarantees the opportunity for equal participation by all voters in the election of state legislators. Diluting the weight of votes because of place of residence impairs basic constitutional rights under the Fourteenth Amendment just as much as invidious discrimination based upon factors such as race.[97]

In the end, Chief Justice Warren sought to turn *Reynolds* into just another Equal Protection case, treating racial discrimination and residential discrimination as first cousins for Equal Protection purposes, even though equating the two turns history on its head. It is, after all, hard to imagine a civil war being fought over residential discrimination and, more to the point, residential discrimination *is* deeply embedded in our constitutional system. The roughly 10 percent of the population living in our smaller states have 40 percent of the votes in the United States Senate. Alaska, Montana, Delaware, North

Dakota, South Dakota, Vermont, and Wyoming have approximately 1.7 percent of the nation's population but have 14 percent of the votes in the U.S. Senate. These smaller states also have a proportionally bigger influence than more populous states in the electoral college since each state's electoral vote is based upon representation in the House of Representatives *and* the Senate.

Reynolds v. Sims was troubling to Justice Harlan, for he saw it as a real attack on the federalism balance. For Harlan, "the Equal Protection Clause was never intended to inhibit the states in choosing any democratic method they pleased for apportionment of their legislatures" and they "are wholly free of constitutional limitations, save such as may be imposed by the Republican Form of Government Clause."[98] Notice how Harlan viewed the Republican Guaranty provision as the appropriate provision for considering malapportionment claims.

Reynolds's requirement that *both* houses of a bicameral state legislature be based upon population was certainly at variance with the federal model approved at the Constitutional Convention and was directly challenged in *Lucas v. Colorado General Assembly*,[99] which was decided on the same day · as *Reynolds*. In *Lucas*, the Court invalidated a Colorado districting plan that had been enacted by the people of Colorado as a constitutional amendment through the initiative process and had been approved by a majority of the voters in each county. The decision drew a strong dissent from Justice Stewart, even though he had concurred in *Reynolds*. Stewart saw a critical distinction between the two cases. For him, the Alabama districting system, which (like the one at issue in Tennessee in *Baker v. Carr*) had not been adjusted in sixty years, was irrational and arbitrary and therefore did not meet the most minimal requirements of the Equal Protection clause. By contrast, Stewart felt that Colorado's system, which divided the assembly into 65 equal population districts and the Senate along regional geographic lines reflecting different interests, made perfect sense. Insisting on equal population for both houses of the legislature troubled Stewart because "it is clear from the record that if per capita representation were the rule in both houses of the Colorado Legislature, counties having smaller populations would have to be merged with larger counties with dissimilar interests."[100] Moreover, because the Colorado Amendment "provides for keeping the apportionment current . . . the majority has consciously chosen to protect the minority's interests. . . . Therefore, there can be no question of frustration of the basic principle of majority will."[101] For Stewart, as long as a state's districting plan did not permit "the systematic frustration of the will of the majority" and was "a rational one given the State's own particular needs," it met the requirements of Equal Protection.

The difference between Warren and Stewart was a deep one. For Warren and the other justices in the majority in *Lucas*, one person–one vote vindicated a fundamental principle of democratic equality, one that transcended concerns about federalism. Not so for Stewart. For him, "there is nothing in the Federal Constitution to prevent a State from choosing any electoral legislative structure it thinks best suited to the interests, temper, and customs of its people,"[102] subject of course to a basic (but not rigid) Equal Protection standard.

Reynolds and *Wesberry* left many issues to be decided, including most importantly the reach of one person–one vote (for example, how did it apply to local elections or elections for special districts) and what amount of deviation, if any, from the equality ideal was permissible for redistricting plans. In a series of subsequent cases, the Court extended the one person–one vote principle to apply to local government elections but not to elections to the boards of special purpose districts like water districts. It also relaxed for state legislative districts, but not congressional districts, the requirement of near perfect mathematical equality.

Was *Baker v. Carr* rightly decided? If so, was one person–one vote the appropriate constitutional rule? As noted earlier, *Baker v. Carr* was revolutionary not only because it led to one person–one vote but also because it ushered in an entirely new era in Supreme Court jurisprudence. *Bush v. Gore*[103] is a direct lineal descendant of *Baker v. Carr*, because once the Court stepped into the world of adjudicating democracy-defining cases, there was no turning back.

One of the most cogent critiques of *Baker v. Carr* was offered by Alexander Bickel in an essay entitled "The Supreme Court and Reapportionment." Bickel wrote:

> The Court could well have held that the question of whether there was a duty to apportion . . . was not a political question but a justiciable one. And the Court could have held that the emanations of the census clause of Article I, Section I, of the Constitution, combined with the republican-form of government clause of Article IV Section 4, were sufficient to authorize the Court to enunciate a rule that each state has a federal constitutional obligation to apportion its legislative bodies or to reexamine its apportionment formula every ten years following the national census.[104]

Bickel did not spell out how the Court was to determine whether a genuine effort at reapportionment had occurred; he was actually proposing a minimalist decision that would have left it to the legislatures to deal with the apportionment issue, subject to the development of some judicial standards to assure that the states had actually engaged in genuine reapportionment. Instead of Bickel's minimalist approach, the Court in *Wesberry*, *Reynolds*, and *Lucas* set forth a rigid mathematical rule for assuring compliance with Equal Protection.

One person–one vote was, from the standpoint of manageability, a standard made in heaven. It was clear, and the extent of any deviation could be ascertained with mathematical precision. This easily manageable standard gained almost immediate public acceptance not only because it seemed to rescue the principle of majority rule but because the textual ("equal protection") perfectly paralleled the mathematical ("one person–one vote"). This was a principle and a remedy that the public could easily understand.

Another approach to the reapportionment problem was offered by Robert Dixon. He suggested that, as an alternative to one person–one vote, the Court could simply have ruled that egregious population deviations were per se unconstitutional, as a violation of due process: "A due process approach would not create, as the Court's rulings based on the equal protection clause have, a never-ending affirmative duty to try to equalize representation on the basis of census figures alone."[105] The appeal of the Dixon approach is that it would have provided a rational constitutional basis for attacking population deviations of the kind the Court faced in *Reynolds* and even *Wesberry* while likely providing for a different result in *Lucas*.

There is one issue that remains open as a result of one person, one vote that is worth a moment's reflection. Congress did not impose a requirement that states create congressional districts for choosing representatives until 1842. Prior to that time, a number of states chose all their representatives at large, meaning by the state as a whole. At-large elections, however, often resulted in one party winning all of the state's congressional seats. This meant that a state, for example, that was 55 percent Whig and 45 percent Democratic would have a 100 percent Whig congressional delegation. Didn't this system, as a practical matter, result in "some voters" having a "greater voice in choosing a congressman than others"? Mathematically, each voter in those statewide elections had an equal voice in determining the result, but the results, when viewed in the aggregate, deprived 45 percent of the voters of any representation by their preferred candidates at all. Would an at-large election system for electing a state's congressional delegation pass constitutional muster today? The issue currently is a theoretical one, because in 1967 Congress enacted a statute prohibiting at-large elections for Congress, which was intended to ensure that the Voting Rights Act of 1965 would not be emasculated by Southern states using winner-take-all at-large districts to nullify the effect of an increase in the number of black voters.

In his comprehensive work on the reapportionment revolution, Robert Dixon wrote, "when political avenues for redressing political problems become dead-end streets some judicial intervention in the politics of the people may be essential in order to have an effective politics."[106] This is the justification for *Baker v. Carr*, and it is a reasonable one. It does not mean, however, that *Wesberry* and *Reynolds* were correct. One's view of the persuasiveness of those cases rests much more on one's sense of the demands for complete numerical equality in the political process.

Does the Government Have a Duty to Protect Us from Each Other?

Oral argument is not usually the occasion for sudden displays of emotion—particularly on the part of one of the justices —but *DeShaney v. Winnebago County*,[107] involving as it did the infliction of permanent brain damage on a four-year-old by his own father was no ordinary case. So it was perhaps not totally surprising when Justice Blackmun, in the middle of the argument, leaned forward and exclaimed, "Poor Joshua," and then repeated the phrase for emphasis. Much later, Blackmun would explain his unusual outburst by stating, "This little boy got a bad shake and nobody seemed much concerned about it."[108]

In the Court's 6–3 decision holding that Joshua had no constitutional right to protection from his father, Chief Justice Rehnquist, writing for the Court, admitted that "The facts of this case are undeniably tragic."[109] No one would dispute that assessment. *Tragic* was the right word not just because of what happened to Joshua but because of all the missed opportunities to help him. And these missed opportunities were what made *DeShaney* an important constitutional case.

The Facts

Joshua DeShaney was born in 1979. His situation first came to the attention of the authorities in January 1982 when his father Randy's second wife (not Joshua's mother) complained to police, at the time of their divorce, that Randy hit the boy and was a "prime case for child abuse." The Winnebago

County Department of Social Services (DSS), the defendant in the case (along with individuals working for DSS), interviewed the father at that time but did not pursue the matter when he denied the charges and agreed to enroll Joshua in a preschool program. A year later, Joshua was admitted to the local hospital with multiple bruises and abrasions. The attending physician suspected child abuse. A DSS team of professionals determined that there was insufficient evidence of child abuse to retain Joshua in the custody of the Court, and for that reason the juvenile court dismissed the child protection case and returned Joshua to his father. A month later Joshua was again admitted to the emergency room with suspicious injuries, but the caseworker, advised of the situation, took no action. For the next six months, the caseworker made monthly visits to the DeShaney household; she observed a number of suspicious injuries on Joshua's head and noticed that he had not been enrolled in school. She still took no action. In November 1983, Joshua was again treated in the emergency room for injuries that emergency room personnel thought was the result of child abuse and notified DSS. On the caseworker's next two visits, she was told that Joshua was too ill to see her. DSS still took no action. Finally, in March 1984, Randy DeShaney beat Joshua so badly that he went into a coma and emerged permanently brain damaged. The father was subsequently convicted of child abuse.

The Lawsuit

Joshua and his biological mother sued the Winnebago County DSS and various individual employees of DSS in United States District Court, alleging that their actions and omissions deprived Joshua of liberty under the Due Process clause of the Fourteenth Amendment by failing to intervene to protect him from his father, a risk, it was alleged, the DSS knew or should have known about. The complaint was dismissed by the district court on the ground that the facts presented by the plaintiff did not establish a case of legal liability even assuming that they were true. Thus, no trial was held. The dismissal was affirmed by the Court of Appeals for the Seventh Circuit in an opinion written by Judge Richard Posner. In his opinion, Judge Posner wrote: "The state does not have a duty enforceable by the federal courts to maintain a police force or fire department, or to protect children from their parents. The men who framed the original Constitution and the Fourteenth Amendment were worried about the government's oppressing the citizenry rather than about its failure to provide adequate social services."[110]

Joshua's attorneys were aware that Judge Posner was correct in his general description of the Fourteenth Amendment. They argued, however, that once the DSS took Joshua into custody even for just a few days, a special relationship had been created between the DSS and Joshua. This special relationship, Joshua's attorneys contended, entitled him to a level of protection from the state, a level of protection he did not receive. Judge Posner in his opinion had rejected this view. Mere knowledge of Joshua's situation, he wrote, was not enough, and cases cited by Joshua's attorneys in which the state, for example, was found to have a constitutional duty to protect prison inmates from one another, were not applicable because the state had custody of the inmates and because the DSS had not placed Joshua in the situation of danger, the original decision to grant the father custody of Joshua having been made by a Wyoming court after Randy's first divorce.

The Opinion of the Court

At the outset, Chief Justice Rehnquist, writing for the Court, stated that neither the language nor the history of the Fourteenth Amendment "requires the State to protect life, liberty and property of its citizens against invasion by private actors,"[111] nor as a general matter does the state have a duty to provide substantive services. The purpose of the amendment, he notes, "was to protect the people from the State, not to ensure that the State protected them from each other."[112] Distinguishing the cases cited by DeShaney's attorneys, Rehnquist wrote, "The affirmative duty to protect arises not from the State's knowledge of the individual's predicament or from its expressions of intent to help him, but from the limitation which it has imposed on his freedom to act on his behalf."[113] Applying this rule to the facts of the case, the chief justice asserted, "While the State may have been aware of the dangers that Joshua faced in the free world, it played no part in their creation, nor did it do anything to render him more vulnerable to them. The most that can be said of the state functionaries in this case," the Court concluded, "is that they stood by and did nothing when suspicious circumstances dictated a more active role for them."[114] Nothing, the Court finally noted, would prevent the State of Wisconsin from imposing a system of liability upon itself through its tort law, but the state "should not have it thrust upon them by this Court's expansion of the Due Process Clause of the Fourteenth Amendment."[115]

Brennan's Dissent (Joined by Marshall and Blackmun)

Justice Brennan looked at the same facts as the majority and came to a radically different conclusion. He criticized the Court for permitting the state to "displace private sources of protection and then, at the critical moment, to shrug its shoulders and turn away from the harm that it has promised to prevent."[116] Justice Brennan would have allowed a trial to go forward to determine whether the state's failure to help Joshua arose "not out of the sound exercise of professional judgment," which would preclude liability, but "from the kind of arbitrariness that we have in the past condemned."[117] For Brennan, knowledge alone could trigger liability because it could amount to a limitation of one's freedom to act or to obtain help from others. "Wisconsin law," he wrote, "invites—indeed, directs—citizens and other governmental entities to depend on local departments of social services such as respondent [DSS] to protect children from abuse"[118] and thus "the State of Wisconsin has relieved ordinary citizens and governmental bodies other than the Department of any sense of obligation to do anything more than report their suspicions of child abuse to the DSS."[119] Brennan looked to the totality of the Wisconsin child-welfare program, an approach that the majority ignored given its view that the Fourteenth Amendment simply does not generally protect citizens from violence from each other.

Blackmun's Dissent

Blackmun's solo dissent reflected his growing frustration with a Court he saw as increasingly indifferent to the human needs that the Fourteenth Amendment was designed to protect. The emotional tone of the opinion sets it apart from the normal disagreements of constitutional law. While Rehnquist in his majority opinion had recognized the "natural sympathy" that the facts of the case evoked, Blackmun saw this as mere "pretense," a "retreat into a sterile formalism which prevents it [the Supreme Court] from recognizing either the facts of the case before it or the legal norms that should apply to these facts."[120] The Court's "formalistic reasoning," he argued, "has no place in the interpretation of the broad and stirring Clauses of the Fourteenth Amendment."[121]

Blackmun's dissent is significant and unusual because it defends an emotionally infused vision of the Fourteenth Amendment, one that embraces the need for a "sympathetic" reading of the amendment that "comports with dictates of fundamental justice and recognizes that compassion need not be exiled from the province of judging."[122]

Did the Conversation End Too Soon?

Whether or not Justice Rehnquist's expression of sympathy was a pretense—and that assessment seems harsh—a finding against the DSS would have raised significant policy questions. For example, one might legitimately question the wisdom of a rule of law, particularly one of constitutional dimension, that arguably biases social workers toward recommending removal of children from their parents for the workers' own legal protection. There are also broad public policy considerations. If *DeShaney* had been decided the other way, might not states with comprehensive social work systems be tempted to pull back the level of these services to minimize the potential for liability? Moreover, the federalism issue raised by the chief justice is not easy to dismiss. The fact is that the State of Wisconsin is free to impose whatever degree of tort liability it might deem appropriate to deal with the kind of facts presented in *DeShaney*. The Court was understandably hesitant to craft a national rule of tort liability in such a delicate area, infused with so many competing considerations and covering a subject matter generally beyond its area of expertise.

And yet it is fair to ask whether the Court could have crafted a different ruling, one that would have left open the possibility of some prophylactic role for the Fourteenth Amendment. Rehnquist's broad opinion fails to consider the most telling point of Justice Brennan's dissent, namely that a child welfare system that preempts the role of other potential protectors such as doctors, nurses, emergency personnel, police, and teachers and places full responsibility for child welfare decisions with a social services department is a form of state action that, when combined with a failure to act on information provided to the agency, can place a child in greater peril than if there had been no child welfare system at all. For example, in the absence of a child welfare system, medical personnel in Joshua's case might well have gone to the police after his further emergency trips to the hospital. The law enforcement attitude toward such situations might well have been more proactive in the absence of a county agency having full responsibility for child welfare. It is hard to believe that there is no set of facts in which a continuing failure to remove a child from danger might rise to the level of a constitutional violation.

Brennan's concern also resonates with an argument advanced by John Goldberg of Vanderbilt Law School. In an article for the *Yale Law Journal*,[123] Goldberg suggests that states and the federal government have a constitutional duty under the Due Process clause to provide for a legal system of redress of private wrongs. Goldberg's main focus is on tort reform legislation, and his aim is to show that there are constitutional limits on how far such legislation can go in limiting private rights of redress. On one level, *DeShaney* is irrelevant to Goldberg's concerns since *DeShaney* involved an attempt to impose liability on the sovereign and did not implicate the right of private citizens to sue each other under a system of tort law. Nevertheless, if Goldberg is correct and embedded in the concept of due process is an affirmative right to a system of redress for private wrongs, would it be unwarranted to extend this principle to a state-created legal system that, if improperly administered, strands a defenseless child in a legal no-man's land—denied meaningful protection from his fellow citizens in their deference to a legal system that ignores his plight? We may be approaching the outer boundary of what the Constitution requires but, if Goldberg is correct in his underlying premise, we may not have crossed it.

Conclusion

Politics is about power. In a democracy, political power is awarded to those who win elections. The Constitution, however, says almost nothing about how elections should actually be conducted. The Constitution's treatment of the election process is typical of its terseness on many subjects. That terseness is a great strength of the Constitution, but it also has left an extraordinary amount to be interpreted: gaps to be filled in, ambiguities to be resolved, soaring phrases and ideas to be applied.

We have seen that the Constitution's terseness extends to the Supreme Court itself. The very judicial supremacy that allows the Court to be the final arbiter of the Constitution was earned, not guaranteed. That continues to be true today because, like so many things in our democracy, judicial supremacy ultimately depends on public acceptance.

The Constitution is not the only thing that makes democracy work. Even more important is the respect that everyone, regardless of their deeply held political differences, holds for the system itself and for each other. That is why the friendships on the Court that transcend ideological differences are both moving and important. We may be able to tolerate Red States and Blue States; we cannot tolerate Red State justices and Blue State justices.

Some might argue that *Bush v. Gore* showed that Red State justices and Blue State justices do exist. We have discussed how ideology in certain cases does matter, and it is therefore perhaps not surprising that *Bush v. Gore* ended as it did. Yet that decision does not seem to have eroded confidence in the Court as an institution or respect for its decisions. Nevertheless, if presidential appointments to the Court continue to be made along strictly ideological lines, then at some point, perhaps in the near future, there will be no centrist justices and the Court will, in important cases, simply mirror the nation's ideological divisions. That would be unfortunate for both the Court and the country.

Shortly after the conclusion of the Constitutional Convention, a friend of Gouverneur Morris is reputed to have congratulated him with the words,

"You have given us a good Constitution," to which Morris is said to have replied, "That depends on how it is construed."[1]

We have discussed some of the many different perspectives on how to interpret and apply the Constitution. Indeed, other than the Bible, it seems safe to say that the Constitution is our nation's most contested document. Because it is so contested, we want it applied in as fair and impersonal a way as possible. We want the rule of law to apply to the Constitution, and therefore we want justices who are perceived to be above politics. That is why we imbue the Court with such respect. This is why, in some senses, it is our most apolitical institution. But we also know that even the Court does not exist in a vacuum and that in a democracy the Court will inevitably reflect over time the election results.

Does this mean that my regret about the possible absence of centrist justices, meaning justices whose positions on cases that involve divisions over deeply held values are not entirely predictable, is misplaced? I do not believe so. Certainly, there is great value in justices like Brennan and Scalia, who bring real sharpness and clarity to the constitutional debate. But for most of the last half century, there have been fine justices—O'Connor, Powell, Stewart—who have provided a certain ballast for the Court. Centrists can also be great justices, particularly with their emphasis on the factual and the pragmatic and their inherent respect for precedent as a real limitation on their freedom of action. They too are justices of strong conviction. One wonders whether a polarized electorate will allow for these kinds of justices in the future.

If we do go through a period where the Court is dominated by one ideological viewpoint, then respect for precedent by the majority will become particularly important, for in some largely unacknowledged way, it is this system that mediates between the Court's political and apolitical character. What was particularly disturbing about the *Citizens United* case was how easily the majority ignored the fact that the legislation it was voiding had been ten years in the making, had been vigorously negotiated by both parties, and had been carefully considered by the Court itself just a few years earlier.

Ultimately, the Court does not decide how successful we are as a nation. As mentioned, it does not set fiscal policy, decide spending priorities, choose between peace and war, react to crises, or make policy on matters like the environment, health care, or energy. But if the Court does not determine our success, it does help define who we are to each other and our relation to governmental power: Can the state require that gays be allowed to participate in the Boys Scouts? Can prayer be required or even allowed in public schools? Should state universities be allowed to discriminate on a racial basis in the interest of diversity? Can the state require a woman to complete her pregnancy? Can wealthy people be denied full use of their resources in influencing political outcomes? Must a visitor walking down the hallway of a public courthouse be allowed to wear a jacket bearing offensive words? Can a community ban pornography? Can the state execute an individual for raping a child? Can the state require the mother but not the father of a child born out of wedlock to consent to the adoption of her child? Do high school students have First Amendment rights while in school? Can teachers in a public university system be required to swear that they are not members of a subversive organization? The list goes on and on; they are the kinds of questions that the Court has been answering for over two centuries (especially the last century) and will continue to have to answer.

There is no standard model for applying the Constitution. Unlike classical physics, there is no set of equations that define constitutional meaning. Indeed, as we have seen, the very notion of an objective Constitution is up for grabs.

The physicist Richard Feynman was once asked: if all scientific knowledge were to be lost to future generations except for one sentence, what information should that sentence contain?[2] How would we answer such a question about the Court? What is the most important thing about the Court that we would want future generations to know? It's a tough question but one I will not try to answer because I believe you are now in a position to begin to develop your own answer.

One thing, however, should now be clear. The development of constitutional law has been a collaborative process among generations of lawyers, judges, politicians, and society at large. The Framers got us started with the Constitution, and it was a good start. Some, however, think it was such a good start that our reference point should always be the meanings of things as they were understood in the founding generation. For them, the Constitution is good as fundamental law only if it commands and limits future generations. Others dispute this. For them, in varying degrees, the Constitution represents something larger than the words of its text and, given these larger purposes and the right of each generation to forge its own identity, the Constitution allows a greater measure of freedom for interpretation.

These contrasting perspectives may reflect something even deeper, a fundamental difference in temperament and outlook between constitutional conservatives, arguably more pessimistic about human nature and consequently looking to the Constitution to restrain the worst in human nature, and constitutional liberals, more optimistic about human nature and therefore more willing to find in the Constitution itself, paradoxically, both a greater guaranty of individual liberties and a broader vision of the power of the national government.

Perhaps the founding generation's greatest contribution has been to have created a document and a governance structure that has allowed our constitutional debate to proceed and to change course over time. In the end, however, as the Civil War attested, the Constitution holds together and lives only through our own deeds as a nation and society. It will only be as durable as the nation it helped create.

Appendixes
Notes
Suggestions for Further Reading
Index

Appendix 1:
Major 5–4 Constitutional Law Decisions, 1869–1999

For all the reasons discussed in Chapter 1, it should not be surprising that the Supreme Court over the years has issued numerous 5–4 constitutional law decisions. Some of the most important (excluding cases cited in Appendix 2) are briefly described here.

Adamson v. California, 332 U.S. 46 (1947). In a case addressing whether the Fifth Amendment privilege against self-incrimination was binding on the states, Justice Black failed by one vote to persuade the Court that the Fourteenth Amendment totally incorporated the Bill of Rights.

Adarand Constructors, Inc. v. Pena, 515 U.S. 200 (1995). Reversed earlier position of the Court that federal set-aside programs to benefit minority contractors did not need to satisfy strict scrutiny under the Equal Protection clause.

Afroyim v. Rusk, 387 U.S. 253 (1967). Held that Congress did not have the power to strip a citizen of citizenship and that loss of citizenship can only be the act of voluntary renunciation.

Associated Press v. Walker, 388 U.S. 130 (1967). Extended to public figures the rule of *New York Times v. Sullivan*, requiring actual malice for a recovery of defamatory falsehood.

Barnes v. Glen Theater, Inc., 501 U.S. 560 (1991). Upheld Indiana statute barring public nudity against a challenge brought by an establishment offering totally nude dancing as a form of live entertainment.

Branzburg v. Hayes, 408 U.S. 665 (1972). Held that the First Amendment does not create a special privilege for journalists to protect their confidential sources; journalists had sought to require a compelling government interest before being forced to reveal information gained from confidential sources.

Cohen v. California, 403 U.S. 15 (1971). Held that First Amendment protected the wearing of a jacket emblazoned with offensive language.

Cruzan v. Director, Missouri Department of Health, 497 U.S. 261 (1990). Upheld decision of Missouri Court requiring proof of clear and convincing evidence of comatose patient's desire not to live in a vegetative state before removing artificial means of life support.

Everson v. Board of Education, 330 U.S. 1 (1947). Despite unanimous agreement that the Establishment clause applied to the states, a 5–4 majority held that the clause was not violated by a taxpayer-supported program that reimbursed parochial school parents, as well as public school parents, for student transportation costs.

Furman v. Georgia, 408 U.S. 238 (1972). Held that death penalty, as then being applied throughout the nation, violated the Eighth Amendment's prohibition against cruel and unusual punishment because imposition was totally random and without any guidelines; decision called a temporary halt to executions nationwide.

Garcia v. San Antonio Metropolitan Transit Authority, 469 U.S. 528 (1985). Held that federal court review of congressional regulation of state activities would no longer seek to distinguish between traditional and nontraditional activities; the Court instead would leave it to the political branches to protect the interest of the states.

Gold Clause Cases, 294 U.S. 240, 294 U.S. 317, 294 U.S. 330 (1935). Upheld congressional power to take United States off the gold standard notwithstanding its effect on obligations under existing contracts.

Hammer v. Dagenhart, 247 U.S. 251 (1918). Voided federal law prohibiting transportation in interstate commerce of goods produced by child labor; decision revived distinction between manufacturing and commerce that had been made in earlier opinions.

Home Building & Loan Association v. Blaisdell, 290 U.S. 398 (1934). Upheld Minnesota law authorizing its state courts to grant moratoriums preventing the foreclosing of mortgages on real property.

Lee v. Weisman, 505 U.S. 577 (1992). Held that Establishment clause prohibits prayer invocation at high school graduation ceremonies.

Legal Tender Cases (Knox v. Lee), 79 U.S. (12 Wall.) 457 (1870). Held that Congress had authority to make paper currency legal tender for all debts, reversing an earlier decision to the contrary.

Lochner v. New York, 198 U.S. 45 (1905). Voided New York law establishing maximum hours of work for bakers.

Michael M. v. Superior Court of Sonoma County, 450 U.S. 464 (1981). Upheld, against an Equal Protection challenge, a California statutory rape law that made male but not female of the same age guilty of statutory rape.

Miller v. California, 413 U.S. 15 (1973). Established criteria for defining obscenity and held that determining whether a particular work was obscene within those criteria was to be determined by local community standards.

Milliken v. Bradley, 418 U.S. 717 (1974). Held that desegregation remedy for one school district could not require merging of that district with another, nonsegregating district; case marked the first time that the Court had denied a request for relief intended to promote integration.

Miranda v. Arizona, 384 U.S. 436 (1966). Held that implementation of Fifth and Sixth Amendment rights of persons taken into custody requires they be informed of their right to remain silent, to avoid self-incrimination, and to the assistance of counsel.

Moore v. East Cleveland, 431 U.S. 494 (1977). Local ordinance that had the effect of preventing a grandmother from living with her two grandsons because the grandsons were cousins, not brothers, held unconstitutional as a violation of right of intimate association protected under the Liberty interest in the Fourteenth Amendment's Due Process clause.

National Labor Relations Board v. Jones & Laughlin Steel Corp., 301 U.S. 1 (1937). Upheld the constitutionality of the National Labor Relations Act

Near v. Minnesota, 283 U.S. 697 (1931). Formally incorporated First Amendment protection for freedom of speech into the Due Process clause of the Fourteenth Amendment and voided a Minnesota statute that had authorized a judge without a jury to halt publication of a newspaper deemed, among other things, scandalous, malicious and defamatory material.

Nollan v. California Coastal Commission, 483 U.S. 825 (1987). Held that requiring a beachfront property owner to grant a public easement allowing access over his beach as a condition for permit to expand his bungalow constituted a taking under the Eminent Domain clause since the expansion was not creating a situation that the easement would remedy and therefore the government was simply seeking a public benefit without paying for it.

Olmstead v. United States, 277 U.S. 438 (1928). Held that wiretapped conversations were not protected by the Fourth and Fifth Amendments; the decision was later overruled by *Katz v. United States.*

Oregon v. Mitchell, 400 U.S. 112 (1970). Held that Congress had the authority to set voting age for federal but not state elections; decision led directly to the Twenty-sixth Amendment.

Planned Parenthood of Southeastern Pennsylvania v. Casey, 505 U.S. 833 (1992). Reaffirmed a woman's right to choose an abortion but allowed for state regulation of the right that did not unduly burden it; the decision abandoned the trimester framework of *Roe v. Wade.*

Plyer v. Doe, 457 U.S. 202 (1982). Decision of the State of Texas to exclude immigrant, undocumented children from public schools held to violate the Equal Protection clause of the Fourteenth Amendment

Pollock v. Farmers Loan & Trust Company, 157 U.S. 429 (1895). Invalidated first U.S. income tax law on ground that it was a direct tax that was required to be apportioned among the States; the decision led to the Sixteenth Amendment.

Printz v. United States, 521 U.S. 898 (1997). Invalidated provision of federal law requiring states to cooperate in background checks of potential gun owners as undue burden on the states.

Regents of the University of California v. Bakke, 438 U.S. 265 (1978). Held that quota system that reserved sixteen spots in a medical school's admission program for minorities violated the rights of a white applicant under the Equal Protection clause since he was totally foreclosed from competing for those spots.

Rosenberger v. Rector and Visitors of the University of Virginia, 515 U.S. 819 (1995). Held that the University of Virginia, which generally provided support for student groups, including religious groups, had engaged in viewpoint discrimination violating the First Amendment when it denied funds for publication by a Christian student group of its newspaper *Wide Awake*.

Rust v. Sullivan, 500 U.S. 173 (1991). Upheld federal regulation forbidding doctors working for family planning clinics receiving federal funds to counsel women on the availability of abortion against challenges that the regulation infringed on a doctor's First Amendment rights and on a woman's right to choose.

San Antonio School District v. Rodriguez, 411 U.S. 1 (1973). Held that Texas's system of financing public school education through the property tax did not violate the Equal Protection clause since education is not a fundamental right and system of financing not irrational.

Shaw v. Reno, 509 U.S. 630 (1993). Applied strict scrutiny to invalidate North Carolina redistricting plan relying on race and held that mere desire to conform to the requirement of majority minority districts in the Voting Rights Act was not a sufficiently compelling state interest to justify the plan.

Slaughterhouse Cases, 83 U.S. (16 Wall.) 36 (1873). Narrowly construed the Privileges and Immunities clause in the Fourteenth Amendment to protect only a few rights (such as the right of access to the Nation's capital) arising out of national, as opposed to state, citizenship.

Texas v. Johnson, 491 U.S. 397 (1989). Upheld right to burn the flag as a form of political expression protected by the First Amendment.

Time, Inc. v. Hill, 385 U.S. 374 (1967). Having unanimously established the principle that an award of damages to a public official for defamation relating to his official conduct requires a showing of actual malice in *New York Times Co. v. Sullivan*, 376 U.S. 254 (1964), the Court extended that principle to require a showing of actual malice in a civil action authorized by statute for violations of privacy where the private individuals were involved in a matter of public interest.

United States v. Lopez, 514 U.S. 549 (1995). Federal law making it a criminal offense to possess a firearm within a school zone voided as outside the scope of Congress's power over interstate commerce.

United States v. Richardson, 418 U.S. 166 (1974). Held that taxpayer lacked standing to sue to challenge law that prohibited disclosure of CIA expenditures.

U.S. Term Limits, Inc. v. Thornton, 514 U.S. 779 (1995). Held that qualifications set forth in the Constitution for members of Congress and U.S. senators were meant to be exclusive and that, consequently, state laws imposing congressional term limits were unconstitutional.

West Coast Hotel Co. v. Parrish, 300 U.S. 379 (1937). Upheld Washington state minimum wage law, explicitly overturning earlier Court decision (*Adkins v. Children's Hospital*) that had invalidated a minimum wage law for women and children.

Appendix 2:
Major 5–4 Constitutional Law Decisions, 2000–2011

The Supreme Court, like many important institutions, has enjoyed periods of relative consensus and periods marked by deep divisions. In Chapter 1 we noted factors that helped explain why, even during the same period, the Court can produce both unanimous and closely divided decisions. When a sufficient consensus exists for a long enough period of time, it may become associated with a particular point of view. Thus, the Marshall Court of the first three decades of the nineteenth century gave constitutional shape to the nationalist impulse that had given rise to the Constitution itself. From the end of the Civil War to the New Deal, an era of Republican hegemony, the Court reinforced the dominant position of business. The Warren Court was dominated by a "liberal" wing that led to historic decisions in the areas of race relations, criminal procedure, reapportionment, free speech, and school prayer. Undoubtedly, the Warren Court reflected the coincidence that following the Democratic dominance of the 1930s and 1940s (during which the party won five consecutive presidential elections), President Eisenhower, a Republican, unwittingly appointed two of the Court's most liberal justices—Earl Warren himself and William Brennan.

While it is true that the last thirteen presidential elections, starting in 1960, have been won seven times by the Republican candidate and six times by the Democrat, and the public itself seems deeply conflicted over issues of constitutional meaning, the extraordinary number of 5–4 decisions during the past ten years—more than sixty—still seems difficult to account for. During this period, Justices Rehnquist, Scalia, Thomas, Alito, and Roberts (who replaced Rehnquist) comprised the "conservative" bloc of the Court and Justices Ginsburg, Stevens, Breyer, Souter, Kagan, and Sotomayor (who replaced Souter) comprised the liberal bloc. Justices Kennedy and O'Connor were regarded as swing votes.

The sixty-three cases described below, in the aggregate, present an interesting picture.

Justice Alito replaced Justice O'Connor on the Court on January 31, 2006. Prior to his ascension, on twelve occasions, at least one liberal or conservative justice crossed over to vote with the other bloc. There have been only three such occasions since Justice O'Connor left the Court. The increased conservative direction of the Court since the retirement of Justice O'Connor is also very clear. Prior to her leaving, there were fourteen cases in which the conservative bloc was in the majority and twelve cases in which the liberal bloc was in the majority, joined by either Justice Kennedy or Justice O'Connor. After her leaving, there were sixteen cases in which the conservative bloc prevailed and only six cases in which the liberal bloc, joined by Justice Kennedy, prevailed. Moreover, of these six cases, three dealt with cruel and unusual punishment, one with habeas corpus, one with Miranda warnings, and one with procedural due process. After Justice O'Connor left, the liberal bloc was in the minority on a huge range of cases, dealing with, among other things, abortion, gun rights, free speech rights of students, campaign finance, preemption, desegregation, and the exclusionary rule.

During the portion of this period when Justice O'Connor was on the bench, the liberal bloc actually enjoyed a plurality of four over three. They needed to attract the vote of only Justices Kennedy or O'Connor to prevail. The essentially conservative bent of both of these justices is shown by the fact that the conservative bloc still prevailed fourteen times, attracting the votes of both Justices Kennedy and O'Connor. The liberal bloc, as noted, prevailed twelve times during the O'Connor portion of the decade with Justice O'Connor herself providing the crucial swing vote on nine occasions and Justice Kennedy three times.

For those interested in examining these voting patterns in more detail, I have indicated for each case described below whether there was a crossover of at least one ideological vote to the "other side" and, if not, which bloc prevailed. The symbols following the description of each case have the following meanings:

"Con." means the conservative bloc prevailed
"Lib." means the liberal bloc prevailed.
"Crossover" means at least one liberal or conservative justice crossed over
     to vote with the other bloc.

In cases in which the liberal bloc prevailed, I have indicated whether Kennedy or O'Connor provided the fifth vote. I have also categorized the cases by constitutional subject matter. Please note that a blank page reference means that a page number had not yet been assigned in the indicated volume of *U.S. Reports* at the time we went to press.

Abortion

Gonzales v. Carhart, 550 U.S. 124 (2007). Upheld federal law outlawing the "partial birth" abortion procedure even though legislation did not make specific exception allowing procedure to protect the health, only the life, of the mother. Writing for the majority, Justice Kennedy argued that the decision was consistent with the right of choice upheld in *Planned Parenthood v. Casey*. Con.

Affirmative Action

Grutter v. Bollinger, 539 U.S. 306 (2003). Affirmative action programs subject to strict scrutiny; Michigan Law School's admissions policy aimed at creating a diverse student body served a compelling government interest, was not a quota system, and emphasized individual review and therefore passed constitutional muster. Lib. (O'Connor voted with the liberal bloc.)

Commerce Clause

Granholm v. Heald, 544 U.S. 460 (2005). Michigan and New York State laws that prohibited out-of-state but not in-state makers of alcohol from selling directly to in-state consumers held unconstitutional as unlawful discrimination under theory of the Dormant Commerce clause. Crossover.

Morrison v. United States, 529 U.S. 598 (2000). Federal Violence against Women Act providing a civil remedy for gender-based violence against women held unconstitutional as beyond the legislative power of Congress. Con.

Constitutional Remedies

Connick v. Thompson, 563 U.S. ____ (2011). Held that district attorney's office, which had failed to turn over potentially exculpatory blood evidence, was not liable to a defendant who spent eighteen years in jail following his conviction; though the Court has held a constitutional requirement to disclose evidence exists, it would not impose liability unless the office was guilty of a clear pattern of failing to train its lawyers properly, a pattern the majority believed had not been established in this case. Con.

Criminal Procedure

Atwater v. City of Lago Vista, 532 U.S. 318 (2001). Fourth Amendment does not limit a police officer's authority to arrest without a warrant for minor criminal offenses he has probable cause to believe have been committed by defendant. Crossover.

Bullcoming v. New Mexico, 564 U.S. ____ (2011). Held that defendant in a driving-while-intoxicated case was entitled, under the Sixth Amendment's confrontation clause, to cross-examine at trial the preparer of a pivotal blood test laboratory report. Crossover.

Herring v. United States, 555 U.S. 135 (2009). Refused to apply exclusionary rule where police search was the result of a database error on theory that exclusionary rule is not an individual right and applies only where its deterrent effect outweighs the cost of letting a guilty defendant go free. Con.

Hiibel v. Sixth Judicial District Court of Nevada, Humboldt County, 542 U.S. 177 (2004). Nevada law making it a crime not to identify oneself to a police officer held not unconstitutional under either the Fourth or Fifth Amendments when applied to an individual who refused to give his name to a police officer reasonably investigating a nearby assault. Con.

Hudson v. Michigan, 547 U.S. 586 (2006). Held that violation of the knock-and-announce rule by police does not, in and of itself, require evidence subsequently seized to be excluded from trial. Con.

J.D.B. v. North Carolina, 564 U.S. ____ (2011). Held that a child's age was relevant in determining when it was constitutionally necessary to give a child Miranda warnings, given that a young child would be less likely to feel free to leave when being questioned by the police, and therefore should be deemed by the police to be in their custody and entitled to Miranda warnings. Lib. (Kennedy voted with liberal bloc.)

Kylo v. United States, 533 U.S. 27 (2001). Use of thermal imaging device to detect relative amounts of heat emanating from a private home without a warrant constituted an unconstitutional search in violation of the Fourth Amendment. Crossover.

Rogers v. Tennessee, 532 U.S. 451 (2001). Supreme Court of Tennessee did not deny defendant due process of law when it retroactively applied a decision to abolish the state's common law rule that had prevented a conviction for murder when victim died more than a year after the attack. Crossover.

Rompilla v. Beard, 545 U.S. 374 (2005). Defendant was deprived of his Sixth Amendment right to effective counsel in a capital case during the sentencing phase of his trial when his counsel did not try to obtain material that prosecution would likely seek to use at the sentencing phase and which also contained evidence supporting mitigation. Lib. (O'Connor voted with the liberal bloc.)

Smith v. Massachusetts, 543 U.S. 462 (2005). The double jeopardy clause is violated when a judge rules midway through a trial that defendant is not guilty of a charge but later attempts to reverse himself. Crossover.

Texas v. Cobb, 532 U.S. 162 (2001). Sixth Amendment right to counsel is offense-specific and did not attach or extend to crimes factually related to those actually charged. Con.

United States v. Gonzalez-Lopez, 548 U.S. 140 (2006). A defendant is automatically entitled to have his conviction overturned if his Sixth Amendment right to counsel of his own choosing is denied. Crossover.

Yarborough v. Alvarado, 541 U.S. 652 (2004). Police not required to consider a suspect's youth in deciding whether he is entitled to Miranda warnings since suspect was not in custody and therefore not entitled to the warnings. Con.

Cruel and Unusual Punishment

Brown v. Plat, 563 U.S. ____ (2011). Held that California prisons were so overcrowded as to constitute cruel and unusual punishment and therefore ordered the state to reduce the prison population to 137.5 percent of capacity, down from 200 percent, within two years. Lib. (Kennedy voted with liberal bloc.)

Kansas v. Marsh, 548 U.S. 163 (2006). A statute that allows for the death penalty when the aggravating and mitigating factors are found to be equal does not violate the Eighth Amendment. Con.

Kennedy v. Louisiana, 554 U.S. 407 (2008). Held that Eighth Amendment bars Louisiana from imposing death sentence for rape of a child where the crime did not result, and was not intended to result, in the victim's death. Lib. (Kennedy voted with liberal bloc.)

Lockyer v. Andrade, 538 U.S. 63 (2003). Twenty-five-year to life sentence for stealing five videotapes from a K-Mart store did not violate Eighth Amendment when imposed pursuant to California's three strikes law even though none of the crimes involved use of weapons or violence and first two crimes could have been reclassified by trial judge as misdemeanors to avoid the harsh effect of the law. (A similar case decided to similar effect by the same vote on the same day was *Ewing v. California*, 538 U.S. 11 (2003).) Con.

Panetti v. Quarterman, 551 U.S. 930 (2007). The Eighth Amendment does not permit the execution of a person whose mental illness prevents him from comprehending the reason for his execution. Lib. (Kennedy voted with liberal bloc.)

Roper v. Simmons, 543 U.S. 551 (2005). Infliction of death penalty on those seventeen and under at time a capital crime was committed violated Eighth Amendment's prohibition against cruel and unusual punishment. Lib. (Kennedy voted with liberal bloc.)

Desegregation

Parents Involved in Community Schools v. Seattle School District No. 1, 551 U.S. 701 (2007). School assignment policy that gave preference to blacks in certain circumstances to maintain racial balance in public schools held unconstitutional given perniciousness of racial classifications and absence of a compelling justification. Con.

Equal Protection

Tuan Anh Nguyen v. Immigration and Naturalization Service, 533 U.S. 53 (2001). Statute imposing different requirements for a child's acquisition of citizenship depending on whether the citizen parent is the mother or father does not violate Equal Protection guarantee embedded in Due Process clause of the 5th Amendment. Crossover.

Establishment of Religion

McCreary County v. American Civil Liberties Union, 545 U.S. 844 (2005). Held that inclusion of Ten Commandments as part of a courthouse exhibit on the "American Legal Tradition" violated the Establishment Clause in light of avowed religious purpose of exhibit. Lib. (O'Connor voted with the liberal bloc.)

Van Orden v. Perry, 545 U.S. 677 (2005). Held that monument inscribed with the Ten Commandments located on grounds surrounding state capital building did not violate the Establishment clause given that the monument had been installed forty years earlier, had not aroused controversy, and was one of 21 historical markers and 17 monuments surrounding the building, none of which had any religious content. (Decided on same day as *McCreary*.) Crossover.

Zelman v. Simmons-Harris, 536 U.S. 639 (2002). Held that Ohio's voucher program, enabling low-income parents to receive tuition aid to send their children to private or public schools, did not violate the Establishment clause, notwithstanding that more than 95 percent of participating parents chose to send their children to religious schools and more than 80 percent of schools participating in the program had a religious affiliation. Con.

Federalism

American Insurance Association v. Garamendi, 539 U.S. 396 (2003). State statute imposing certain obligations on insurance companies doing business in the state to provide information to aid Holocaust victims interfered with federal government's authority over foreign affairs and was therefore preempted. Crossover.

Board of Trustees v. Garrett, 531 U.S. 356 (2001). Suit to recover money damages against the state for violation of Title I of Americans with Disabilities Act barred by the Eleventh Amendment since authorization of the suit was not within Congress's Fourteenth Amendment enforcement powers: Court held that Congress had not established that states were engaging in systematic discrimination against the disabled. Con.

Central Virginia Community College v. Katz, 546 U.S. 356 (2006). Held that Congress's enumerated power under section 8 of Article I to make uniform rules relating to bankruptcy supersedes state's claim of sovereign immunity, thus allowing the bankrupt estate to sue for a debt owed by the community college. Lib. (O'Connor voted with the liberal bloc.)

Chamber of Commerce of United States of America v. Whiting, 563 U.S. ____ (2011). Arizona law providing for suspension or revocation of licenses of businesses employing illegal aliens held not preempted by federal immigration laws. (This was a 5–3 decision that divided along ideological lines, with Justice Kagan taking no part in the consideration of the case.) Con.

Federal Maritime Commission v. South Carolina State Ports Authority, 535 U.S. 743 (2002). Held that a federal administrative agency tasked with enforcing the federal maritime law did not have jurisdiction over a state authority clothed with the sovereign immunity of the state. Con.

Pliva v. Mensing, 564 U.S. ____ (2011). State tort lawsuit against a manufacturer of generic drugs for an inadequate warning label held preempted by a federal requirement that generic manufacturers use same label as the parallel brand name drug. Con.

Tennessee v. Lane, 541 U.S. 509 (2004). Held that a suit to require a government to provide access to its facilities, based on the due process clause of the Fourteenth Amendment, did not violate a state's sovereign immunity since, unlike the Garrett case described above, Congress had ample evidence of a denial of access when it authorized such suits. Lib. (O'Connor voted with the liberal bloc.)

Freedom of Expression

Ashcroft v. American Civil Liberties Union, 542 U.S. 656 (2004). Held that the federal Child Online Protection Act likely violated the First Amendment because it was overly broad, denying adults material to which they would be entitled under the First Amendment, given that there were likely other means available to protect children, such as blocking software. Crossover.

Boy Scouts of America v. Dale, 530 U.S. 640 (2000). Held that discrimination by Boy Scouts of America against gays is protected under freedom of expressive association given the organization's message that homosexuality is wrong. Con.

Garcetti v. Ceballos, 547 U.S. 410 (2006). Held that First Amendment does not protect a public employee's right of free speech unless it is engaged in as a private citizen. Con.

Legal Services Corp. v. Velazquez, 531 U.S. 533 (2001). Held that funding restrictions on Legal Services Corp. that prevented attorneys from representing clients to challenge or amend existing welfare laws or regulations violated First Amendment. Lib. (Kennedy voted with the liberal bloc.)

Lorillard Tobacco v. Reilly, 533 U.S. 525 (2001). Held that attorney general of Massachusetts failed to show that advertising regulations for smokeless tobacco and cigars were not more extensive than necessary to advance the state's interest in preventing underage tobacco use. Con.

Morse v. Frederick, 551 U.S. 393 (2007). Held that public school officials did not violate a student's First Amendment rights when it sanctioned him for displaying a sign at a school sponsored event that could have been interpreted as endorsing the use of illegal drugs. Con.

Thompson v. Western States Medical Center, 535 U.S. 357 (2002). Held that the First Amendment rights of certain licensed pharmacists who specialized in providing compounded drugs were violated by a prohibition in the federal Food and Drug Administration Modernization Act against advertising or promotion of such drugs since there was no evidence that less severe restrictions might not have served the government's interest in avoiding interference with the drug approval process. Crossover.

Gun Ownership Rights

District of Columbia v. Heller, 554 U.S. 570 (2008). Held that the Second Amendment provides for an individual right to bear arms. Con.

Immigration

Demore v. Kim, 538 U.S. 510 (2003). Civil detention without bail authorized by the Immigration and Nationality Act, pending the deportation hearing of a resident alien, did not violate alien's Liberty interest protected by the Due Process clause of the Fourteenth Amendment; alien had been convicted of a crime constituting an aggravated felony under the act. Con.

Native American Rights

Idaho v. United States, 533 U.S. 262 (2001). Executive Order was clear enough that national government held title to underlying portion of river and lake beds in trust for Coeur d'Alene tribe; dissent argued that the Order was not clear enough to divest a State of its sovereign interest in land. Lib. (O'Connor voted with the liberal bloc.)

Political Process/Campaign Finance Reform

Arizona Free Enterprise v. Bennett, 564 U.S. ____ (2011). Declared unconstitutional the provision in Arizona's campaign finance law providing additional funds for publicly financed candidates facing wealthy, privately financed candidates. Con.

Bush v. Gore, 531 U.S. 98 (2000). Put a halt to the statewide recount ordered by the Florida State Supreme Court on theory that Florida intended to meet federal law that would allow Florida's electoral votes to go unchallenged if the votes were filed with Congress by December 12 and therefore there was no time left for the recount. Con.

Citizens United v. Federal Election Commission, 558 U.S.____ (2010). Voided as a violation of the First Amendment a provision in Bi-Partisan Campaign Reform Act of 2002 that prohibited independent corporate expenditures prior to primary and general elections and overruled earlier holdings of the Court to the contrary. Con.

Davis v. Federal Election Commission, 554 U.S. 724 (2008). Voided an amendment to the Campaign Finance Law that allowed less wealthy candidates to accept higher contribution amounts when running against a wealthy, self-financing candidate. Con.

Federal Election Commission v. Colorado Republican Federal Campaign Committee, 533 U.S. 431 (2001). Held that a political party's coordinated expenditures may be restricted to minimize circumvention of federal campaign contribution limits without violating the First Amendment. Lib. (O'Connor voted with the liberal bloc.)

Federal Election Commission v. Wisconsin Right to Life, 551 U.S. 449 (2007). Upheld as an applied challenge to a provision of campaign finance law that prohibited advertisements by corporations within sixty days of a general election on ground that ad was a genuine issue ad and therefore protected by the First Amendment; effectively eliminated bright line rule established by the prohibition. Con.

McConnell v. Federal Election Commission, 540 U.S. 93 (2003). Upheld all major provisions of the Bi-Partisan Campaign Reform Act of 2002 against First Amendment challenges; partially overturned by *Citizens United v. Federal Election Commission*. Lib. (O'Connor voted with the liberal bloc.)

Republican Party of Minnesota v. White, 536 U.S. 765 (2002). Held that a canon of conduct for candidates for judicial office in Minnesota that prohibits candidates from stating their position on contested legal and political matters unconstitutionally infringes on candidates' right of free expression. Con.

Procedural Due Process

Board of Education v. Earl, 536 U.S. 822 (2002). Requiring all students who participate in competitive extracurricular activities to submit to a blanket drug testing program did not violate the Fourth Amendment's prohibition of unreasonable searches and seizures. Crossover.

Caperton v. Massey, 556 U.S. ____ (2009). Refusal of state high court judge to recuse himself from a case in which one of the litigants had provided him with a huge amount of financial support held to violate other litigant's due process rights under the Fourteenth Amendment. Lib. (Kennedy voted with liberal bloc.)

Dusenberry v. United States, 534 U.S. 161 (2002). The FBI satisfied due process when it sent a certified letter to a prisoner's place of incarceration notifying him of an impending cash forfeiture; the prisoner never received the notice. Con.

Property Rights

Kelo v. City of New London, 545 U.S. 469 (2005). Upheld condemnation of 19-acre parcel of land comprising a mixed neighborhood of commercial and residential properties for an economic development project intended to revitalize downtown area; project had been challenged as not being a public use for which eminent domain was appropriate. Lib. (Kennedy voted with the liberal bloc.)

Philip Morris USA v. Williams, 549 U.S. 346 (2007). Held that punitive damage award against Philip Morris for wrongful death of longtime smoker violated due process because, while jury could consider harm to nonparties in weighing outrageousness of defendant's behavior, it could not award punitive damages based on the actual harm to nonparties—dissent argued that this was a distinction without a difference. Crossover.

Sentencing

United States v. Booker, 543 U.S. 220 (2005). A defendant's right to a trial by jury is unconstitutionally denied when an enhanced sentence is rendered under the U.S. Sentencing Guidelines based on a fact not reviewed by a jury; the guidelines themselves are constitutional only to the extent that they are advisory, not mandatory. Crossover.

Separation of Powers

Boumediene v. Bush, 553 U.S. 723 (2008). Voided federal law that purported to withdraw habeas corpus jurisdiction from federal courts with respect to Guantanamo prisoners, citing critical role of judiciary in such proceedings and historic importance of habeas corpus. Lib. (Kennedy voted with the liberal bloc.)

Standing

Arizona Christian School Organization v. Winn, 563 U.S. ____ (2011). Held that taxpayers did not have standing to challenge an Arizona law providing tax credits for contributions to school tuition organizations, which applied the funds to subsidize religious education. Con.

Hein v. Freedom from Religion Foundation, 551 U.S. 587 (2007). Taxpayers do not have standing to bring an Establishment clause challenge against executive branch actions funded by appropriations for general and administrative expenses. Con.

State Action

Brentwood Academy v. Tennessee Secondary School Association, 531 U.S. 288 (2001). Statewide association incorporated to regulate interscholastic athletic competition among public and private secondary schools engaged in state action when it enforced a rule against a member school. Lib. (O'Connor voted with the liberal bloc.)

Notes

1. Some Foundational Ideas

1. Oliver Wendell Holmes Jr., "The Path of Law" 10 *Harvard L. Rev.* 457, 461 (1896–97).

2. *Id.* at 459.

3. Keith E. Whittington, *Constitutional Interpretation* 8 (University Press of Kansas 1999).

4. *Rumsfeld v. Forum for Academic and Institutional Rights, Inc.*, 547 U.S. 47 (2006).

5. *Id.* at 58.

6. *Id.* at 59–60.

7. *Crane v. Kentucky*, 476 U.S. 683 (1985).

2. The Constitution and Its Amendments: An Overview

1. Howard Fineman, *The Thirteen American Arguments* 42 (Random House 2008).

2. Gordon S. Wood, *The Creation of the American Republic* 405 (University of North Carolina Press 1998).

3. *Id.* at 473.

4. *The Federalist No. 1*, at 89 (Alexander Hamilton) (Benjamin F. Wright ed., 1961).

5. David O. Stewart, *The Summer of 1787* 163 (Simon & Schuster 2007).

6. Carol Berkin, *A Brilliant Solution* 131 (Harcourt 2003).

7. *Id.* at 150.

8. *Id.*

9. David Brian Robertson, *The Constitution and America's Destiny* 101 (Cambridge University Press 2005).

10. *Id.*

11. James Madison, *Notes of Debates in the Federal Convention of 1787*, at 25 (intro. by Adrienne Koch, Ohio University Press 1966).

12. *Id.*

13. *Id.* at 123.

14. Jack N. Rakove, *Original Meanings* 19 (Alfred A. Knopf 1996).

15. *Id.* at 172.

16. *Ware v. Hilton*, 3 Dall. (3 U.S.) 199 (1796).

17. See, for example, *Goodridge v. Department of Public Health*, 440 Mass. 309 (2003).

18. Rakove, *supra* note 14, at 134.

19. Gregory E. Maggs, "A Concise Guide to the Federalist Papers as a Source of the Original Meaning of the United States Constitution," 87 B.U.L.Rev. 801, 802 (2007).

20. *U.S. Term Limits, Inc. v. Thornton*, 514 U.S. 779 at 846 (1995).

21. Akhil Reed Amar, *America's Constitution: A Biography* 5 (Random House 2005).

22. For a cogent presentation of this perspective, see Robert A. Dahl, *How Democratic Is the American Constitution* (Yale University Press 2001).

23. Sortoris Barber, "Constitutional Failure: Ultimately Attitudinal," in The Limits of Constitutional Democracy 27 (Jeffrey K. Tulis and Stephen Macedo eds., Princeton University Press 2010).

24. Henry Mayer, *All on Fire: William Lloyd Garrison and the Abolition of Slavery* 313 (St. Martin's Press 1998).

25. 9 Charles Francis Adams, *The Works of John Adams* 377–78 (1856) quoted in Donald Grier Stephenson Jr., *The Right to Vote* 60 (ABC-Clio 2004).

26. A letter from Adams to Jefferson quoted in Robert W. Bennett, "Counter-Conversationalism and the Sense of Difficulty," 95 *Nw.U.L.R.* 845, 858 n. 50 (2000–2001).

27. Harvey Strum, "Property Qualifications and Voting Behavior in New York, 1807–1816," *J. of the Early Republic* 347, 348 (1981).

28. Charles A. Beard, *An Economic Interpretation of the Constitution of the United States* 324 (intro. by Forrest McDonald, Free Press 1986).

29. Introductory Statement of Akhil Reed Amar in "Coloquium,"115 *Yale L.J.* 2009 (2006).

30. David McCullough, *John Adams* 564 (Simon & Schuster 2001).

31. During the balloting, one of the Federalist representatives, William Cooper, the father of James Fenimore Cooper, wrote "Had Burr done anything for himself, he would long ere have been President." Quoted in Edward J. Larson, *A Magnificent Catastrophe* 266 (Free Press 2007).

32. *The Federalist No. 51, supra* note 4, at 357.

33. *The Federalist No. 10, supra* note 4 at 135.

34. *Id.* at 131.

35. *Id.*

36. *Id.* at 136.

37. Tinsley Yarbrough, *John Marshall Harlan: Great Dissenter of the Warren Court* 149 (Oxford University Press 1992).

38. From an Address given by Justice Harlan on August 9, 1964, *id.* at 149.

39. Leonard W. Levy, *Origins of the Bill of Rights* 39 (Yale University Press 1999).

40. James Madison, Speech before Congress on June 8, 1789, in *The Annals of America* vol. 3 (Encyclopedia Britannica 1976) at 361.

41. Akhil Reed Amar, *The Bill of Rights* 29 (Yale University Press 1998).

42. Madison, *supra* note 11, at 360.

43. Quoted in Ralph Ketchem, *James Madison: A Biography* 291 (University Press of Virginia 1990).

44. The rejected Second Amendment provided that any change in congressional compensation would not be effective until after the next congressional election. Admirers of persistence will draw great comfort from the history of this proposal, which after lying dormant for 200 years, was finally ratified as the Twenty-seventh Amendment.

45. Levy, *supra* note 39.

46. *District of Columbia v. Heller,* 554 U.S. 570 (2008).

47. *Griswold v. Connecticut,* 381 U.S. 479 (1965).

48. Levy, *supra* note 39, at 242.

49. *Id.* at 254.

50. *Calder v. Bull,* 3 U.S. 386 at 388.

51. *Id.* at 399.

52. Charles L. Black, Jr., *A New Birth of Freedom: Human Rights Named and Unnamed* 38 (Yale University Press 1997).

53. Michael Stokes Paulsen, "How to Interpret the Constitution (and How Not to)" 115 *Yale L.J.* 2037, 2047–48 (2006).

54. "Tenth Amendment," in *The Oxford Companion to the Supreme Court of the United States*, 2nd ed., 1007 (Oxford University Press 2005).

55. *Hammer v. Dagenhart*, 247 U.S. 251 (1917).

56. *Id.* at 275.

57. *United States v. Darby Lumber Co.*, 312 U.S. 100, at 124 (1941).

58. U.S. Senate, *Confirmation of Federal Judges: Hearings before the Committee on the Judiciary of the United States Senate*, 97th Cong., 2nd sess., 1982, 92 quoted in James B. Staab, *The Political Thought of Justice Scalia* 230 (Rowman & Littlefield 2006).

59. See *Pollock v. Farmers' Loan Trust Co.*, 158 U.S. 601 (1895).

60. *Minor v. Happersett*, 88 U.S. (21 Wall.) 162 (1875).

61. *Chisholm v. Georgia*, 2 U.S. (2 Dall.) 419 (1793).

62. John V. Orth, *The Judicial Power of the United States* 34 (Oxford University Press 1987).

63. *Id.* at 41.

64. *Osborn v. United States Bank*, 22 U.S. (9 Wheat.) 738 (1824).

65. *Louisiana ex rel. Elliot v. Jumel*, 107 U.S. 711 (1883).

66. *Id.* at 727–28, quoted in Orth, *supra* note 62, at 67.

67. *Hans v. Louisiana*, 134 U.S. 1 (1890).

68. *Ex Parte Young*, 209 U.S. 123 (1908).

69. *Id.* at 160, quoted in Orth, *supra* note 62, at 129–30.

70. *Edelman v. Jordan*, 415 U.S. 651 (1974).

71. *Seminole Tribe v. Florida*, 517 U.S. 44 (1996).

72. *Alden v. Maine*, 527 U.S. 706 (1999).

73. William P. Marshall, "Understanding Alden," 31 *Rutgers L.J.* 803. (2008).

74. *Jones v. Alfred H. Mayer Co.*, 392 U.S. 409 (1968).

75. *United States v. Harris*, 106 U.S. 629 (1883).

76. *Jones*, *supra* note 74, at 442.

77. *Giles v. Harris*, 189 U.S. 475, 488 (1903).

78. *Id.* at 488.

79. Michael Kent Curtis, *No State Shall Abridge* 31 (Duke University Press 1986).

80. *Barron v. Mayor and City of Baltimore*, 32 U.S. 243 (1833).

81. Curtis, *supra* note 79, at 23.

3. The Fourteenth Amendment

1. *U.S. v. Wong Kim Ark*, 169 U.S. 649 (1898).

2. *Lochner v. New York*, 198 U.S. 45 (1905).

3. *Lawrence v. Texas*, 539 U.S. 558 (2003).

4. Eric Foner, *Reconstruction* 257 (Harper & Row 1988).

5. Joseph B. James, *The Ratification of the Fourteenth Amendment* 2 (Mercer University Press 1984).

6. For a detailed description of the Black Codes see Foner, *supra* note 4, at 199–201.

7. *Id.* at 203–5.

8. *Id.* at 240.

9. Garrett Epps, *Democracy Reborn* 99 (Henry Holt and Co. 2006).

10. Eric Foner, *The Story of American Freedom* 105 (W. W. Norton 1998).

11. *Corfield v. Coryell*, 6 Fed. Cases 546, 551 (C.c.e.D. Pa. 1823).

12. *Cong. Globe*, 39th Cong., first sess., 2765–66 (1866), quoted in Michael Kent Curtis, *No State Shall Abridge* 88 (Duke University Press 1986).

13. Milton R. Konvitz, *Fundamental Rights* 23 (Rutgers University Press 2001).

14. *The Slaughterhouse Cases*, 83 U.S. (16 Wall.) 36 (1873).

15. *Id.* at 78.

16. *U.S. v. Cruikshank*, 92 U.S. 542 (1975).

17. *Romer v. Evans*, 517 U.S. 620 (1996).

18. *United States Department of Agriculture v. Moreno*, 413 U.S. 528 (1973).

19. *O'Lone v. Estate of Shabazz*, 482 U.S. 342, 357 (1987).

20. Michael Klarman, "An Interpretive History of Modern Equal Protection," 90 *Michigan L. Rev.* 213, 216 (1991).

21. *Bolling v. Sharpe*, 347 U.S. 497 (1954).

22. *U.S. v. Singleton*, 109 U.S. 3 (1883).

23. *Id.* at 58.

24. *Heart of Atlanta Motel v. United States*, 379 U.S. 241 (1964).

25. *U.S. v. Harris*, 106 U.S. 629 (1883).

26. *Shelley v. Kraemer*, 334 U.S. 1 (1948).

27. *Jackson v. Metropolitan Edison Co.*, 419 U.S. 345 (1974).

28. *Burton v. Wilmington Parking Authority*, 365 U.S. 715 (1961).

29. *Id.* at 722.

30. Laurence H. Tribe, *Constitutional Choices* 246 (Harvard University Press 1985).

31. *Caperton v. A. T. Massey Coal Co.*, 556 U.S. ____ (2009).

32. *Id.* at 15.

33. *Id.* at 16.

34. *Joint Anti-Fascist Refugee Committee v. McGrath*, 341 U.S. 123 (1951).

35. *Goldberg v. Kelly*, 397 U.S. 254 (1970).

36. *Board of Regents v. Roth*, 408 U.S. 564 (1972).

37. *Perry v. Sindermann*, 408 U.S. 593 (1972).

38. See *Chicago, Burlington and Quincy Railroad Co.*, 166 U.S. 226 (1897).

39. See *Gitlow v. New York*, 268 U.S. 652 (1925).

40. *Palko v. Connecticut*, 302 U.S. 319 (1937).

41. *Id.* at 325.

42. *Id.*

43. See *Benton v. Maryland*, 395 U.S. 784 (1969).

44. *Malloy v. Hogan*, 378 U.S. 1 (1964).

45. *Adamson v. California*, 332 U.S. 46 (1947).

46. *Id.* at 89.

47. Quoted in Ralph A. Rossum, *Antonin Scalia's Jurisprudence* 167 (University Press of Kansas 2006).

48. *Poe v. Ullman*, 367 U.S. 497 at 542 (1961).

49. *Id.* at 539.

50. *Roe v. Wade*, 410 U.S. 113 (1973).

51. For Exhibit A in the case of humanity v. Justice McReynolds, see *The Forgotten Memoir of John Knox*, a memoir of a year spent with McReynolds by one of his law clerks. The book was edited by Dennis Hutchinson and David J. Garrow and published by the University of Chicago Press in 2002.

52. *Meyer v. Nebraska*, 262 U.S. 390 (1923).

53. Konvitz, *supra* note 13, at 62.

54. *Meyer*, 262 U.S. at 399.

55. *Pierce v. Society of Sisters*, 268 U.S. 510 (1925).

56. *Id.* at 535.

57. Melvin I. Urofsky, *Louis D. Brandeis: A Life* 399 (Pantheon Books 2009).

58. *Lochner, supra* note 2, at 45.

59. *Holden v. Hardy*, 169 U.S. 366 (1898).

60. *Lochner, supra* note 2, at 56.

61. *Coppage v. Kansas*, 236 U.S. 1 (1915).

62. *West Coast Hotel Co. v. Parrish*, 300 U.S. 379 (1937).

63. *Washington v. Glucksburg*, 521 U.S. 702 (1997).

64. *Id.* at 789.

65. *Id.* at 735.

66. *Lawrence v. Texas*, 539 U.S. 558 (2003).

67. *Bowers v. Hardwick*, 478 U.S. 186 (1986).

68. *Lawrence*, 539 U.S. at 562.

69. *Id.* at 578.

70. *Id.*

71. *Duncan v. Louisiana*, 391 U.S. 182 (1967).

72. *Id.* at 173.

73. *Carrington v. Rash*, 380 U.S. 89, 98–99 (1964).

74. *Kelo v. City of New London, Connecticut*, 545 U.S. 125 (2005).

75. *Id.* at 475.

76. See Martin E. Gold and Lynne B. Sagalyn, "The Use and Abuse of Blight in Eminent Domain," 38 *Fordham Urban L.J.* 1119 (2011).

77. *City of Boerne v. Flores*, 521 U.S. 507, 520 (1997).

78. *Board of Trustees of the University of Alabama v. Garrett*, 531 U.S. 356 (2001).

79. *Id.*

80. *Tennessee v. Lane*, 541 U.S. 509 (2004).

4. The Supreme Court in the Constitutional Structure

1. James Madison, *Notes of Debates in the Federal Convention of 1787*, 73 (intro. by Adrienne Koch, Ohio University Press 1966).

2. *Id.* at 344.

3. See Jack Rakove, *Original Meanings* 246 (Alfred A. Knopf 1996).

4. Madison, *supra* note 1, at 61.

5. *Raines v. Byrd*, 521 U.S. 811 (1997).

6. *Clinton v. City of New York*, 524 U.S. 417 (1998)

7. *Hein v. Freedom from Religion Foundation, Inc.*, 551 U.S. 1 (2007).

8. *Id.* at 2.

9. See *Flast v. Cohen*, 392 U.S. 83 (1968).

10. *Arizona Tuition School Organization v. Winn*, 563 U.S. ___ (2011).

11. *Marbury v. Madison*, 5 U.S. 137, 170 (1803).

12. *Baker v. Carr*, 369 U.S. 186 (1962).

13. *Id.* at 217.

14. See *Davis v. Bandemer*, 478 U.S. 109 (1986) and *Vieth v. Jubelirer*, 541 U.S. 267 (2004).

15. *Baker v. Carr*, 369 U.S. 186, 217 (1962).

16. Bob Woodward and Scott Armstrong, *The Brethren* 126 (Simon and Schuster 1979).

17. See *Luther v. Borden*, 48 U.S. (7 Howard) 1 (1849).

18. See *Charlton v. Kelly*, 229 U.S. 447 (1913).

19. See *Goldwater v. Carter*, 444 U.S. 996 (1979).

20. *Swift v. Tyson*, 41 U.S. (16 Pet.) 1 (1842).

21. *Erie Railroad v. Tompkins*, 304 U.S. 64 (1938).

22. *The Federalist No. 78*, at 490 (Alexander Hamilton) (Benjamin F. Wright ed., 1961).

23. *Id., No. 81*, at 508.

24. *Worcester v. Georgia*, 31 U.S. (6 Pet.) 515 (1832).

25. Abraham Lincoln, *Executive Message to Congress*, July 4, 1861, at 17, in *The Portable Abraham Lincoln* 216 (Andrew Delbanco ed., Viking Penguin 1992).

26. See *Norman v. Baltimore and Ohio Railroad Company*, 294 U.S. 240 (1935) and *Nortz v. United States*, 294 U.S. 317.

27. *Powell v. McCormick*, 395 U.S. 486 (1969).

28. *Youngstown Sheet & Tube Co. v. Sawyer*, 343 U.S. 579 (1952).

29. *United States v. Nixon*, 418 U.S. 683 (1974).

30. *New York Times Co. v. United States*, 403 U.S. 713 (1971).

31. *Bowsher v. Synar*, 478 U.S. 714 (1986).

32. *Clinton*, 524 U.S. at 417.

33. *Immigration & Naturalization Service v. Chadha*, 462 U.S. 919 (1983).

34. Marian McKenna, *Franklin Roosevelt and the Great Constitutional War* 96 (Fordham University Press 2002).

35. Keith E. Whittington, *Constitutional Construction* 70 (Harvard University Press 1999).

36. *Marbury v. Madison*, 5 U.S. (1 Cr.) 137 (1803).

37. *Stuart v. Laird*, 5 U.S., (1 Cr.) 299 (1803).

38. Bruce Ackerman, *The Failure of the Founding Fathers* 9 (Belknap Press 2005).

39. *Id.* at 194.

40. *Id.* at 193–94.

41. *Id.* at 9.

42. *Id.*

43. *Martin v. Hunter's Lessee*, 14 U.S. (1Wheat.) 304 (1816).

44. *Fairfax's Devisee v. Hunter's Lessee*, 11 U.S. (7 Cranch) 603 (1813).

45. *Martin*, 14 U.S. (1 Wheat.), at 344.

46. *Brown v. Board of Education*, 347 U.S. 483 (1954).

47. *Cooper v. Aaron*, 358 U.S. 1 (1958).

48. *Id.* at 18.

49. Larry Kramer, *The People Themselves* 69 (Oxford University Press 2004).

50. *Id.* at 91.

51. *Id.* at 92.

52. *The Federalist No. 78, supra* note 22, at 491.

53. Quoted in *John Marshall: Major Opinions and Other Writings* 16 (Bobbs-Merrill Co. 1967).

54. For an excellent analysis of this internal discussion, see H. Jefferson Powell, *A Community Built on Words* 11–30 (University of Chicago Press 2002).

55. See *Dalton v. Specter*, 511 U.S. 462, 475 (1994) in which Chief Justice Rehnquist noted that discretionary decisions of the president, whether the discretion is derived from a statute or from the Constitution, are not subject to judicial review.

56. Alexander M. Bickel, *The Least Dangerous Branch* 18 (Bobbs-Merrill Co. 1962).

57. *Id.* at 16–17.

58. John Hart Ely, *Democracy and Distrust* 1 (Harvard University Press 1980).

59. Robert A. Dahl, "Decision-Making in a Democracy: The Supreme Court as a National Policy-Maker," 6 *J. of Public L.* 294 (1957).

60. *Id.* at 283.

61. Christopher L. Eisgruber, *Constitutional Self-Government* 58–59 (Harvard University Press 2001).

62. *Id.*

63. Frederick Schauer, "The Supreme Court 2005 Term, Forward: The Court's Agenda and the Nation's" 120 *Harvard L. Rev.* 5, 20 (2006).

64. *Id.* at 50.

65. Robert C. Post, "The Supreme Court 2002 Term, Forward: Fashioning the Legal Constitution: Culture, Courts, and Law" 117 *Harvard L. Rev.* 7 (2003–4).

66. Keith E. Whittington, *Political Foundations of Judicial Supremacy* 25 (Princeton University Press 2007).

67. Jeffrey Rosen, *The Most Democratic Branch* 210 (Oxford University Press 2006).

68. "A Conversation with Earl Warren" quoted in *Judges on Judging: Views from the Bench* 30 (David M. O'Brien ed., Chatham House 1997).

69. Bruce Allen Murphy, *The Legend and Life of William O. Douglas* 179–80 (Random House 2003).

70. Joyce Murdoch and Debby Price, *Courting Justice: Gay Men and Lesbians v. the Supreme Court* 43 (Basic Books 2001).

71. *Id.* at 53.

72. Richard Allan Baker, "The United States Congress Responds to Judicial Review," in *Constitutional Justice under Old Constitutions* 73 (Eivind Smith ed., Kluwer Law International 1995).

73. Murdoch and Price, *supra* note 70, at 115.

74. The information in this paragraph was compiled from entries in "Brief Biographies" section in Joan Biskupic and Elder Witt, *The Supreme Court at Work* (Congressional Quarterly 1997).

75. Justice Souter served only very briefly before being nominated to the Supreme Court but had served as a justice of the Supreme Court of New Hampshire from 1983 to 1990.

76. For a detailed record of Supreme Court nominations, see Denis Rutkus, Maureen Bearden, Sam Garrett, and Elizabeth Rybicki, *Supreme Court Nominations 1789– 2005* (The Capital Net 2007).

77. *Id.* at 7.

78. Jack E. Bronston, "A Citizen's Guide to the Supreme Court" (2006) (unpublished manuscript).

79. Christopher L. Eisgruber, *The Next Justice* (Princeton University Press 2007).

80. See *United States v. Butler,* 297 U.S. 1 (1936) (voiding the Agricultural Adjustment Act) and *Carter v. Carter Coal Company,* 298 U.S. 238 (1936) (voiding the Bituminous Coal Conservation Act).

81. See *N.L.R.B. v. Jones & Laughlin Steel Co., et al.,* 300 U.S. 1 (1937).

82. See *Steward Machine Company v. Davis,* 301 U.S. 548 (1937) (upholding by a 5–4 vote the Social Security Act's framework for unemployment compensation) and *Helvering et al. v. Davis,* 301 U.S. 619 (1937) (upholding by a 7–2 vote the retirement benefits program).

83. William H. Rehnquist, *The Supreme Court* 58–59 (Alfred A. Knopf 2001).

84. *Ledbetter v. Goodyear Tire,* 550 U.S. 618 (2007).

85. *Wabash, St. Louis and Pacific Railway Co. v. Illinois,* 118 U.S. 557 (1886).

86. *Employment Division, Department of Human Resources of Oregon v. Smith,* 494 U.S. 872 (1990).

87. *City of Boerne v. Flores,* 521 U.S. 507 (1997).

88. *Zurcher v. Stanford Daily,* 436 U.S. 547 (1978).

89. *Id.* at 567.

90. *Cutter v. Wilkinson,* 544 U.S. 709 (2005).

5. What the Court Does: The Stuff of Judicial Review

1. *McCulloch v. Maryland*, 17 U.S. (4 Wheat.) 316 (1819).

2. *Id.* at 421.

3. *Gibbons v. Ogden*, 22 U.S. (9 Wheat.) 1 (1824).

4. *Fletcher v. Peck*, 10 U.S. (6 Cr.) 87 (1810).

5. *Sturges v. Crowinshield*, 17 U.S. (4 Wheat.) 122 (1819).

6. *Charles River Bridge v. Proprietors of Warren Bridge*, 36 U.S. 420 (1837).

7. *Prigg v. Pennsylvania*, 16 Peters (41 U.S.) 539. For an excellent account of this case, see Paul Finkelman, *Story Telling on the Supreme Court: Prigg v. Pennsylvania and Justice Story's Judicial Nationalism*, 1994 *Sup. Ct. Rev.* 247 (1994).

8. *Hepburn v. Griswold*, 75 U.S. (8 Wall) 603 (1870).

9. *Knox v. Lee*, 79 U.S. 457, 542 (1870).

10. *Champion v. Ames*, 188 U.S. 321 (1903).

11. *United States v. E. C. Knight Co.*, 156 U.S. 1 (1895).

12. *Id.* at 16.

13. *Swift & Co. v. United States*, 196 U.S. 375 (1905).

14. *Id. at* 398.

15. *Northern Securities Co. v. United States*, 193 U.S. 197 (1904).

16. Hammer v. Dagenhart, 247 U.S. 251 (1918).

17. *Id.* at 280.

18. *Carter v. Carter Coal Co.*, 298 U.S. 238 (1936).

19. *NLRB v. Jones & Laughlin*, 301 U.S. 1 (1937).

20. *Wickard v. Filburn*, 317 U.S. 111 (1942).

21. *United States v. Lopez*, 514 U.S. 549 (1995).

22. *United States v. Morrison*, 529 U.S. 598 (2000).

23. Ernest A. Young, "Just Blowing Smoke?" in *The Supreme Court Review 2005*, at 2 (University of Chicago Press 2005).

24. *Reno v. Condon*, 528 U.S. 141 (2000).

25. *Gonzales v. Raich*, 545 U.S. 1 (2005).

26. Mark Tushnet, *A Court Divided* 277 (W.W. Norton 2005).

27. *United States v. Butler*, 297 U.S. 1 (1936).

28. *South Dakota v. Dole*, 483 U.S. 203 (1987).

29. Thomas Lundmark, *Power and Rights in U.S. Constitutional Law* 19 (Oxford University Press 2008).

30. *New York v. United States*, 326 U.S. 572 (1946).

31. *National League of Cities v. Usery*, 426 U.S. 833 (1976).

32. *Garcia v. San Antonio Metropolitan Transit Authority*, 469 U.S. 528 (1985).

33. *Id.* at 556.

34. *Printz v. United States*, 521 U.S. 898 (1997).

35. *New York v. United States*, 505 U.S. 144 (1991).

36. *Warner-Lambert Co. v. Kent*, 552 U.S. 440 (2008).

37. *Cooley v. Board of Wardens of the Port of Philadelphia et al.*, 53 U.S. (12 Howard) 299 (1851).

38. *Id.* at 319.

39. *Maine v. Taylor*, 477 U.S. 131 (1986).

40. See, for example, *Bibb v. Navajo Freight Lines, Inc.*, 359 U.S. 520 (1959).

41. *Humphrey's Executor v. United States*, 295 U.S. 602 (1935).

42. *Bowsher v. Synar*, 478 U.S. 714, 726–27 (1986).

43. *Clinton v. Jones*, 520 U.S. 681 (1997).

44. *Morrison v. Olson*, 487 U.S. 654 (1988).

45. *Clinton v. City of New York*, 524 U.S. 417 (1998).

46. *Immigration and Naturalization Service v. Chadha*, 462 U.S. 919 (1983).

47. *Boumedienne v. Bush*, 553 U.S. 723 (2008).

48. *Id.* at 797.

49. *Id.* at 827.

50. *Id.* at 828.

51. *Id.* at 842.

52. *Finstuen v. Crutcher*, 496 F.3d 1139 (10th Cir. 2007).

53. *Nevada v. Hall*, 440 U.S. 410 (1979).

54. *San Antonio Independent School Dist. v. Rodriguez*, 411 U.S. 1 (1973).

55. See, for example, *Turner v. Safley*, 482 U.S. 78 (1987) (upholding the right of prisoners to marry even though prison regulations are generally subject only to rational basis review).

56. *Wooley v. Maynard*, 430 U.S. 705, 713 (1977).

57. *Roth v. United States*, 354 U.S. 476 (1957).

58. *Jacobellis v. Ohio*, 378 U.S. 184, 197 (1964).

59. *Paris Adult Theater v. Slaton*, 413 U.S. 49 (1973).

60. *Id.* at 112–13.

61. *Korematsu v. United States*, 323 U.S. 214 (1944).

62. *Id.* at 239.

63. *Masses Publishing Co. v. Patten*, 244 F. Supp. 535 (S.D.N.Y.) 1917, reversed, 246 F. 24 (2d Cir. 1917).

64. Gerald Gunther, *Learned Hand and the Origins of Modern First Amendment Doctrine* 27 Stan. L. Rev. *719* (1975).

65. *Abrams v. United States*, 250 U.S. 616 (1919).

66. *Brandenburg v. Ohio*, 395 U.S. 444 (1969).

67. *Id.* at 447.

68. *Chaplinsky v. New Hampshire*, 315 U.S. 568 (1942).

69. *Cohen v. California*, 403 U.S. 15 (1971).

70. *Gooding v. Wilson*, 405 U.S. 518 (1972).

71. *New York Times v. Sullivan*, 376 U.S. 254 (1964).

72. *Beauharnais v. Illinois*, 343 U.S. 250 (1952).

73. *Id.* at 252.

74. See, for example, *Saxe v. State College Area School District*, 240 F.3d 200 (3d Cir. 2001).

75. *Virginia v. Black*, 538 U.S. 343 (2003).

76. See *United States v. O'Brien*, 391 U.S. 367 (1968).

77. *Cal. Democratic Party v. Jones*, 530 U.S. 567 (2000).

78. See *Hurley v. Irish-American Gay, Lesbian and Bisexual Group of Boston, Inc.*, 515 U.S. 557 (1995) and *Boy Scouts of America v. Dale*, 530 U.S. 640 (2000).

79. *Romer v. Evans*, 517 U.S. 620 (1996).

80. See *Edwards v. California*, 314 U.S. 160 (1941).

81. See *Saenz v. Roe*, 526 U.S. 489 (1998).

82. *Id.*

83. *Chandler v. Florida*, 449 U.S. 560 (1981).

84. *Bartnicki v. Vopper*, 532 U.S. 514 (2001).

85. *Snyder v. Phelps*, 562 U.S. ____ (2011).

86. *Frisby v. Schultz*, 487 U.S. 474 (1988).

87. *Good News Club v. Millford Central School*, 533 U.S. 98 (2001).

88. *State Farm Mutual Automobile Insurance Co. v. Campbell*, 538 U.S. 408, 425 (2003).

89. *Lockyer v. Andrade*, 538 U.S. 63 (2003).

90. *Id.* at 83.

91. *Mapp v. Ohio*, 367 U.S. 643 (1961).

92. *Miranda v. Arizona*, 384 U.S. 436 (1966).

93. *J.D.B. v. North Carolina*, 564 U.S. ____ (2011).

94. *Terry v. Ohio*, 292 U.S. 1 (1968).

95. *United States v. Wade*, 388 U.S. 218 (1967).

96. *Wesberry v. Sanders*, 376 U.S. 1 (1964); *Reynolds v. Sims*, 377 U.S. 533 (1964).

97. *Citizens United v. Federal Election Commission*, 558 U.S. ____ (2010).

98. *U.S. Term Limits, Inc. v. Thornton*, 514 U.S. 779 (1995).

99. *Elrod v. Burns*, 427 U.S. 347 (1976).

100. See the Shaw line of cases beginning with *Shaw v. Reno*, 509 U.S. 630 (1993).

101. *Bush v. Gore*, 531 U.S. 98 (2000).

102. *Munro v. Socialist Workers Party*, 479 U.S. 189 (1986).

103. *Jenness v. Fortson*, 403 U.S. 341 (1971).

104. *Davis v. Bandemer*, 478 U.S. 109 (1986); *Vieth v. Jubelirer*, 541 U.S. 267 (2004).

105. *Arkansas Educational Television Commission v. Forbes*, 523 U.S. 666 (1998).

106. *Republican Party of Minnesota v. White*, 536 U.S. 765 (2002).

107. For a recitation of cases favoring the major parties, see Walter M. Frank, *Individual Rights and the Political Process* 35 S.U.L.Rev. 47, 48 n. 4 (2005).

108. *Clingman v. Beaver*, 544 U.S. 581 (2005).

109. *Tashjian v. Republican Party of Connecticut*, 479 U.S. 208 (1986).

110. *U.S. Term Limits*, 514 U.S. 779.

111. *Id.* at 803.

112. *Id.* at 849.

113. Robert H. Jackson, *The Supreme Court in the American System of Government* 81 (Harper & Row 1955).

114. Robert G. McClosky, *The American Supreme Court* 64 (3rd ed., University of Chicago Press 2000).

115. Gerald Rosenberg, *The Hollow Hope: Can Courts Bring about Social Change?* 336 (University of Chicago Press 1993).

116. Michael J. Klarman, "*How Great Were the 'Great' Marshall Court Decisions?*" 87 *Va. L. Rev.* 1111, 1181–82 (2001).

117. *Olmstead v. United States*, 277 U.S. 438 at 478 (1928).

118. Noah Feldman, *Scorpions* 185 (Grand Central Publishing 2010).

119. *Reno v. American Civil Liberties Union*, 521 U.S. 844 (1997).

120. *Euclid v. Amber Realty Co.*, 272 U.S. 365 (1926).

121. Randall L. Kennedy, "Race and the Fourteenth Amendment" 282, in *A Less Than Perfect Union* (Jules Lobel ed., 1988).

122. Quoted in Louis Fisher, *Constitutional Dialogues* 11 (Princeton University Press 1988).

123. Jim Newton, *Justice for All: Earl Warren and the Nation He Made* 426–28 (Riverhead Books 2006).

124. *Bouie v. City of Columbia*, 378 U.S. 347, 367 (1964).

6. The Federal Judicial System

1. *Crowell v. Benson*, 285 U.S. 22 (1932).

2. *Pennoyer v. Neff*, 95 U.S. 714 (1877).

3. David P. Currie, *The Constitution in the Supreme Court: 1789–1888*, at 366 (University of Chicago Press 1985).

4. *J. McIntyre Machinery, Ltd. v. Nicastro*, 564 U.S. ____ (2011).

5. See Erwin C. Surrency, *History of the Federal Courts* 23 (Oceana Publications 2002).

6. *Id.* at 5.

7. *Herring v. United States*, 555 U.S. 135 (2009).

8. Quoted from article by Adam Liptak, "Supreme Court Edging Closer to Repeal of Evidence Ruling," *N. Y. Times*, January 31, 2009, at A1.

9. *Herring*, 555 U.S. at 9.

10. *Kitzmiller v. Dover Area School District*, 400 F. Supp. 2d 707 (2005).

7. Life on the Court

1. Linda Greenhouse, "Courtside Seat," *N.Y. Times*, Week in Review, July 13, 2008, at 1.

2. Todd C. Peppers, *Courtiers of the Marble Palace* 191 (Stanford University Press 2006).

3. *Id.* at 209.

4. *Id.* at 211.

5. Lucas A. Powe Jr., *The Warren Court and American Politics* 140 (Harvard University Press 2000).

6. Artemus Ward, *Deciding to Leave* 209 (S.U.NY. Press 2003).

7. Marian McKenna, *Franklin Roosevelt and the Great Constitutional War* 130 (Fordham University Press 2002).

8. Noah Feldman, *Scorpions* 386–88 (Grand Central Publishing 2010).

9. William O. Douglas, *The Court Years 1939–1975*, at 18 (Random House 1980).

10. Christopher L. Eisgruber, *Constitutional Self-Government* 59 (Harvard University Press 2001).

11. Jeffrey Toobin, *The Nine* 128–29 (Doubleday 2007).

12. Melvin Urofsky, *Felix Frankfurter: Judicial Restraint and Individual Liberty* 47 (Twayne Publishers 1991).

13. *Id.* at 48.

14. In conference, Potter Stewart once remarked, Justice Frankfurter often spoke for fifty minutes if a case really interested him, the exact length of his lecture class (Urofsky, *supra* note 12, at 48).

15. Earl Warren, *The Memoirs of Earl Warren* 286 (Doubleday 1977).

16. Richard Kluger, *Simple Justice* 702 (Vintage Books 2004).

17. Melvin I. Urofsky, *Louis D. Brandeis, A Life* 480 (Pantheon Books 2009).

8. The Litigation Process: From Complaint to Supreme Court Opinion

1. Richard Kluger, *Simple Justice* (Vintage Books 2004).

2. *The National Association for the Advancement of Colored People v. Button*, 371 U.S. 415 (1963).

3. *Id.* at 429.

4. *Plessy v. Ferguson*, 163 U.S. 537 (1896).

5. Peter Irons, *The Courage of Their Convictions* 31 (Penguin Books 1990).

6. *Near v. Minnesota*, 183 U.S. 697 (1931).

7. Richard Allan Baker, "The United States Congress Responds to Judicial Review," in *Constitutional Justice under Old Constitutions* 55 (Eivind Smith ed., Kluwer Law International 1995).

8. *Gideon v. Wainwright*, 372 U.S. 335 (1963).

9. H. W. Perry Jr., *Deciding to Decide* 163 (Harvard University Press 1991).

10. *Id.* at 170.

11. See Jeffrey A. Segal and Harold J. Spaeth, *The Supreme Court and the Attitudinal Model* 252–55 (Cambridge University Press 2002).

12. The Rule of Four was probably adopted after the passage of the Judiciary Act of 1891 as a way of dealing with the Court's newly awarded discretionary jurisdiction.

13. *Id.* at 157.

14. Neal Devins and Louis Fisher, *The Democratic Constitution* 36 (Oxford University Press 2004).

15. Paul M. Collins Jr., *Friends of the Supreme Court: Interest Groups and Judicial Decision Making* (Oxford University Press 2008).

16. *Runyon v. McCrary*, 427 U.S. 160 (1976).

17. James F. Simon, *The Center Holds* 40 (Simon & Schuster 1995).

18. *Id.* at 40–42.

19. *Grutter v. Bollinger*, 539 U.S. 306 (2003).

20. *Terry v. Ohio*, 392 U.S. 1 (1968).

21. See a discussion of Amicus Brief by Stephen L. Wasby, in *The Oxford Companion to the Supreme Court of the United States*, 2nd ed. (Kermit Hall ed., Oxford University Press 2005) at 38.

22. Collins, *supra* note 15, at 27.

23. Maurice Baxter, *Daniel Webster and the Supreme Court* 173 (University of Massachusetts Press 1966).

24. Letter from Story to Stephen White, March 3, 1819, quoted in *id.* at 175.

25. Quoted in Richard N. Current, "The Dartmouth College Case," in *Quarrels That Have Shaped the Constitution* 33 (John Garrity ed., Harper & Row 1962).

26. *Id.*

27. Retold by David O'Brien in *Judges on Judging* 43 (D. M. O'Brien ed., Chatham House 1997).

28. Bernard Schwartz, *Decision* 16 (Oxford University Press 1996).

29. John M. Harlan, "Address before the Judicial Conference of the Fourth Circuit, Asheville, North Carolina, June 24, 1955," in *The Supreme Court: Views from Inside* 57 (Alan Westin ed., Greenwood Press 1961).

30. *Id.*

31. *Id.* at 58.

32. See Timothy R. Johnson, Paul Wahlbeck, and James Spriggs II, *The Influence of Oral Arguments on the U.S. Supreme Court*, 100 *Am. Pol. Sci. Rev.* 99, 101 (February 2006).

33. *Id.* at 99.

34. Schwartz, *supra* note 28, at 89.

35. *R.A.V. v. St. Paul*, 505 U.S. 377, at 415. (1992).

36. Samuel Estreicher and Tristan Pelham-Webb, "The Wisdom of Soft Judicial Power: Mr. Justice Powell Concurring" (N.Y.U. Public Law and Legal Theory Working Papers 102 (2008), which can be found online at http://lsr.nellco.org/nyu/plltwp/papers/102.

37. *Branzburg v. Hayes*, 408 U.S. 665 (1972).

38. See Haig Bosmajian, *Metaphor and Reason in Judicial Opinions* 49 (Southern Illinois University Press 1992).

39. Robert H. Jackson, "The Supreme Court as a Unit of Government," in Westin, *supra* note 29, at 27.

40. Speech of Justice Scalia given at Supreme Historical Society on June 13, 1994, quoted in Forrest Maltzman et al., *Crafting Law on the Supreme Court* 61 (Cambridge University Press 2000).

41. *Id.* at 16.

42. Andrew L. Kaufman, *Cardozo* 477–78 (Harvard University Press 1998).

43. *Furman v. Georgia*, 408 U.S. 238 (1972).

44. *Gregg v. Georgia*, 428 U.S. 153 (1976).

45. *Planned Parenthood of Southeastern Pennsylvania v. Casey*, 505 U.S. 833 (1992).

46. Maltzman et al., *supra* note 40, at 69.

47. *Id.*

48. Remarks of Justice Powell at the Southwest Legal Conference, May 1, 1980, reprinted in O'Brien, *supra* note 27, at 84.

49. Remarks of Chief Justice Rehnquist for the Ninth Annual Will E. Orgain Lecture at the University of Texas School of Law, May 12, 1976, reprinted in O'Brien, *supra* note 27, at 89–90.

50. *Citizens United v. Federal Election Commission*, 558 U.S. ____ (2010).

51. *Safford Unified School District No. 1 v. April Redding*, 557 U.S. ____ (2009).

9. The Toolbox for Judicial Decision Making

1. Sotirios A. Barber and James E. Fleming, *Constitutional Interpretation* 5 (Oxford University Press 2007).

2. William O. Douglas, *The Court Years 1939–1975*, at 8 (Random House 1980).

3. For an argument as to why Black's reliance on the Privileges and Immunities clause is not persuasive, see Akhil Reed Amar, *The Bill of Rights* 174–80 (Yale University Press 1998).

4. *Muller v. Oregon*, 208 U.S. 412 (1908).

5. See *Schaefer v. United States*, 251 U.S. 466 (1920); *Pierce v. United States*, 252 U.S. 239 (1920); and *Gilbert v. State of Minnesota*, 254 U.S. 325 (1920).

6. Quoted in *Brandeis on Democracy* 234 (Philippa Strum ed., University Press of Kansas 1995).

7. George D. Braden, "The Search for Objectivity in Constitutional Law," in *Judicial Review and the Supreme Court* 197 (Leonard W. Levy ed., Harper Torchbooks 1967).

8. William J. Brennan, *"Speech to the Text and Teaching Symposium of Georgetown University delivered October 12, 1985,"* in *Originalism: A Quarter-Century of Debate* 56 (Steven G. Calabresi ed., Regnery 2007).

9. James F. Simon, *The Center Holds* 49–50 (Simon & Schuster, 1995).

10. James B. Staab, *The Political Thought of Justice Scalia* 2 (Rowman and Littlefield 2006).

11. Joan Biskupic, *American Original: The Life and Constitution of Supreme Court Justice Antonin Scalia* 21 (Farrar, Straus and Giroux 2009).

12. Charles L. Black Jr., *Structure and Relationship in Constitutional Law* 7 (Louisiana State University Press 1969).

13. William Blackstone, *Commentaries*, 1:60, quoted in Jonathan O'Neill, *Originalism in American Law and Politics* 14 (Johns Hopkins University Press 2005).

14. *Id.*

15. Akhil Reed Amar, "America's Constitution and the Yale School of Constitutional Interpretation" 115 *Yale L.J.* 1997, 2009 (2006).

16. *Kelo v. City of New London, Connecticut*, 545 U.S. 469 at 479–80 (2005).

17. David A. Strauss, "Common Law Constitutional Interpretation," 63 *U. Chi. L. Rev.* 877, 881 (1996).

18. Quoted in introduction to James Madison, *Notes of Debates in the Federal Convention of 1787*, at xxiii (intro. by Adrienne Koch, Ohio University Press 1966).

19. The Library of America has published a comprehensive two-volume collection of materials on the ratification process entitled *The Debate on the Constitution*. Bernard Bailyn wrote the headings and notes for the documents appearing in the volumes.

20. Antonin Scalia, *A Matter of Interpretation: Federal Courts and the Law* 38 (Princeton University Press 1997) with Commentary by Amy Gutmann (ed.), Gordon S. Wood, Lawrence H. Tribe, Mary Ann Glendon, and Ronald Dworkin.

21. *Nixon v. Administrator of General Services*, 433 U.S. 425 at 475 (1977).

22. Cass Sunstein, *Constitution of Many Minds* 47 (Princeton University Press 2009).

23. *United States v. Morrison*, 529 U.S. 598, 618.

24. See *Gaffney v. Cummings*, 412 U.S. 735 (1973).

25. For an argument that excessive incumbent protection raises a justiciable constitutional claim, see Walter Frank, "Help Wanted: The Constitutional Case against Gerrymandering to Protect Congressional Incumbent," 32 *Ohio N. U. L. Rev.* 227 (2006).

26. The leading case is *Elrod v. Burns*, 427 U.S. 347 (1976).

27. *Parham v. J. R.*, 442 U.S. 584 (1979).

28. Michael J. Gerhardt, *The Power of Precedent* 68 (Oxford University Press 2008).

29. Harold J. Spaeth and Jeffrey A. Segal, *Majority Rule or Minority Will* 308–15 (Cambridge University Press 1999).

30. *Id.* at 7.

31. *Id.* at 287.

32. Gerhardt, *supra* note 28, at 94.

33. Eileen Braman, *Law, Politics and Perception: How Policy Preferences Influence Legal Reasoning* 166 (University Press of Virginia 2009).

34. Statement of Thomas W. Merrill, in Calabresi, *supra* note 8, at 224.

35. *Planned Parenthood v. Casey* 505 U.S. at 854.

36. Gerhardt, *supra* note 28, at 45.

37. Statement of David Strauss, in Calabresi, *supra* note 8, at 249.

38. Felix Frankfurter, "The Process of Judging in the Supreme Court," in *The Supreme Court: Views from Inside* 43 (Alan Westin ed., Greenwood Press 1961).

39. *Id.* at 43–44.

40. *Lee v. Weisman*, 505 U.S. 577 (1992).

41. *Id.* at 596.

42. *United States v. Lopez*, 514 U.S. 549 (1995).

43. *Id.* at 574.

44. *Swain v. Alabama*, 380 U.S. 202 (1965).

45. *Batson v. Kentucky*, 476 U.S. 79 (1986).

46. *National League of Cities v. Usery*, 426 U.S. 833 (1976).

47. *Garcia v. San Antonio Metropolitan Transit Authority*, 469 U.S. 528 (1985).

48. *Gideon v. Wainwright*, 372 U.S. 335 (1963).

49. *Mitchell v. W. T. Grant Co.*, 416 U.S. 600, 636 (1974).

50. Mark Tushnet, *Making Constitutional Law* 36 (Oxford University Press 1997).

51. *Lawrence v. Texas*, 539 U.S. 558 (2003).

52. *Id.* at 578.

53. *Tinker v. Des Moines Independent Comm. School District*, 393 U.S. 503 (1969).

54. *Id.* at 506.

55. *Bethel School District v. Fraser*, 478 U.S. 675 (1986).

56. *Id.* at 683.

57. *Hazelwood School District v. Kulheimer*, 484 U.S. 260 (1988).

58. *Morse v. Frederick*, 551 U.S. 393, 401 (2007).

59. William O. Douglas, from an address given before the Section on Judicial Administration of the American Bar Association, September 9, 1948, in *The Supreme Court: Views from Inside* 54 (Alan Westin ed., Greenwood Press 1961).

60. Michael W. McConnell, "Book Review," 119 *Harvard Law Review* 2387, 2394–97 (2006), quoted in Richard Posner, *How Judges Think* 343 (Harvard University Press 2008).

61. *Id.*

62. *Dickerson v. United States*, 530 U.S. 428 (2000).

63. *Id.* at 443.

64. Douglas, *supra* note 2, at 135–36.

65. Laurence H. Tribe, *The Invisible Constitution* 9 (Oxford University Press 2008).

66. *Nevada v. Hall* 440 U.S. 410 at 433 (1979).

10. Crafting a Constitution

1. *Brown v. Board of Education,* 347 U.S. 483, 492–93 (1954).

2. Quoted in Jeffrey Rosen, *The Supreme Court: The Personalities and Rivalries That Defined America* 88 (Times Books 2006).

3. Colloquium, *115 Yale L.J.* 1972 (2005–6).

4. Ronald Dworkin, *Freedom's Law: The Moral Reading of the Constitution* 7 (Harvard University Press 1996).

5. Richard H. Fallon, *Implementing the Constitution* 19 (Harvard University Press 2001).

6. David Strauss, *The Living Constitution* 59 (Oxford University Press 2010).

7. Thomas M. Keck, *The Most Activist Supreme Court in History* 204–14 (University of Chicago Press 2004).

8. Richard H. Fallon Jr., "How to Choose a Constitutional Theory," 87 *Cal. L. Rev.* 535, 552 (1992).

9. *U.S. v. Carolene Products Co.*, 304 U.S. 144 (1938).

10. John Hart Ely, *Democracy and Distrust: A Theory of Judicial Review* 181 (Harvard University Press 1980).

11. *New York v. United States*, 326 U.S. 572, 583 (1946).

12. *Goldman v. Weinberger*, 475 U.S. 503 (1986).

13. *Connick v. Myers*, 461 U.S. 138 (1983).

14. Herbert Wechsler, "Toward Neutral Principles of Constitutional Law," 73 *Harv. L. Rev.* 1 (1959).

15. *Chambers v. Florida*, 309 U.S. 227 at 241 (1940).

16. Christopher L. Eisgruber, *The Next Justice* 20 (Princeton University Press 2007).

17. *Id.* at 21.

18. Cass Sunstein, *One Case at a Time: Judicial Minimalism on the Supreme Court* 10 (Harvard University Press 1999).

19. *Id.* at 11.

20. Cass R. Sunstein, "Second Order Perfectionism." 75 *Fordham L. Rev.* 2867, 2868 (2007).

21. Earl Warren, *The Memoirs of Earl Warren* 6 (Doubleday 1977).

22. Richard A. Posner, *Law, Pragmatism and Democracy* 351 (Harvard University Press 2003).

23. *Id.* at 353.

24. David A. Strauss, "Common Law Constitutional Interpretation," 63 *U. Chi. L. Rev.* 877, 887 (1996).

25. *Id.* at 894.

26. *Brown v. Plata*, 563 U.S. ____ (2011).

27. Comment, Kory A. Langhofer, 115 *Yale L.J.* 1823 (2005–6).

28. Laurence H. Tribe and Michael C. Dorf, *On Reading the Constitution* 17 (Harvard University Press 1991).

29. Fallon, *supra* note 5, at 33.

30. *Id.* at 48.

31. *Id.* at 35.

32. *Id.* at 66.

33. Antonin Scalia, "Originalism: The Lesser Evil," 57 *U. Cin. L. Rev.* 849, 856 (1989).

34. Quoted in Jeremy Waldron, "The Core of the Case against Judicial Review," 115 *Yale L.J.* 1346, 1350 (2005–6).

11. The Court in Action: Contemporary Constitutional Controversies

1. *Everson v. Board of Education*, 330 U.S. 1 (1947).

2. See *Engel v. Vitale*, 370 U.S. 421 (1962) and Abington School District v. Schempp 374 U.S. 203.

3. See Alison Gash and Angelo Gonzalez, "School Prayer," in *Public Opinion and Constitutional Controversy* 73–74 (Nathaniel Persily et al. eds., Oxford University Press 2008).

4. *Id.* at 69.

5. *Wallace v. Jaffree*, 472 U.S. 38 (1985).

6. Christopher L. Eisgruber and Lawrence G. Sager, *Religious Freedom and the Constitution* (Harvard University Press 2007).

7. *Lemon v. Kurtzman*, 403 U.S. 602 (1971).

8. *Zelman v. Simmons-Harris*, 536 U.S. 639 (2002).

9. *Rosenberger v. Rector and Visitors of the University of Virginia*, 515 U.S. 819 (1995).

10. *Epperson v. Kansas*, 393 U.S. 97, 104 (1968).

11. *McCreary County v. American Civil Liberties Union of Kentucky*, 545 U.S. 844 (2005).

12. *Van Orden v. Perry*, 545 U.S. 677 (2005).

13. *McCreary* 545 U.S. at 896–97.

14. *Id.* at 894.

15. *Id.*

16. *Id.* at 893.

17. *Id.* at 877.

18. *Id.* at 880.

19. *Id.* at 879.

20. *Id.* at 881.

21. *Van Orden v. Perry*, 545 U.S. 677, 700.

22. *Id.* at 704.

23. Stephen Breyer, *Active Liberty* 122–24 (Alfred A. Knopf 2006).

24. *Regents of Univ. of California v. Bakke*, 438 U.S. 265 (1978).

25. *Grutter v. Bollinger*, 539 U.S. 306, 326 (2003).

26. *Id.* at 330.

27. *Id.* at 330–31.

28. *Id.* at 334.

29. *Id.* at 340.

30. *Gratz v. Bollinger*, 539 U.S. 244, 276 (2003).

31. *Id.* at 277.

32. James F. Simon, *The Center Holds* 119 (Simon & Schuster, 1995).

33. *Grutter,* 539 U.S. at 349.

34. *Id.* at 360.

35. *Id.*

36. *Id.* at 340.

37. *Gratz,* 539 U.S. at 301.

38. *Id.*

39. *Parents Involved in Community Schools v. Seattle School District No. 1,* 551 U.S. 701 (2007).

40. *Id.* at 787.

41. *Id.* at 797.

42. *Id.* at 803.

43. *Id.* at 865–66.

44. *N.Y. Times,* January 27, 2010, A16.

45. Hanna was a leading Republican conservative in late-nineteenth-century America. He served as President McKinley's campaign manager and was reputed to be thinking of challenging Theodore Roosevelt for the Republican presidential nomination when he suddenly died in 1904.

46. For most of the nineteenth century, political parties financed their activities in large part through the spoils system. People were awarded government jobs for their service to the party and were expected to pay part of their salary to the party in the form of assessments. This connection was broken at the federal level by the passage of the Pendleton Civil Service Act of 1873. Much later, the Hatch Act prohibited federal employees from engaging in political activities in response to fears that a politicized federal bureaucracy could jeopardize public support for New Deal programs. The Supreme Court itself in 1976 provided the final coup de grace to the patronage system in *Elrod v. Burns* (427 U.S. 347 (1976)) when it found that employees (other than those in policy making positions) in Illinois state government could not be fired because of their political affiliation since such an action would violate their First Amendment right to be free from compelled speech.

47. The spending limit for House primary and general election races was $70,000 each; for the Senate it was the greater of $100,000 or eight cents per voter for primary races, and $150,000 or twelve cents per voter for the general election. Candidates were also prevented from contributing substantial amounts to their own campaigns.

48. *Buckley v. Valeo,* 424 U.S. 1 (1976).

49. *Id.* at 19.

50. *Randall v. Sorrell,* 548 U.S. 230, 277 (2006).

51. *Buckley,* 424 U.S., at 57.

52. Frank J. Sorauf, *Inside Campaign Finance: Myths and Realities* (1992), quoted in Samuel Issacharoff, *The Constitutional Logic of Campaign Finance Regulation* 238 (*N.Y.U. Pub. L. and Legal Theory Working Papers* 96 (2008), which can be found online at http://lsr.nellco.org/nyu/plltwp/papers/96.

53. *McConnell v. Federal Election Commission,* 540 U.S. 93 (2003).

54. *Citizens United v. Federal Election Commission,* 558 U.S. ____ (2010), slip opinion of Stevens, J. at 2.

55. *Id.* at 51.

56. *Id.* at 57.

57. *Id.* at 90.

58. Owen M. Fiss, *The Irony of Free Speech* 13 (Harvard University Press 1996)

59. Jack M. Balkin, "*Roe v. Wade* Engine of Controversy," in *What Roe v. Wade Should Have Said* 7 (New York University Press 2005).

60. *Roe v. Wade*, 410 U.S. at 153.

61. *Id.*

62. *Id. at* 156.

63. *Id.* at 158.

64. *Id.* at 159.

65. *Id.* at 163.

66. Michael Stokes Paulsen quoted in *What Roe v. Wade Should Have Said, supra* note 59, at 207.

67. *Id.*

68. *Id.* at 213.

69. *Planned Parenthood of Southeastern Pa. v. Casey,* 505 U.S. 833, 979 (1992).

70. *Id.*

71. Ronald Dworkin, *Freedom's Law* 121 (Harvard University Press 1996).

72. *Planned Parenthood,* 505 U.S., at 985.

73. *Id.* at 992.

74. *Id.* at 996.

75. Archibald Cox, *The Court and the Constitution* 334 (Houghton Mifflin 1987).

76. *Id.*

77. *Id.* at 333.

78. *Gonzales, Attorney General v. Carhart,* 550 U.S. 124 (2007).

79. Just as in our presidential election, in a county unit system a candidate can win a statewide election without winning a majority of the popular vote. This system was held unconstitutional by the Supreme Court in *Gray v. Sanders,* 372 U.S. 368 (1963).

80. A chart with these findings is found in Andrew Hacker, *Congressional Districting* 3 (Brookings Institution 1964).

81. Gene Graham, *One Man One Vote* 15 (Little, Brown 1972).

82. *Id.* at 18.

83. *Colegrove v. Green,* 328 U.S. 549 (1946).

84. *Luther v. Borden,* 48 U.S. (7 How.) 1 (1849).

85. *Pacific States Telephone and Telegraph Co. v. Oregon,* 223 U.S. 151 (1912).

86. "We have no question," wrote Justice Brennan, "decided, or to be decided, by a political branch of government coequal with this Court. Nor do we risk embarrassment of our government abroad, or grave disturbance at home if we take issue with Tennessee as to the constitutionality of her action here challenged. Nor need the appellants, in order to succeed in this action, ask the Court to enter upon policy determinations for which judicially manageable standards are lacking. Judicial standards under the Equal Protection Clause are well developed." *Baker v. Carr,* 369 U.S. 186, 226 (1961).

87. David M. O'Brien, *Storm Center: The Supreme Court in American Politics* 287 (W. W. Norton 1986).

88. *Baker,* 369 U.S. at 323.

89. *Wesberry v. Sanders,* 376 U.S. 1 (1964).

90. *Id.* at 7–8.

91. *Id.* at 13–14.

92. *Id.* at 21.

93. *Id.* at 27.

94. *Reynolds v. Sims,* 377 U.S. 533 (1964).

95. *Id.* at 568.

96. *Id.* at 562–63.

97. *Id.* at 565–66.

98. *Id.* at 590–91.

99. *Lucas v. Colorado General Assembly* 377 U.S. 713 (1963).

100. *Id.* at 757.

101. *Id.* at 759.

102. *Id.* at 754.

103. *Bush v. Gore,* 531 U.S. 98 (2000).

104. Alexander M. Bickel, "The Supreme Court and Reapportionment," in *Reapportionment in the 1970s,* at 61 (Nelson W. Polsby ed., University of California Press 1971).

105. Robert G. Dixon Jr., "The Court, The People, 'One Man, One Vote,'" in Polsby, *supra* note 105, at 17.

106. Robert G. Dixon Jr., *Democratic Representation—Reapportionment in Law and Politics* 8 (Oxford University Press 1968).

107. *DeShaney v. Winnebago County Department of Social Services,* 489 U.S. 189 (1988).

108. Quoted in Lynne Curry, *The DeShaney Case* 121 (University Press of Kansas 2007).

109. *DeShaney,* 489 U.S. at 191.

110. *DeShaney v. Winnebago County Department of Social Services,* 812 F. 2d 298, 301 (1987).

111. *DeShaney,* 489 U.S. at 195.

112. *Id.* at 196.

113. *Id.* at 200.

114. *Id.* at 203.

115. *Id.*

116. *Id.* at 212.

117. *Id.* at 211.

118. *Id.* at 208.

119. *Id.*

120. *Id.* at 212.

121. *Id.*

122. *Id.* at 213.

123. John C. P. Goldberg, "The Constitutional Status of Tort Law: Due Process and the Right to a Law for the Redress of Wrongs," 115 *Yale L.J.* 524 (2005–6).

Conclusion

1. This story is recounted in H. Jefferson Powell, *A Community Built on Words* 9 (University of Chicago Press 2002).

2. His answer was the atomic hypothesis—that all matter is made up of atoms.

Suggestions for Further Reading

The Constitution at Inception

There are many excellent works on the Constitutional Convention. Two recent ones are: *A Brilliant Solution* by Carol Berkin and *The Summer of 1787* by David Stewart. Berkin's book also contains a useful appendix containing brief biographies of each of the delegates to the convention. *The Creation of the American Republic* by Gordon Wood provides a detailed, persuasive account of the events leading up to the Constitutional Convention. A more recent volume, covering the Revolutionary period and highly recommended by Professor Wood, is *Revolutionaries: A New History of the Invention of America by* Jack Rakove. A highly valued collection of articles by eminent scholars entitled *Essays on the Making of the Constitution* edited by Leonard Levy (second edition) brings together a number of viewpoints on the motivations and intent of the Framers. It contains, among other things, several articles attacking and defending Beard's thesis respecting the self-interest of the Framers in drafting the Constitution and also a famous article by the historian John Roche emphasizing the role of local politics and loyalties in shaping constitutional positions. *Negotiating the Constitution* by Joseph Lynch follows the struggle to fill out the meaning of the Constitution in its earliest years. Another excellent study is *The Constitution and America's Destiny* by David Robertson. Of course, there is nothing like reading primary materials, which for the Constitutional Convention means *Notes of Debates in the Federal Convention* by James Madison. The Ohio University Press edition has a valuable introduction by Adrienne Koch.

For those interested in the struggle over ratification of the Constitution, Pauline Maier's *Ratification*, published in 2010, will undoubtedly be the standard work on the subject for years to come, in addition to being highly readable. Jack Rakove's book, *Original Meanings*, also provides an important perspective on the ratification struggle and an exceptional description of the politics at work at the Constitutional Convention.

American Law

For those wanting an overview of American law in general, Lawrence Friedman's *American Law in the Twentieth Century* is a worthy introduction. A much older but still very valuable work is a series of essays entitled *Talks on American Law*, edited by the late Harold J. Berman, a wonderful man whom I had the pleasure of knowing from a very young age. While we have avoided extensive discussions of democratic theory, *The Limits of Constitutional Democracy*, edited by Jeffrey K.

Tulis and Stephen Macedo, comprises a series of essays of major scholars asking, among other things, what we should expect of our Constitution and how we should judge whether it is succeeding or failing. The essays are uniformly excellent, and a concluding essay by Chris Eisgruber brings them together with insights of its own.

Interpreting the Constitution

A slim volume entitled *Constitutional Interpretation: The Basic Questions* by Sotirios Barber and James E. Fleming might be an excellent first choice for further reading on this subject as it sets forth in a highly readable but not oversimplified way the major interpretive issues in modern constitutional law. Another excellent work aimed more at the nonlawyer is *On Reading the Constitution* by Laurence Tribe and Michael Dorf.

Books that contain more than one point of view are also good beginning points for exploring this topic. *A Matter of Interpretation* by Justice Antonin Scalia contains an introductory essay by the Supreme Court justice that focuses on statutory as well as constitutional interpretation, followed by comments from four major scholars of decidedly different viewpoints—Laurence Tribe, Gordon Wood, Mary Glendon, and Ronald Dworkin. A response by Justice Scalia concludes the book, which totals less than 150 pages. Another good book entitled *Originalism: A Quarter Century of Debate* features speeches and transcripts of panel discussions on various aspects of Originalism. The panel discussions include a number of non-Originalists and provide a good sense of the differing viewpoints on this controversial mode of interpretation.

Among the best works advocating particular approaches to constitutional interpretation are *Democracy and Distrust* by John Hart Ely, arguing that the Supreme Court should vigilantly police the democratic process for constitutional violations but should otherwise be extremely wary of overturning statutes on constitutional grounds; *The Least Dangerous Branch* by Alexander Bickel, arguing for deference to elected bodies; *Active Liberty* and *Making Our Democracy Work*, both works by Justice Stephen Breyer, arguing the need for a strong pragmatic element in constitutional decision making; *One Case at a Time* by Cass Sunstein, arguing for narrowly focused, fact-based constitutional decisions; and *Constitutional Self-Government* by Christopher Eisgruber, defending a robust view of judicial review. A book I admire greatly is Richard Fallon's *Implementing the Constitution*, perhaps because it comes closest to expressing my own views but also because of its clarity and concision. A collection of essays by Ronald Dworkin entitled *Freedom's Law* gives a good sense of his highly influential perspective on constitutional law. Two works which argue the case for locating unenumerated or natural rights in the Constitution but from very different perspectives are Charles Black's *A New Birth of Freedom* and Hadley Arkes's *Constitutional Illusions and Anchoring Truths*. A rigorous, dense, but highly rewarding work entitled *Constitutional Interpretation*, by Keith Whittington, defends Originalism as a constitutional theory. A recent work by Cass Sunstein, *A Constitution of Many Minds*, also provides an interesting perspective on constitutional interpretation.

America's Constitution: A Biography by Akhil Amar provides not only a detailed tour of the historical basis of the constitutional text but many original insights as well.

Some historians and scholars have come increasingly to emphasize the role of political forces in shaping constitutional meaning. In this connection, the works of two scholars with very different perspectives on the Constitution stand out. Keith Whittington's *Constitutional Construction* describes a number of clashes, including the impeachment of Samuel Chase, the Nullification Crisis, and Andrew Johnson's impeachment and trial, which in Whittington's view developed constitutional meaning in profound ways. *We the People* by Bruce Ackerman is a two-volume (projected to be three-volume) work of history and political theory that, among other things, attempts to show how profoundly our understanding of the Constitution and indeed the Constitution itself has been changed by political developments. It is a controversial but fascinating approach to the Constitution. The first volume is entitled *Foundations*, the second *Transformations*.

Narrative Surveys of Supreme Court Constitutional Decisions

Several straightforward but highly readable accounts giving a broad sweep of the development of constitutional law from the beginning are *The American Supreme Court* by Robert McCloskey, *A History of the Supreme Court* by the late Bernard Schwartz, and *The Supreme Court: An Essential History* by Peter Hoffer, William-james Hoffer, and N. E. H. Hull. A more provocative look at the Court's history, emphasizing its support of establishment interests, is provided in *The Supreme Court and the American Elite* by Lucas Powe Jr. The late Chief Justice William Rehnquist wrote a worthwhile account of constitutional development entitled *The Supreme Court* which, of course, draws added interest by virtue of the author himself.

What many regard as the best law book ever written is *Simple Justice* by Richard Kluger. This 750-page work reads like a novel. It is perhaps the only real page turner on the law I've ever read and details the decades-long struggle for the recognition of black constitutional rights and the many ingenious ways the South attempted to get around the rulings issued by the Court prior to *Brown v. Board of Education*. It is, however, Kluger's descriptions of the litigants and lawyers themselves and their compelling personal dramas that elevates this to a work of literature.

The Modern Court

There are a number of excellent works focusing on the Warren and post-Warren Courts. *The Warren Court: Justice Rulings and Legacy* by Melvin Urofsky provides a good introduction to the Warren Court. A much more comprehensive and highly readable study is provided by *The Warren Court and American Politics* by Lucas A. Powe Jr. It is particularly valuable in the way it shows how Court decisions influence, and in turn are influenced by, the politics and history of their times. Bernard Schwartz has written an excellent account of the Burger Court entitled *The Ascent of Pragmatism*. James Simon wrote an interesting history of the Rehnquist Court about midway through Rehnquist's tenure entitled *The Center Holds*. A more complete accounting of the Rehnquist Court is provided by Mark Tushnet's book, *A Court Divided: The Rehnquist Court and the Future of Constitutional Law*.

How the Court Works

One of the best books on the Court itself, now in its sixth edition, is *Storm Center: The Supreme Court in American Politics* by David M. O'Brien, which contains excellent descriptions of how the Court chooses what cases to hear and how it goes about reaching its decisions. Another excellent work on the Court as a working institution is *Decision* by Bernard Schwartz. Linda Greenhouse's book *Becoming Justice Blackmun* gives one a great feel for the human side of Court life as well as telling a fascinating story of one justice's evolution. Two works, H. W. Perry's *Deciding to Decide* and Walter Murphy's *Elements of Judicial Strategy*, provide excellent analyses of the Court's institutional perspective on accepting and deciding cases.

Some important works focus on specific features of the Court and its processes. Among the best are *Deciding to Leave: The Politics of Retirement from the United States Supreme Court* by Artemus Ward, *Friends of the Court: Interest Groups and Judicial Decision Making* by Paul M. Collins Jr., which examines the influence of amicus briefs, *Oral Argument and Decision Making on the United States Supreme Court* by Timothy R. Johnson and *Concurring Opinion Writing on the U.S. Supreme Court* by Pamela Corley. For those interested in learning more about the attitudinal account of Supreme Court decision making, I would especially recommend Eileen Braman's *Law, Politics and Perception*.

Three books that give a good sense of the inner dynamics of Court life are: *The Brethren* by Bob Woodward and Scott Armstrong, a journalistic window on Court life during the first six years of Chief Justice Burger's tenure, based on interviews with clerks and some justices, most notably Potter Stewart; *The Nine* by Jeffrey Tobin, a very entertaining read that focuses on the more recent Court; and *Making Constitutional Law: Thurgood Marshall and the Supreme Court, 1961–1991* by Mark Tushnet, an enjoyable, more academic work that gives a real sense of the Court's decision-making processes.

The best view of the Court can sometimes come from statements by justices themselves. David M. O'Brien has edited a wonderful collection of reflections, speeches, and excerpts by the justices entitled *Judges on Judging*, which not only addresses many of the major topics in Constitutional law but also provides an excellent overview of the federal judicial system as a whole. In the text, there was a brief discussion of the role that the lower federal courts play in constitutional law. No book shows this more clearly or dramatically than *58 Lonely Men* by J. W. Peltason, which tells the story of the forty-eight district court and ten circuit court judges, mainly Southerners, who were charged with the duty of enforcing the Supreme Court's decision in *Brown v. Board of Education*.

Judicial Biographies and Memoirs

One avenue for learning about the Court in the context of American history is through biographies. I would highly recommend *Justice Brennan: Liberal Champion* by Seth Stern and Stephen Wermiel; *Louis D. Brandeis: A Life* by Melvin Urofsky; *American Original: The Life and Constitution of Supreme Court Justice Antonin Scalia* by Joan Biskupic; and *Justice for All: Earl Warren and the Nation*

He Made by Jim Newton. A biography by Tinsley Yarbrough of the second Justice John Harlan gives a fascinating look at the Warren Court through the eyes of its most formidable critic and is aptly titled *John Harlan: Great Dissenter of the Warren Court*. Another biography, *Felix Frankfurter: Judicial Restraint and Individual Liberties* by Melvin Urofsky, also focuses mainly on his Court years and describes how a brilliant justice's personality severely undermined his influence with his colleagues. Two broader biographies, one of Justice Cardozo (*Cardozo* by Andrew Kaufman) the other of John Marshall (*John Marshall: Definer of a Nation* by Jean Smith) provide real insight into the workings of the Court during two of its most important moments. Justice Black was another important and controversial justice whose life and career are the subject of Gerald T. Dunne's excellent *Hugo Black and the Judicial Revolution*.

Memoirs are always a bit tricky and need to be taken with a grain of salt. Nevertheless, the second volume of William O. Douglas's autobiography entitled *The Court Years* is well worth the time. A fascinating but somewhat frightening memoir (because of what it reveals about its subject) is provided by John Knox's account of his year clerking for Justice McReynolds. The volume is entitled *The Forgotten Memoir of John Knox* and was edited by Dennis J. Hutchinson and David J. Garrow.

The Bill of Rights

For an excellent discussion of the legal background for each of the amendments, there is Leonard Levy's *Origins of the Bill of Rights*. The distinguished Yale Law School professor Akhil Amar has written a book entitled *The Bill of Rights*, which argues that the Bill of Rights was originally less concerned about individual rights than about assuring that the states and the people were adequately protected against the power of the federal government. Our view, he argues, of the Bill of Rights understandably shifted with the final vindication of national supremacy through the medium of the Civil War. *In Our Defense: The Bill of Rights in Action* by Ellen Alderman and Caroline Kennedy gives the Bill of Rights concrete meaning through real live cases; those dealing with Fifth and Sixth Amendment rights are particularly interesting.

There are a number of concise works that provide a good beginning for further reading on the First Amendment. *War and Liberty* by Geoffrey Stone is a short version of a longer work by a noted First Amendment scholar that examines how the Court has attempted to balance First Amendment rights under the stress of wartime conditions, including the Cold War and today's battle with terrorism. Another short work by the Pulitzer Prize–winning author Anthony Lewis, *Freedom for the Thought We Hate*, also gives us a readable brief history of the First Amendment from a somewhat broader vantage point. In *The Irony of Free Speech*, Owen Fiss, another important scholar, argues that restricting certain forms of speech can actually further First Amendment values. A good starting point for further exploration of the First Amendment religion clauses is *Religious Freedom and the Constitution* by Christopher Eisgruber and Lawrence Sager, who argue that a variant of equal protection analysis is actually the best way to decide religion cases.

The Fourteenth Amendment

Democracy Reborn by Garrett Epps is a good introduction to the politics behind the Fourteenth Amendment and *No State Shall Abridge* by Michael Kent Curtis makes a compelling case that the Fourteenth Amendment was intended to incorporate the Bill of Rights. Perhaps the best overall history of the Amendment is found in *The Fourteenth Amendment* by William Nelson.

Individual Cases

If you wish to learn more by focusing on individual cases, you should consult the Landmark Law Cases & American Society Series of the University of Kansas Press. Each title in the series focuses on a particular case and is about 200 to 250 pages in length. You can review the catalog for the series online by going to the Press's web site.

Reference Works

The Oxford Companion to the Supreme Court of the United States, second edition, edited by Kermit Hall is, in my view, the best, most comprehensive single-volume reference work on the Supreme Court and Constitutional Law. Another worthwhile one is *A Practical Companion to the Constitution* by Jethro K. Lieberman, a really monumental achievement for a sole scholar. In addition to excellent subject entries, it also has an extremely useful time chart that allows you to determine the composition of the Court for any given year and also a brief biographical note for each justice.

Law at Ground Level

I wouldn't want to omit from any list of suggested readings a few personal favorites that have some relevance to our topic. The first book I ever read about the law, a fortuitous choice, was *My Life in Court*, by Louis Nizer. Nizer was a highly acclaimed trial lawyer who describes a number of his most interesting cases in this work. A couple of the cases actually have strong constitutional overtones. While Nizer's self-regard permeates these pages, it is never at the expense of, and in fact in an odd way enhances, the enjoyment of the book. Written more than forty years ago, it still provides the best look at trial law I've ever read. Another terrific work along these lines of more historical interest is Clarence Darrow's *The Story of My Life*. Two more books that give a good look at legal battles before they reach the Supreme Court are *To Set the Record Straight* by Judge John Sirica of Watergate fame and a biography, *Judge Frank M. Johnson Jr.*, by Robert Kennedy Jr., about the federal district judge from Alabama who bravely authored decisions assisting the civil rights movement in the 1960s. A riveting account of the integration struggles in Boston in the early 1970s entitled *Common Ground* by Anthony Lukas reminds us of how profoundly the law can impact everyday lives. Finally, a work of narrative history that reads like a novel is *Stories of Scottsboro* by James Goodman, as harrowing a description of what happens when law is the handmaiden of hate as one is ever likely to read.

Index

Walter M. Frank retired from his position as chief of commercial litigation for the Port Authority of New York and New Jersey in 2005. Since that time he has taught, lectured, and written on various aspects of constitutional law, focusing particularly on electoral process issues.